WEB-BASED SYSTEMS

& NETWORK MANAGEMENT

Kornel Terplan

Series Editor-in-Chief
Saba Zamir

CRC Press
Boca Raton   London   New York   Washington, D.C.

Acquiring Editor:	Jerry Papke
Project Editor:	Joanne Blake
Marketing Managers:	Barbara Glunn, Jane Lewis, Arline Massey, Jane Stark
Cover design:	Dawn Boyd
PrePress:	Walt Cerny
Manufacturing:	Carol Slatter

Library of Congress Cataloging-in-Publication Data

Terplan, Kornel.
     Web-based systems and network management / Kornel Terplan.
          p.   cm. — (Advanced and emerging communications technologies)
     Includes bibliographical references and index.
     ISBN 0-8493-9598-4 (alk. paper)
     1. Computer networks—Management. 2. World Wide Web (Information retrieval system) 3. Web
servers. I. Title. II. Series.
TK5105.5.T475 1999
004.6—dc21   98-55545
                                                                                          CIP

The CRC Press
Advanced and Emerging Communications Technologies Series
Series Editor-in-Chief: Saba Zamir

Dedication

To my God daughter, Borcsa Sághi Vass.

Foreword

Web-based technology is very rapidly penetrating many business areas. Systems and network management are no exception. The new technology is based on the internet and offers a number of benefits in terms of unification and simplification of systems and network management. The ability to use a universal browser to access management functions, device status, performance metrics, statistics, and to configure remote managed objects from anywhere at anytime is a realistic and significant dream of many managers.

The book deals critically with this new technology. It evaluates its applicability for typical management processes and functions. It concludes that this technology is expected to be used in combination with existing technologies of data collection, such as SNMP (simple network management protocol) and remote monitoring (RMON), data processing, data analysis, planning and design. Carefully deployed, this technology offers lower total cost of ownership of management tools. Training is easy and less expensive, mobility of management teams is much improved, and rapid access to information is guaranteed from anywhere.

This book is not about Web basics. It uses the experiences of early implementations, but does not go into details. It addresses various implementation models, such as embedding Web servers into managed objects or extending management platforms with Web server capabilities.

The purpose of this book is to improve the effectivity of current processes and tools of systems and network management. It is very useful for network managers, systems administrators, operators, performance analysts, designers and change managers. It can also be used as reference material for management platforms, management applications, and Web-based management standards.

Chapter 1 gives an overview of the present management technology, applied to systems and network management. It highlights the differences between systems and network management. It also addresses innovative management tools to be applied in combination with Web-based technologies. This chapter also includes user requirements in relation to management and a realistic list of present capabilities of suppliers.

Chapter 2 focuses on the first critical view of the applicability of Web-based technology for principal management processes, such as collecting, processing and analyzing management data, information distribution, design and planning. The conclusion is that the primary targets are information distribution and data analysis. It is unlikely that data collection will be exclusively supported by Web technologies.

Chapter 3 goes one step further and investigates the applicability of Web technology for practically all management functions. Four areas, such as description of the function, support of the function, most likely used tools for the function, and support by Web technologies, are under evaluation for each management function.

The conclusion is that approximately 35% of the total of 84 functions gets high and very high marks for applicability, 19% good marks, 35% limited marks, and 11% signals no support by Web technologies.

Chapter 4 is devoted to Web basics. Principal components, such as Web servers, Web browsers, addressing schemas, and Web protocols are addressed, in addition to HTML (HyperText Markup Language). Unsophisticated examples from the systems and network management domains help the reader to understand the terms: pages, links, and structures. This chapter also covers the recent extensions of HTML towards DHTML (dynamic HTML) and XML (extended Markup Language). Early implementation examples complete this chapter.

Chapter 5 presents the current status of Web-based technology standards for systems and network management. There are actually two directions: JavaManagement API and WBEM (Web-based Enterprise Management). They complement each other. Effectivity is the highest when they are used in combination with each other. Java applets are extremely useful to support thin management clients; WBEM is at its best advantage when management architectures must be built and supported on the basis of CIM (Common Information Model). Based on the standards, enabling technologies are also addressed in this chapter. They show the first results of using Web servers in managed objects or in management platforms. Both have advantages and disadvantages that are discussed and compared in this chapter.

Chapter 6 identifies the attributes of current management platforms. Each of the key suppliers, such as Cabletron, Computer Associates, Hewlett Packard, IBM/Tivoli, Microsoft, and Sun is interested in extending its platforms with Web server capabilities. The technical solutions may differ, but the principal goal is to offer access to management data from universal browsers. In certain cases, two-way communication is also supported that is extremely useful for change management. It is expected that push-technology will be combined with Web servers to guarantee on-time delivery of relevant management information to selected users. Also Web innovations and the attributes of future management frameworks are addressed in this chapter.

Chapter 7 helps readers to review existing management applications that also support Web technology. Both device-dependent (3Com, Bay, Cabletron, Cisco, Ungermann Bass) and device-independent applications (trouble ticketing, analysis and reporting, application and storage management, server management, service management) are shown. The depth of the implementation of Web technology is different, but the typical attributes are the same. They allow easy access from universal browsers, offer dynamic page updates, accept user requests for certain management actions, and support a relatively wide range of distribution alternatives for management information to users. For most management applications, Web technology offers flexible access, including conversion to or from DBMSs. Push technology is expected to be used here the same way it is used with management platforms.

The use of Web technology for systems and network management must not cause any bottlenecks in systems and networks. Page contents, access networks and servers must be properly designed and sized. Chapter 8 introduces tools and services to increase the efficiency of Web-based applications by using state-of-the-art content management tools, log file analyzers and software- or hardware-based load balancers.

Chapter 9 summarizes the expected trends with the use of Web-based technology for systems and network management. It emphasizes the combination of emerged management technologies with this new way of simplifying and unifying management. It also contains entries for business cases by outlining cost justification components, such as the changing corporate culture, use of a universal front-end for all management applications and tools, and fewer expenses for maintenance. Finally, specific recommendations are given to increase overall effectivity by combining both Web-based technology standards, using advanced agent technologies and deploying more security features.

Acknowledgments

I would like to thank Jerry Papke, retired senior editor of CRC Press, who initiated this book. I would also like to thank Josephine Gilmore, senior editor, and Dawn Mesa, associate editor, from CRC Press for their continuous support of this title.

I am particularly grateful to Joanne Blake for the excellent copyediting, Adam Szabo for the preparation of all the figures and tables, and my Ph.D. student, Endre Sara at Stevens Institute of Technology, for supporting me with secondary research results.

Contents

1 Basics of Systems and Network Management

Networks and systems will get faster and more virtual in nature over the next decade. The result is that management is getting more difficult and alternatives must be found for controlling the technology.

New applications force a rapid migration to high-speed technologies to connect systems, including fast Ethernet, switched broadband networks, Gigabit Ethernet, digital subscriber lines, and Asynchronous Transfer Mode (ATM).

In designing interconnected information systems, there is always a trade-off between spending more on systems or on networks. As network capacity is expected to become cheaper, it will make sense to accept higher network ownership costs for significantly lower server and support costs.[8]

The major challenges of systems and network management remain, particularly the following:

- Unification and simplification of systems and network management
- Integration of certain management functions, tools, and databases
- Distribution of certain management functions, tools, and databases

More importantly, these challenges are expected to be met at the same time, whereby integration and distribution may seem to be contradictory in some situations.

1.1 UNIFICATION AND SIMPLIFICATION OF SYSTEMS AND NETWORK MANAGEMENT

In order to improve the economy of scale in terms of human resources and management tools, unification of network and systems management has long been on the agenda of many enterprises. But this unification is a very difficult task for various reasons, including:

- Network and systems management have been separate tasks for many years. Each of them is supported by its own staff with different training and skill sets.
- The tasks are different, as well. Monitoring, control, and configuring devices and communication links are similar to each other. But, in the networking area, more responsibilities have been left over to suppliers and vendors.

1

- Even when the tasks are similar, the volumes are not. Systems management needs more integration and automation. Otherwise, the human resources demand would rise exponentially.
- In the systems area, the number of managed objects is very high. With networks, the gigantic throughput rates force managers to re-equip basic traffic measurement, troubleshooting, and accounting.
- Enterprises have collected more experience with network management tools. Network equipment comes usually with built-in management agents or monitoring software. Certain systems, primarily desktops, have not yet been designed for management.
- Prices of support tools vary greatly. Enterprises are willing to spend more to manage networks than systems. Even in the networking environment, prices vary depending on whether wide area networks (WANs) or local area networks (LANs) are managed.
- Standards differ for networks and systems. Simple network management protocol (SNMP) and remote monitoring (RMON) have made the breakthrough for managing networks, but desktop management interface (DMI) is far away from this status for systems. However, it does not mean that each hardware and software component has been provided with SNMP agents.

Figure 1.1 shows the demarcation lines between systems and networks. Web-based technology may offer a universal interface contributing to unification and simplification.

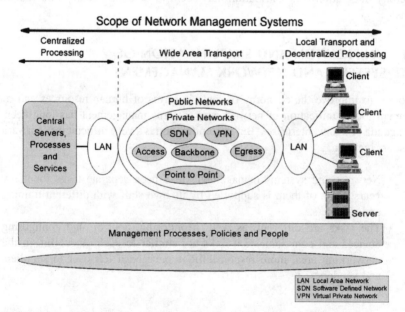

FIGURE 1.1 Demarcation line between systems and network management.

1.2 EXPECTATIONS OF USERS

The expectations of users may be summarized as follows:

- Powerful solutions: meeting all of the needs with reasonable costs and optimal capacity of tools.
- Scalability: the solution can grow with growing number of network and systems components.
- Maturity: the product has been utilized in multiple environments, and the deployment experiences have been good.
- High level of integration: frameworks, platforms, and management applications are integrated.
- Excellent user interface: mostly graphical with easy navigation and help features; universal front-end, such as a browser, is welcome.
- Low maintenance needs: inspections and preventive maintenance are very rarely needed.
- Reasonable costs: operating expenses are extremely low.
- Use of relatively open standards: the use of defacto standards is desired, but open standards are the ultimate goal.
- Small number of vendors to deal with: users prefer strategic vendors who can address multiple management areas with solutions.
- Willingness to pay for professional services: as part of outsourcing deals, users are considering out-tasking and outsourcing.

1.3 OFFERS BY VENDORS

On the other hand, hardware manufacturers and software vendors are willing to deliver:

- SNMPv1 support: manufacturers are careful not to invest too early into unstable standards.
- Proprietary solutions: custom solutions are offered for better performance and for user dependence on the product.
- Willingness to customize and integrate: offering custom solutions with fine-tuned performance.
- Common management information protocol (CMIP) support for specific solutions: in particular for the telecommunication industry, vendors offer special protocol support and robust management applications.
- Strategy of integrating with the market leaders: for the sake of stability, vendors build strategic relationships with platform and framework suppliers.
- Acquisitions, mergers, and joint ventures: management applications suites can be offered this way to meet user expectations.
- Offering professional services: in addition to products, vendors want to enter this area for additional revenues and for tighter relationships with the users.

1.4   WHERE HAVE INTEGRATION CONCEPTS FAILED?

Big integration projects and approaches have failed over the last few years. Figure 1.2 depicts three different directions of integration without success.

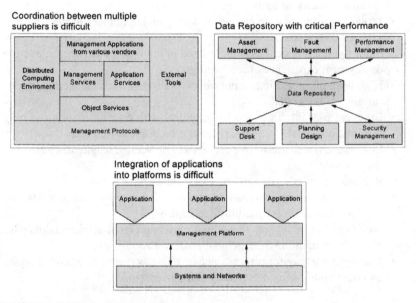

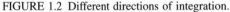

FIGURE 1.2 Different directions of integration.

The DME (distributed management environment) has failed because leading manufacturers were not able to work together honestly. DME could not consolidate the best pieces of many products, such as from Hewlett Packard, IBM, Bull, Tivoli, etc. In addition, management policies and company interests could not be brought onto a level of mutual interests. The use of a data repository by many management functions and management tools has failed for performance reasons. Database management systems could simply not meet the requirements. Maybe the timing was unfortunate, and certain internal tools were missing. Integration on the database level may be revisited as data warehouses and data mining tools are getting more mature and more widely spread. Using the management platform as the integrator has been showing some successes, but it assumes that management applications can be deeply integrated into the platforms, and that is not always the case. In addition, integration is expensive. In most cases, integration is shallow, and does not let management applications talk to each other. Web technology can contribute greatly to integrating and accessing management data and distributing reports.

Managing client/server-structures needs the distribution of certain management functions, especially display devices and databases. Distribution requires that communications are kept alive among managing entities and that central control is not lost. There are multiple approaches in this area. None of them offers a complete solution, but most of them are in use:[11]

- Using X-Windows to promote remote access to several users. Users may reside at different geographical locations. This technique is simple to implement, but bandwidth requirement may become critical. Security is poor, and performance can be critical, unless outband technology is used for data export and import.
- Using multiple graphical clients to distribute the views of status and performance. Graphical clients may be separated from servers, and implemented in a distributed fashion in the network. Scalability and performance are better than with X-Windows. Bandwidth requirements are lower because just the updated information needs to be transmitted.
- Using smart agents to distribute data collection tasks. It saves bandwidth and processing power by localizing data collection. Hierarchical control can be promoted by a combination of SNMP management platforms and third-party data collection applications. But in these cases a complicated management network configuration must be maintained. Figure 1.3 shows this structure.

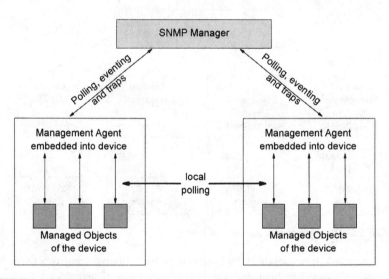

FIGURE 1.3 Use of smart agents.

- Using domain managers to increase reliability and distribute functions. This concept allows automatic backup of domain servers. It can also be used to consolidate and correlate alarms across multiple domains. It also reduces the bandwidth demand over WANs. But domain managers need to communicate with each other, requiring standard or proprietary solutions. Scalability is limited because bilateral communication links between managers must be maintained. Figure 1.4 shows this alternative.
- Using a manager of managers to offer a complete management architecture. This concept permits centralized control over multiple SNMP platforms across wide areas. Also non-SNMP managed objects can be

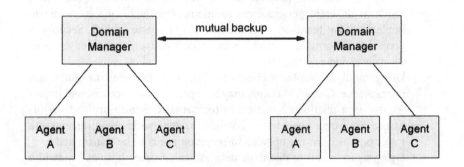

FIGURE 1.4 Use of domain managers. Agents A, B, and C represent various managed objects, such as hubs, routers, switches, multiplexers, etc.

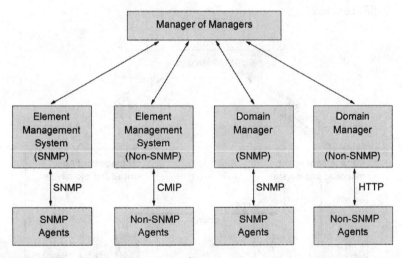

FIGURE 1.5 The concept of a manager of managers.

included. It consolidates and automates many management functions. It is well suited to manage large hybrid structures of networking devices and systems. This solution (Figure 1.5) is expensive, and its implementation and maintenance are complicated.

Web-technology may offer an additional alternative to using universal browsers to access management information from anywhere, enabling local execution of configuration, troubleshooting, and reporting tasks.

1.5 INTEREST OF DEVICE MANUFACTURERS AND PLATFORM SUPPLIERS

Unification on the basis of Web technology may simplify the management environment. The early reaction to this unification is different by vendors. If device vendors want their management applications to run on all the widely used management platforms — and there are many — developers must write different versions of the same management application for each one. This is an expensive exercise for both vendors and users. Device vendors would welcome the unification on the Web server level. Whether or not the server is built into the device or maintained separately is a different issue.

Platform vendors, however, may think differently. If Web servers are able to offer the same or at least similar functionality for less money, they may lose their market segment completely. Now, they are opening their platforms for information access by browsers. But they do not redesign their platform architecture. They may consider later on to integrate the Web server into their platforms. Technically, it is doable without any major redesign.

1.6   SUMMARY

The Web-based unification and simplification of network and systems management must somehow collaborate with innovative technologies used in management applications. These technologies are:

- Object orientation: in order to improve efficiency of design and development, platform and management applications have become object oriented. Most of the benefits are on the side of developers and less on the side of users. Users may benefit from performance gains and from more efficient use of storage spaces.
- Service level orientation: monitoring and measurements are put together under the umbrella of service level agreements (SLAs). They are helpful to quantify and control performance of the internal and external service providers.
- Use of mobile agents: in distributed management environments, managers may send agents to managed objects to execute certain functions, such as data collection or execution of presentation programs. After completing their jobs, they return to the manager. In particular, they can work with thin clients or network computers very well.
- Use of push technology: users or clients can be notified selectively about status changes in networks and systems. It is similar to the technique widely used in software distribution. In this case, the distributor checks status and conditions. If they match for certain predefined client profiles, they push the data to the targeted receivers.
- Policy-based management: this is the ability to establish policies for how networks and systems will be managed, e.g., what applications will be launched based on certain events, or establishing access rights based on user profiles, or automating management as the ultimate goal.

- Rules-based intelligence: it enables automated management by initiating alarms and corrective actions via predefined rules, programmed into a management station by the user or by the management tool vendor.
- Case-based reasoning: the tools supporting it are essentially a repository or library of problem-solving expertise of the users or of SolutionPaks of the vendors. They enable the user to view present cases or develop a case and decide how to solve a problem based on information stored in the repository.

These technologies are somewhat interrelated. Web-based technology should help to take better advantage of them and make them accessible to a broader community of users.

The standardization on Web-based technology brings the following benefits:

- Simplification of management tasks
- Extensions for missing elements
- Offering practical solutions
- Use of universal browsers to administer devices and applications
- Support for practically all devices and applications
- Use of existing standards and protocols
- Unification of data models
- Saving costs by standardizing on browsers instead of workstations
- Simplification of training for the management team

2 Web-Based Technology Is Supporting Basic Management Functions

2.1 INTRODUCTION

This chapter is based on the work of Dr. Jeffrey Case, one of the founders of the SNMP protocol.[3] His basic statements are valid despite progress made with dynamic HTML pages, push technologies, and better content management.

The initial success stories about Web technology, including ease of use supported by universal browsers, platform and operating system independence, and unifying access to management data sources may indicate that all management functions should be supported by this technology. This is definitively not the case: there is no urgent need to replace existing processes and successfully implemented solutions.

Web technology will have to cooperate with others already in use. The best results may be accomplished when Web technology addresses gray areas of network and systems management. Basically, management functions can be broken down into data collection, processing, analyzing data, information distribution, design and planning. Each of these principal functions will be reviewed to determine whether Web technology is the right choice or not. More detailed analysis will follow in subsequent chapters.

2.2 MANAGEMENT DATA COLLECTION

In order to get status information, data should be gathered in and around managed objects. The existing internet standard approach for defining and collecting data is the SNMP structure of management information (SMI) and the use of standard MIBs (management information bases). Figure 2.1 shows an example with MIB entries.

Also, the desktop management task force (DMTF) is busy in defining management information structures for systems, in particular for desktops. They standardize around MIFs (management information formats). Figure 2.2 shows an example with MIF entries.

The presentation of status and performance data for managed objects in HTML format is easy and unsophisticated. But, at this time, it assumes a pull technology. The user has to read the information when the managed object is experiencing a problem. The universal browser offers views for one or for a small number of managed objects at a time.

Unless a standard data definition language — such as SMI of CMIP or SNMP — is used, interoperability among management platforms, systems, and applications

GetStatusEntry
getStatusLineState
getStatusPaperState
getStatusInterventionState
getStatusNewMode
getStatusNewMode
getStatusConnectionTerminationAck
getStatusPeripheralError
getStatusPaperOut
getStatusPaperJam
getStatusTonerLow
getStatusPagePunt
getStatusMemoryOut
getStatusIOActive
getStatusBusy
getStatusWait
getStatusInitialize
getStatusDoorOpen
getStatusPrinting
getStatusPaperOutput
getStatusReserved
getStatusNovBusy
getStatusTcpBusy
getStatusAtBusy
getStatusLlcBusy

FIGURE 2.1 An example of management information base (MIB) entries: hpjetdirect status.

from multiple vendors is impossible. When each vendor presents device status or other management data to a Web page on a server in a nonstandard format, the data are programmatically useless to every management system except those supplied by the individual device vendor.

Any user may be able to read and interpret the data, but it will be impossible for any other vendor's management application to process and change the data along with management data from other vendor's devices. As a result, automation is very difficult to achieve.

Over the last decade, both vendors and users have made significant investments into management platforms, management applications, and into their interoperability. In order to save investments, Web technology should expand, but not replace, these investments.

2.3 MANAGEMENT DATA PROCESSING

In most cases today, agents maintain their own MIBs and MIFs. In critical cases, alerts can be sent to the manager. In the usual case, however, agents are periodically polled by super-agents or managers for data (Figure 2.3). In order to reduce overhead, adaptive polling is also used. HTML pages are not well suited for polling due to

Component ID:
- Manufacturer
- Product
- Version
- Serial number
- Installation
- Verification

System resources description:
- Device count
- System resource count

System resources:
- Device ID
- Resource number
- Resource type
- Resource base
- Resource size
- Resource flags
- Group ID

Network Adapter 802 Port Group:
- Port index
- Permanent network address
- Current network address
- Connector Type
- Data rate
- Total packets transmitted
- Total bytes transmitted
- Total packets received
- Total bytes received
- Total transmit errors
- Total receive errors
- Total host errors
- Total wire errors

802 Alternate Address Group:
- Alternate address index
- Port index
- Address type
- Alternate address

Network ADAPTER Driver Group:
- Driver index
- Driver software name
- Driver software version
- Driver size
- Driver interface type

- Driver interface version
- Driver interface description

Network Adapter Hardware Group
- Network topology
- Transmission capability
- Network adapter RAM size
- Bus type
- Bus width

Operational State:
- Operational state instance index
- Device group index
- Operational status
- Usage state
- Availability status
- Fatal error count
- Major error count
- Warning error count

Field Replaceable Unit:
- FRU index
- Device group index
- Description
- Manufacturer
- Model
- Part number
- FRAU serial number
- Revision level
- Warranty start date
- Warranty duration
- Support phone number

Boot ROM Configuration
- Boot ROM description
- Boot ROM version
- Remote boot protocol type
- Remote boot protocol version

Boot ROM Capabilities:
- Capability index
- Capability description
- Capability status

LAN Adapter Extensions:
- MIF and instrumentation filename

FIGURE 2.2   An example of management information format (MIF) entries: Intel TokenExpress PRO LAN Adapter.

the lack of programmability of reloads. In addition, HTML is not a good address to receive alerts from components due to the problem of dynamic page updates. To the point views and limited data transfer may be supported, but not bulk transfer of data via Web technology. HTML via hypertext transfer protocol (HTTP) is connection-oriented; SNMP is connectionless. Analytical studies and field experiments have shown that connection-oriented protocols may cause more problems with transmitting data.[3]

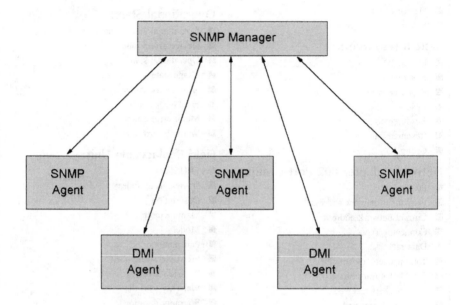

FIGURE 2.3 Processing data collected by SNMP agents.

2.4 ANALYZING MANAGEMENT DATA

SNMP and DMI have helped to collect and transfer data to the management platform for further processing. But these standards have left a lot of room for analyzing, correlating, and reporting management data. Existing third-party tools are usually limited to certain hardware and software environments. Platform vendors usually do not provide guidelines for data repositories and data warehouses.

Web technology in general, supported by Java applications, may help in this area a lot by providing a front-end to many different data sources and databases, as shown in Figure 2.4. Web interfaces do exist for a number of relational and legacy databases. But the intelligent interpretation of data remains the responsibility of the performance analysts.

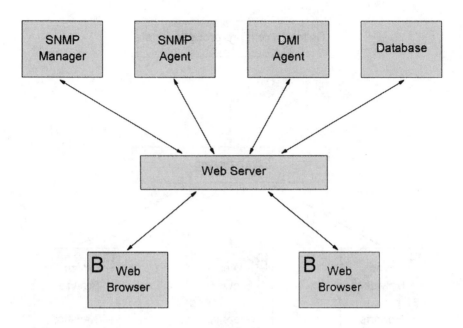

FIGURE 2.4 Web server as focal point to analyze data.

2.5   INFORMATION DISTRIBUTION

This may be the optimal use of Web technology. Publishing data in HTML is an effective and simple way to distribute information. But also in this case, receivers are expected to read the pages prepared on the Web server (Figure 2.5). Efficient pushing technologies may change this in the near future. HTML and HTTP are platform independent, but can be connected to platforms to receive and convert information. The lack of dynamic capabilities may limit the actuality of information for real-time use. Java can help a lot here by introducing dynamic features.

2.6   DESIGN AND PLANNING

Design and planning may be considered as a continuation of analyzing data provided by other tools. Making data, statistics, trends and other statistics available in Web pages for planners helps them to focus on their real task, such as sizing resources and predicting performance. These tasks can be supported by modeling devices, but using them is beyond the scope of Web technology.

In this area, the convenient, flexible and inexpensive access of data (Figure 2.6) is the big benefit for using Web technology. Practically, there are no limits to data to be displayed on Web pages. Also the results of the design and planning processes may be presented via Web pages.

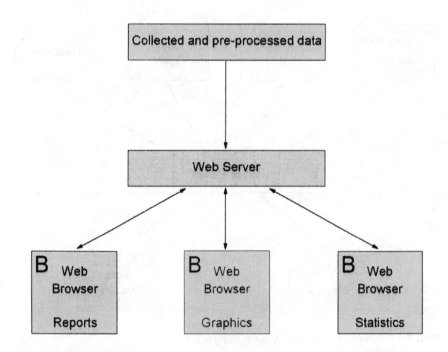

FIGURE 2.5 Web server as focal point to distribute information.

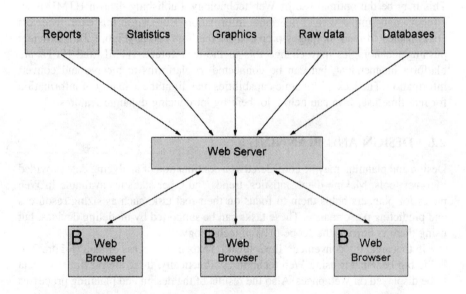

FIGURE 2.6 Web server as focal point for data repository.

2.7   SUMMARY

Web management technology offers new opportunities for systems and network management. Most likely, existing tools need not be replaced, and investments can be saved. But opportunities are different depending on the targeted management functions. Table 2.1 summarizes the results of this early assessment.

TABLE 2.1
Management Functions and Web Technology

Opportunities	Great	Good	Fair	Poor
Management data collection				x
Management data processing			x	
Analyzing management data		x		
Information distribution	x			
Design and planning			x	

3 Principal Functions of Systems and Network Management

3.1 INTRODUCTION

On the basis of the first orientation about applicability of Web technology for systems and network management, this chapter addresses each of the typical functions of management processes. As a result, the reader and the practical user of this book can better evaluate which management functions should be webified first.

Critical success factors for systems and network management are those few key areas of activity in which favorable results are absolutely necessary for the network management organization to reach its goals. Critical success factors for network management are:

- Processes: sequence of application steps, including guidelines for how to use tools to execute systems and network management functions.
- Instruments: hardware and software, or both, for collecting, compressing, databasing, correlating network management related information, and for predicting the future performance and utilization of systems and network components.
- Standards: agreements for how to store, process, and transmit systems and network management related information.
- Human resources: all individuals involved in supporting systems and network management functions. This relates to the organization of the company and depends on the degree to which systems and networking resources are shared as a function of various business objectives.

3.2 BUSINESS MODEL OF SYSTEMS AND NETWORK MANAGEMENT

Before starting with the discussion of principal management functions, the business model of the processes will be shown first. The logical model mirrors the usual distribution of management functions among different departmental organizations. In order to avoid duplications, management functions are allocated to a single business area only. Assuming shared management knowledge, information integrity may be guaranteed between business areas.

Figure 3.1 shows the logical model, highlighting business areas and the major information flows between them. This model is based on Reference 25. The scope of business areas is based on an average corporation, but it is not the model of a particular corporation.

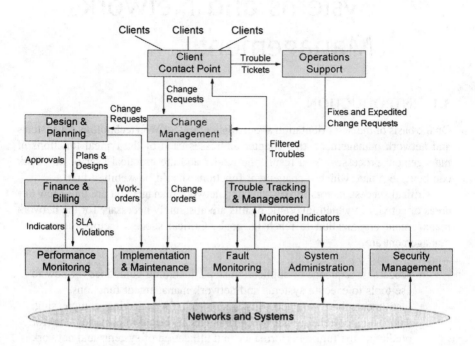

FIGURE 3.1 The business model of systems and network management.

The functions of network and systems management processes are described using four attributes:

1. Short description of the function
2. How the function is supported, manually or automatically
3. What tools are most likely used
4. How the function can be supported by Web technology

These functions represent an average set for average corporations. The purpose is to get a realistic view, where Web-based technology can be utilized first and best. After addressing each individual function, a summary table will give an overview of the depth of support by Web-based technologies.

The entry point into the model is the client. Clients represent internal or external customers or any other users of management services. Clients may report problems, request changes, order equipment or facilities, or just want to get information. This interface is the client contact point, implemented as the single point of contact to handle all client-related problems, changes, orders and inquiries.

3.3   CLIENT CONTACT POINT PROCESSES

Principal functions include:

- Receive problem report
  1. Short description of the function: users send in reports on various problems with applications, software, and hardware.
  2. Support of the function: manual support by taking phone calls. Registration could be automatic. Computer telephony integrated (CTI) implementation is likely. Mail and fax could also be automated.
  3. What tools are most likely used: phone, fax, e-mail, and special customized products.
  4. Support by Web technology: very high by using browsers, assuming information is converted into Web format.

- Handling calls
  1. Short description of the function: receipt of phone calls from users on problems, change requests, orders, and information inquiries.
  2. Support of the function: usually manual, but CTI may be considered.
  3. What tools are most likely used: usually phones, automated call distributors (ACDs), and CTI.
  4. Support by Web technology: very low.

- Inquiry handling
  1. Short description of the function: users want to get information on the status of managed objects, their performance, progress of trouble resolution, and change schedules.
  2. Support of the function: manual support by taking phone calls. Registration could be automatic. CTI implementation is likely. Mail and fax could also be automated.
  3. What tools are most likely used: phone, fax, e-mail, and special customized products.
  4. Support by Web technology: high with browsers, assuming information is converted into Web format. But push technology may be required to alarm the client contact point.

- Receive change requests
  1. Short description of the function: users are sending in change requests for applications, software, and hardware.
  2. Support of the function: manual support by taking phone calls. Registration could be automatic. CTI implementation is likely. Mail and fax could also be automated.
  3. What tools are most likely used: phone, fax, e-mail, and special customized products.
  4. Support by Web technology: very high with browsers, assuming the use of Web-forms for change requests.

- Handling orders
  1. Short description of the function: administrative activity to handle orders to purchase equipment or execute service requests.
  2. Support of the function: manual support by taking phone calls. Registration could be automatic. CTI implementation is likely. Mail and fax could also be automated.
  3. What tools are most likely used: phone, fax, e-mail, and special customized products.
  4. Support by Web technology: very high, and it points towards electronic commerce.

- Make service requests
  1. Short description of the function: based upon user's requests, administrators contact other organization units for implementing service orders. Information exchange is usually based on electronic documents.
  2. Support of the function: manual support by making phone calls or sending messages via fax or e-mail to other functional units. Registration could be automatic. CTI implementation is likely.
  3. What tools are most likely used: phone, fax, e-mail, and special customized products.
  4. Support by Web technology: could be high with browsers, assuming smart poll techniques.

- Opening and referring trouble tickets
  1. Short description of the function: as a result of registered problems, opening a trouble ticket, if the problem is not absolutely trivial.
  2. Support of the function: mostly still manual, supported by on-the-fly decision support systems, including consolidation and correlation of events, alarms, and messages.
  3. What tools are most likely used: third-party special tools are in use.
  4. Support by Web technology: very high, if the receiver is notified to read the entry in the Web server.

- Closing trouble tickets
  1. Short description of the function: if problem resolution has been confirmed, the trouble ticket can be closed.
  2. Support of the function: mostly still manual, supported by on-the-fly decision support systems, including consolidation and correlation of events, alarms, and messages.
  3. What tools are most likely used: third-party special tools are in use.
  4. Support by Web technology: could be high, using universal browsers as part of the management process.

3.4 OPERATIONS SUPPORT PROCESSES

Operations support receives trouble tickets from the client contact point. Major functions of operations support include:

- Problem isolation and determination by handling trouble tickets
  1. Short description of the function: on the basis of information provided by users, by the client contact point, consolidation and correlation of events, messages, alarms to conclude what happened.
  2. Support of the function: creative activity with semiautomation.
  3. What tools are most likely used: many management platforms with a number of device-dependent and device-independent management applications.
  4. Support by Web technology: the chances are good that the Web technology is embedded into the process. Embedding may happen at the device or platform level.

- Problem diagnosis
  1. Short description of the function: on the basis of information provided by users, by the client contact point, consolidation and correlation of events, messages, alarms to conclude why something happened.
  2. Support of the function: creative activity with semiautomation.
  3. What tools are most likely used: many management platforms with a number of device-dependent and device-independent management applications.
  4. Support by Web technology: low.

- Taking corrective actions to resolve fault
  1. Short description of the function: on the basis of information provided by users, by the client contact point, consolidation and correlation of events, messages, alarms to decide and execute actions to resolve problems.
  2. Support of the function: creative activity with semiautomation.
  3. What tools are most likely used: many management platforms with a number of device-dependent and device-independent management applications.
  4. Support by Web technology: good for device level changes, assuming vendor is offering device-related HTML pages.

- Repair and replacement
  1. Short description of the function: on the basis of information provided by users, by the client contact point, consolidation and correlation of events, messages, alarms to execute very concrete actions.
  2. Support of the function: in most cases manual dispatch supported by workforce management systems.
  3. What tools are most likely used: testing tools.

    4. Support by Web technology: some support by displaying work orders in home pages plus device-level repair actions can be well supported.

- Fault referral to third parties
  1. Short description of the function: on the basis of trouble ticketing entries, decision on the dispatching targets.
  2. Support of the function: manual activity supported by various instruments, such as workforce management.
  3. What tools are most likely used: workforce management systems.
  4. Support by Web technology: some support by displaying work orders in home pages.

- Backup and reconfiguration
  1. Short description of the function: activating backup components as required by the problem resolution process. Also, reconfiguring devices and routes may be required with and without backup.
  2. Support of the function: manual activity, but to a limited extent, self-healing automatics may be supported.
  3. What tools are most likely used: built-in features of managed objects, plus application packages provided by the vendors.
  4. Support by Web technology: limited, but information publication and distribution are possible plus device-level execution is good.

- Recovery
  1. Short description of the function: process of returning to normal operating conditions.
  2. Support of the function: high level of automation is possible, in particular with systems administration.
  3. What tools are most likely used: provided by suppliers of managed objects.
  4. Support by Web technology: low.

- Logging events and corrective actions
  1. Short description of the function: in order to promote further analysis, every essential event must be registered.
  2. Support of the function: in most cases, it can be automated.
  3. What tools are most likely used: third-party tools are used in combination with built-in tools provided by vendors.
  4. Support by Web technology: low for logging, high for the distribution of logs.

- Proactive problem management
  1. Short description of the function: by continually monitoring the network and its systems components, early warnings on status changes and quality deterioration can be determined. Acting instead of reacting helps to hide problems from users.

2. Support of the function: highly automatic for data collection and processing; creative for interpretation.
3. What tools are most likely used: many third-party tools.
4. Support by Web technology: high for viewing, but not for collecting and processing capabilities.

- Chronic trouble and fault identification
  1. Short description of the function: careful evaluation of trouble will reveal chronic problems with network and systems components. This will identify the faults, their reasons, and most probable causes.
  2. Support of the function: automatic for processing and correlation, manual for final conclusions.
  3. What tools are most likely used: trouble ticketing systems, extended by expert-like systems for consolidation and correlation.
  4. Support by Web technology: low.

- Periodic fault reporting
  1. Short description of the function: processed data are presented periodically or ad hoc, using different groupings such as by hardware, by software, by applications, and user caused.
  2. Support of the function: highly automatic.
  3. What tools are most likely used: many databasing and reporting tools from third-party vendors.
  4. Support by Web technology: very high for publication and distribution.

- Vendor performance reporting
  1. Short description of the function: processed data are presented periodically or ad hoc, using different groupings such as by vendor, by hardware, by software, by applications, and user caused.
  2. Support of the function: highly automatic.
  3. What tools are most likely used: many databasing and reporting tools from third-party vendors.
  4. Support by Web technology: very high for publication and distribution.

- Establish thresholds and alarm rates
  1. Short description of the function: in order to promote automation and the use of decision support systems, thresholds and alarm rates are defined, measured, and deployed.
  2. Support of the function: preparation of data is automatic, but decision about the thresholds and rates is manual.
  3. What tools are most likely used: registration, monitoring, and statistical tools.
  4. Support by Web technology: very high for publishing the thresholds and alarm rates.

This business area may be further subdivided into second- and third-level support, support by vendors and by third-party maintainers. As a result of their troubleshooting work, change requests for fixes are sent to change control. Not only clients, but also monitors may report problems to operations support. In this case, trouble tickets are opened in Fault Monitoring, and forwarded to operations support via fault tracking.

3.5 FAULT TRACKING PROCESSES

The principal functions of fault tracking concentrate on:

- Tracking manually reported or monitored faults
  1. Short description of the function: progress control of trouble tickets.
  2. Support of the function: could be highly automated.
  3. What tools are most likely used: trouble ticketing products and applications.
  4. Support by Web technology: limited to viewing capabilities via home pages.

- Tracking the status and progress and escalating problems if necessary
  1. Short description of the function: periodic checks on open trouble tickets to determine status and progress. If thresholds are violated, escalation steps are triggered.
  2. Support of the function: in most cases automatic.
  3. What tools are most likely used: trouble ticketing products, extended by third-party applications.
  4. Support by Web technology: very high for viewing and distributing information.

- Referral
  1. Short description of the function: triggered by tracking status, progress and escalation, it may be defined that different targets — usually technicians or external companies — should be contacted electronically.
  2. Support of the function: mostly manual, some automation is possible by trouble ticketing systems.
  3. What tools are most likely used: trouble ticketing tools and workforce management systems.
  4. Support by Web technology: marginal; limited to information distribution.

- Dispatch and coordinate technicians
  1. Short description of the function: optimal use of human resources on-site or at the central site.
  2. Support of the function: could be automated.
  3. What tools are most likely used: workforce management systems.

    4. Support by Web technology: marginal, limited to viewing capabilities.

- Create and maintain a trouble ticketing database
  1. Short description of the function: trouble tickets maintain very valuable information on trouble tracking and resolution processes. The professional maintenance in a database is very important in order to develop and deploy expert and decision support systems. Also case-based reasoning is very helpful.
  2. Support of the function: creation is manual, but some processing of data entries in trouble tickets can be automated.
  3. What tools are most likely used: database management and trouble ticketing tools.
  4. Support by Web technology: high for offering viewing capabilities supported by browsers and common gateway interfaces (CGIs).

This is a very central activity, playing a key role in supervising and correcting service quality-related problems.

3.6 CHANGE CONTROL PROCESSES

Change control deals with:

- Managing moves, adds, and changes
  1. Short description of the function: service requests usually include moves, adds, and changes. Management means the whole life cycle from request until completion.
  2. Support of the function: coordination is manual; single functions may be automated.
  3. What tools are most likely used: change and asset management tools.
  4. Support by Web technology: high for displaying and distributing information.

- Testing completed service orders (moves, adds, and changes)
  1. Short description of the function: process of testing deployed media access (MACs).
  2. Support of the function: tests can be highly automated; evaluation is usually manual.
  3. What tools are most likely used: testing tools.
  4. Support by Web technology: low.

- Routing service orders
  1. Short description of the function: the proper dispatching of orders to the right person or group(s) of persons.
  2. Support of the function: mostly manual, supported by workforce management systems.
  3. What tools are most likely used: workforce management systems.

    4. Support by Web technology: marginal, limited to information distribution.

- Maintaining the configuration database
  1. Short description of the function: databases may help to track history of moves, adds, and changes. It helps to accelerate trouble-shooting. It helps to return to a safe status, if moves, adds, and changes fail.
  2. Support of the function: creation is manual, but processing and reporting can be automated.
  3. What tools are most likely used: database management and trouble ticketing tools.
  4. Support by Web technology: high for offering viewing capabilities supported by browsers and common gateway interfaces.

- Supervising the handling of changes
  1. Short description of the function: it is actually a control function to manage the whole change cycle.
  2. Support of the function: in most cases can be automated.
  3. What tools are most likely used: change management tools, extended by third-party management applications.
  4. Support by Web technology: limited to viewing and information distribution capabilities.

- Equipment provisioning
  1. Short description of the function: process of order, receive, test and deployment of equipment.
  2. Support of the function: the whole process can be supported by state-of-the-art workflow management tools.
  3. What tools are most likely used: workflow management tools.
  4. Support by Web technology: high for information display and for supporting electronic commerce.

The results of these activities are validated change requests sent to planning and design.

3.7 PLANNING AND DESIGN PROCESSES

This management area supports design and planning functions, such as:

- Needs analysis
  1. Short description of the function: depending on the resource demand of new applications, needs for hardware, software, and communications are determined.
  2. Support of the function: in most cases manual, combined with monitoring present utilization.
  3. What tools are most likely used: monitors for present utilization.

    4. Support by Web technology: low, but can be used for information collection from users who work with browsers. Home pages are expected to receive uploads.

- Projecting application load
  1. Short description of the function: depending on the business needs, growth rates of present applications and the load of new applications are estimated.
  2. Support of the function: manual techniques, supported in certain cases with statistical tools.
  3. What tools are most likely used: statistical packages.
  4. Support by Web technology: low, but can be used for information collection from users who work with browsers. Home pages are expected to receive uploads.

- Sizing resources
  1. Short description of the function: depending on the aggregate load, resources must be sized for optimal performance.
  2. Support of the function: in most cases, analytical modeling and simulation can be helpful.
  3. What tools are most likely used: modeling and simulation packages.
  4. Support by Web technology: low, just for the presentation of the results.

- Authorizing and tracking changes
  1. Short description of the function: change requests with significant resource demand must be evaluated in depth. In most cases, impact analysis is pursued.
  2. Support of the function: the administrative part is automatic; the decision support is manual.
  3. What tools are most likely used: change management tools.
  4. Support by Web technology: medium; change requests can be collected by Web-based tools. Home pages are expected to receive uploads.

- Raising purchase orders
  1. Short description of the function: as a result of the previous steps, resources may be short. In these cases, additional resources must be ordered.
  2. Support of the function: the administrative part is automatic.
  3. What tools are most likely used: order processing and asset management packages.
  4. Support by Web technology: high, if the partners are supporting e-commerce.

- Producing implementation plans
  1. Short description of the function: changes must be carefully planned for execution. Depending on the impacts, implementation plans may become very detailed.
  2. Support of the function: in most cases manual, sometimes workforce management packages can be utilized.
  3. What tools are most likely used: workforce and workflow management tools.
  4. Support by Web technology: electronic forms can be created and distributed via Web technologies.

- Establishing company standards
  1. Short description of the function: it is vital that orders and purchases follow standards.
  2. Support of the function: it is a long and manual process.
  3. What tools are most likely used: the basis is given in standards for hardware, software, and communications.
  4. Support by Web technology: none, with one exception that results can be published via the Web.

- Quality assurance
  1. Short description of the function: it is an ongoing process of defining, measuring, and evaluating quality metrics.
  2. Support of the function: Open Systems Interconnected (OSI) 9000 and total quality management (TQM) guidelines are available.
  3. What tools are most likely used: no particular tools are under consideration.
  4. Support by Web technology: none.

The results of the work of this group are distributed to finance and billing, and to implementation and maintenance. Implementation and maintenance implements changes and work orders sent by planning and design, and by change control.

3.8 IMPLEMENTATION AND MAINTENANCE PROCESSES

- Implementing change requests and work orders
  1. Short description of the function: this function means the physical implementation of changes in hardware, software, and in communication facilities.
  2. Support of the function: workflow and workforce tools can help to automate the administration, but hardly the execution.
  3. What tools are most likely used: workforce and workflow management tools.
  4. Support by Web technology: very limited.

- Maintaining resources
  1. Short description of the function: ad hoc and preventive maintenance help to assure high availability and reliability of resources.
  2. Support of the function: it is a mixture of manual and automated procedures.
  3. What tools are most likely used: measurement and inspection tools are available.
  4. Support by Web technology: limited to distributing schedules via Web-based forms.

- Inspection
  1. Short description of the function: ad hoc and preventive inspections help to assure high availability and reliability of resources.
  2. Support of the function: it is mostly a manual process.
  3. What tools are most likely used: very limited opportunities for using tools.
  4. Support by Web technology: limited to distributing schedules via Web-based forms.

- Maintaining a configuration database
  1. Short description of the function: this function means continuous updating and synchronizing of the configuration database.
  2. Support of the function: could be automated up to a high level.
  3. What tools are most likely used: built-in database management tools.
  4. Support by Web technology: limited to particular cases, where CGIs are used to convert updates.

- Provisioning services
  1. Short description of the function: an extension of change management; not only single equipment, but also facilities are considered together in order to establish services.
  2. Support of the function: the process flow can be automated up to a very high level.
  3. What tools are most likely used: workflow management tools.
  4. Support by Web technology: Web-based forms can be very successfully utilized.

By continuously monitoring systems and networks, status and performance information is collected.

3.9 FAULT MONITORING PROCESSES

Fault monitoring is responsible for:

- Proactively detecting problems

1. Short description of the function: using monitoring techniques, most of the problems can be detected prior to serious performance degradations.
2. Support of the function: highly automated by properly setting thresholds and alarm levels.
3. What tools are most likely used: WAN and LAN monitors.
4. Support by Web technology: very high by providing status information on a Web page in the managed object or in the management platform.

- Opening trouble tickets
1. Short description of the function: depending on the detected problems, trouble tickets may be opened automatically by the management platform or by management applications.
2. Support of the function: a high level of automation is possible.
3. What tools are most likely used: trouble ticketing tools.
4. Support by Web technology: high, by the support of Web-based trouble ticketing tools.

- Referring trouble tickets
1. Short description of the function: trouble tickets may have to be referred to different subject matter experts.
2. Support of the function: a high level of automation is possible.
3. What tools are most likely used: trouble ticketing tools.
4. Support by Web technology: high by using Web-based trouble ticketing tools.

3.10 PERFORMANCE MONITORING PROCESSES

Performance monitoring deals with:

- Identifying monitoring needs; which data to be collected
1. Short description of the function: in order to efficiently monitor networks and systems, indicators and periodicity of monitoring should be decided, first. Impacting factors are the environment and service level agreements.
2. Support of the function: manual.
3. What tools are most likely used: none.
4. Support by Web technology: low.

- Monitoring the systems and networks performance
1. Short description of the function: monitoring includes the continuous tracking of indicators for network and systems components. Monitoring results are processed and stored in databases.
2. Support of the function: in most cases automatic.

3. What tools are most likely used: a large number of network and systems monitors that could be both hardware and software based.
4. Support by Web technology: altogether good; Web servers may be integrated into managed devices or into management platforms.

- Monitoring service level agreements
  1. Short description of the function: monitoring includes the continuous tracking of SLA indicators for network and systems components. Monitoring results are processed and stored in databases.
  2. Support of the function: in most cases automatic.
  3. What tools are most likely used: a large number of network and systems monitors that could be both hardware and software based.
  4. Support by Web technology: altogether good; Web servers may be integrated into managed devices or into management platforms.

- Monitoring third party and vendor performance
  1. Short description of the function: monitoring includes the continuous tracking of indicators representing vendor performance. Monitoring results are processed and stored in databases.
  2. Support of the function: in most cases automatic.
  3. What tools are most likely used: a large number of network and systems monitors that could be both hardware and software based.
  4. Support by Web technology: altogether good; Web servers may be integrated into managed devices or into management platforms.

- Maintaining a performance metric database
  1. Short description of the function: in order to recognize trends and support capacity planning, performance metrics should be collected and monitored.
  2. Support of the function: collection, processing, and populating the database could be automated.
  3. What tools are most likely used: WAN, LAN and systems monitors.
  4. Support by Web technology: limited to viewing metrics, assuming that database entries can be converted into HTML format.

- Optimization, modeling, and tuning
  1. Short description of the function: performance could be improved by changing key indicators or parameters. A combination of activities is needed.
  2. Support of the function: the creating part is manual; all support can be given by automated procedures.
  3. What tools are most likely used: modeling tools.
  4. Support by Web technology: high for distributing results for viewing and evaluation.

- Reporting on usage statistics and trends to management and to users (availability, utilization, exception)
  1. Short description of the function: process of determining indicators, monitoring process, and finally reporting.
  2. Support of the function: in most cases automated.
  3. What tools are most likely used: a large combination of tools, dominated by reporting and statistical packages.
  4. Support by Web technology: very high for distributing reports by push or pull techniques.

- Performance thresholds and alarms
  1. Short description of the function: in order to promote automation and the use of decision support systems, thresholds and alarm rates are defined, measured and deployed.
  2. Support of the function: preparation of data is automatic, but decisions about the thresholds and alarm rates are manual.
  3. What tools are most likely used: registration, monitoring, and statistical tools.
  4. Support by Web technology: very high for publishing the thresholds and alarm rates.

- Performance analysis for managed objects
  1. Short description of the function: trending is important for capacity planning purposes. Keeping track of the history of managed objects is important for future product decisions.
  2. Support of the function: data collection can be automated. Interpretation is manual.
  3. What tools are most likely used: a large combination of monitoring and modeling tools.
  4. Support by Web technology: low.

- Define which data are accessible by customers
  1. Short description of the function: not all data are accessible to everyone. It is necessary to analyze data for as needed basis by customers.
  2. Support of the function: manual in design, but automated in execution.
  3. What tools are most likely used: filtering and authentication tools.
  4. Support by Web technology: limited to the distribution of information to authorized users.

Performance monitoring is informing finance and billing with status of service quality and service level violations. Fault monitoring is opening trouble tickets and sending them to fault tracking.

3.11   SECURITY MANAGEMENT PROCESSES

Security management is responsible for ensuring secure communication and for protecting the management system. The following functions are supported:

- Threat analysis, including proactive security measures
  1. Short description of the function: this function should be continuously pursued. This function includes four steps: identification of sensitive information, discovering weak components, closing the gaps against potential security violations, and analyzing effectiveness of security measures.
  2. Support of the function: partially manual, partially automatic.
  3. What tools are most likely used: security logs.
  4. Support by Web technology: limited to access security logs.

- Administration (access control, passwords, partitioning, encryption, authentication)
  1. Short description of the function: definition and implementation of access control techniques, passwords, partitioning solutions, encryption technologies and devices, and authentication techniques.
  2. Support of the function: strong support for automation.
  3. What tools are most likely used: access control, password, partitioning, encryption, and authentication tools.
  4. Support by Web technology: good opportunities to access device status, and information exchange between users with browsers.

- Develop and deploy violation indicators
  1. Short description of the function: security indicators must be continuously supervised. In case of violations, alarms are triggered. Indicators must be powerful, but must not overload security officers.
  2. Support of the function: it is a manual process requiring human creativity.
  3. What tools are most likely used: none.
  4. Support by Web technology: none.

- Detection (evaluating services and solutions)
  1. Short description of the function: ongoing supervision of security indicators for violations.
  2. Support of the function: this function is usually supported by monitors.
  3. What tools are most likely used: security monitors.
  4. Support by Web technology: none.

- Recovery (evaluating services and solutions)
  1. Short description of the function: procedures should be prepared prior to security problems and to breakdowns due to security violations.
  2. Support of the function: the recovery process can be automated.
  3. What tools are most likely used: few tools are available to support recovery.
  4. Support by Web technology: none.

- Create and maintain security logs
  1. Short description of the function: all major access activities should be logged. Logs can be continuously or on-demand processed and evaluated.
  2. Support of the function: processing can be automatic; interpretation remains manual.
  3. What tools are most likely used: logging and processing tools.
  4. Support by Web technology: none.

- Security reporting
  1. Short description of the function: on the basis of thresholds and logs, security violations are expected to be reported.
  2. Support of the function: automatic to a high degree.
  3. What tools are most likely used: reporting tools.
  4. Support by Web technology: very high for creating and distributing reports.

- Ongoing security analysis and security plans
  1. Short description of the function: this function should be continuously pursued. This function includes four steps: identification of sensitive information, discovering weak places, closing the gaps against potential security violations, and analyzing effectiveness of security measures.
  2. Support of the function: partially manual, partially automatic.
  3. What tools are most likely used: security logs.
  4. Support by Web technology: limited to information exchange between users with universal browsers.

- Protecting the management systems
  1. Short description of the function: unauthorized access to network management systems can cause a lot of harm. These systems must have a high protection level.
  2. Support of the function: ongoing protection can be automated.
  3. What tools are most likely used: protection tools.
  4. Support by Web technology: very limited to distribution of information on violations.

3.12   SYSTEMS ADMINISTRATION PROCESSES

Systems administration is responsible for administering the whole distributed processing environment. Principal functions include:

- Software version control
  1. Short description of the function: the actual status of software — operating systems and applications — must be maintained continuously.

2. Support of the function: combination of manual and automated procedures.
3. What tools are most likely used: asset management tools.
4. Support by Web technology: limited to information distribution capabilities.

- Software distribution
  1. Short description of the function: distribution of software — operating systems and applications — using the push or pull or a combination of both technologies.
  2. Support of the function: high level of automation is possible.
  3. What tools are most likely used: number of tools supporting this function.
  4. Support by Web technology: high applicability, in particular for the pull technology.

- Systems management (upgrades, disk space management, job control)
  1. Short description of the function: accurate status information is the basis for evaluating utilization and trend figures.
  2. Support of the function: combination of manual and automated tools.
  3. What tools are most likely used: monitors for utilization measurement and reporting tools.
  4. Support by Web technology: good for built-in Web servers to report status; good for the distribution of reports.

- Server administration
  1. Short description of the function: accurate status information on the utilization of servers, in particular UNIX and NT.
  2. Support of the function: high level of automation is possible.
  3. What tools are most likely used: systems monitors are available for UNIX and NT.
  4. Support by Web technology: good for built-in Web servers; good for the distribution of reports.

- Administering the user definable tables (user profiles, router tables, security servers)
  1. Short description of the function: continuous activity for updating user related information.
  2. Support of the function: mostly manual, supported by few tools.
  3. What tools are most likely used: few tools.
  4. Support by Web technology: limited to information distribution and data sharing.

- Local and remote configuring resources
  1. Short description of the function: support of implementing moves, adds and changes.

   2. Support of the function: high level of automation is possible.
   3. What tools are most likely used: device vendors are providing device-dependent solutions.
   4. Support by Web technology: very high, if Web servers are built into the devices.

- Names and address management
  1. Short description of the function: in order to avoid confusion in complex networks, the identification of resources and users is extremely useful. This activity is getting even more important when considering intranets and extranets.
  2. Support of the function: manual administration supported by few services.
  3. What tools are most likely used: few tools, and a number of service alternatives.
  4. Support by Web technology: limited to sharing data and distributing information.

- Applications management
  1. Short description of the function: the rapid growth of applications requires powerful administration techniques. In terms of procedures, there are many similarities with managing hardware and other software components.
  2. Support of the function: combination of manual and automated process steps.
  3. What tools are most likely used: management instruments, including MIB tools.
  4. Support by Web technology: good, when Web servers are built into applications.

Applications management is a key activity requiring the coordination of many instruments that are probably new. The focal point of receiving status indicators, service level violations, plans, designs, major change requests and invoices from third parties is finance and billing.

3.13 FINANCE AND BILLING PROCESSES

- Asset management — create and manage the asset database
  1. Short description of the function: accurate status of assets may save a lot of money for businesses.
  2. Support of the function: high level of automation is possible.
  3. What tools are most likely used: asset management tools.
  4. Support by Web technology: limited to information distribution and data sharing.

- Costing services
  1. Short description of the function: accurate information is required on how the budget is spent. Usual breakdown of costs are hardware, software, infrastructure, communication, and people.
  2. Support of the function: in most cases, manual activity.
  3. What tools are most likely used: very few tools.
  4. Support by Web technology: none.

- Receive and process accounting data
  1. Short description of the function: consolidation of accounting information from multiple sources.
  2. Support of the function: this function can be automated.
  3. What tools are most likely used: in most cases, customized tools.
  4. Support by Web technology: limited to information distribution. In certain cases, HTML forms may be prepared for uploading data.

- Bill clients and deploy the payment process
  1. Short description of the function: on the basis of resource utilization data, costs are distributed between users.
  2. Support of the function: high level of automation is possible.
  3. What tools are most likely used: billing packages.
  4. Support by Web technology: limited to bill distribution; standards are in the works for Web-based billing.

- Usage and outage collection
  1. Short description of the function: in order to support the use of SLAs, usage and outage data are collected. The results are considered for billing and reimbursement of users.
  2. Support of the function: collection can be highly automated.
  3. What tools are most likely used: monitors.
  4. Support by Web technology: good when Web servers are built into managed objects.

- Calculating rebates to clients
  1. Short description of the function: depending on usage and outage data, rebates are calculated.
  2. Support of the function: calculation can be automated.
  3. What tools are most likely used: individual, home-grown tools.
  4. Support by Web technology: none.

- Bill verification
  1. Short description of the function: incoming bills from vendors should be verified before payments.
  2. Support of the function: combination of manual and automated tasks.
  3. What tools are most likely used: few home-grown tools.
  4. Support by Web technology: limited to information distribution.

- Create and manage usage resource database
  1. Short description of the function: database would offer an excellent information source for rapid deployment of many billing functions.
  2. Support of the function: manual process for creating; some automation is possible for maintenance.
  3. What tools are most likely used: in most cases, home-grown tools.
  4. Support by Web technology: very limited; CGIs are required for conversion.

- Software license control
  1. Short description of the function: in order to determine the right number of licenses, the use of packages should be monitored carefully. The goal is to serve users, but not to pay too much for licenses.
  2. Support of the function: in most cases, manual activity.
  3. What tools are most likely used: home-grown tools.
  4. Support by Web technology: none.

- Create and deploy accounting management reports
  1. Short description of the function: in order to support various functions of the accounting department, reports about costs and billing should be created and deployed. The reports contain the breakdown of costs into hardware, software, infrastructure, communications, and people.
  2. Support of the function: creation is manual; deployment can be automated to a certain degree.
  3. What tools are most likely used: home-grown tools.
  4. Support by Web technology: altogether good for distributing reports.

3.14 SUMMARY

In summary, Web-based technology is useful for certain management processes and functions, but not for all of them. The optimal support of processes and functions requires a combination of many technologies. Table 3.1 shows the depth of support of management functions by Web technologies. This table gives a most likely scenario. Changes are expected in many areas, when Web technology is successfully implemented for many functions. If in doubt whether to use Web technology, this table may be of help.

The client contact point is heavily based on client care and support processes. Here, Web technology can help to simplify and unify the client interface.

Reactive and proactive fault management and fault monitoring show a mixed result. Web technology is very promising for accessing and presenting information. The opportunities for using the technology are limited in cases of in-depth technical work. Further penetration is expected in areas where the operator is working directly with various managed objects, assuming managed objects are supporting HTML forms.

The industry sees good opportunities with change management, in particular, where managed objects are directly accessed. In other change management areas, opportunities are somewhat limited.

Planning and design is not the real target of Web-based technology. Help is provided by the Web technology everywhere with information presentation and distribution needs. A little more penetration is expected with implementation and maintenance, in particular, where electronic documents are distributed.

Performance monitoring shows again a mixed picture. Support is expected for all functions. The depth of penetration is different, however: deeper for reporting, shallower for monitoring functions.

Security management, with the exception of reporting, is again not the real target of Web-based technology. Just the opposite is true with systems administration, accounting and billing. The Web technology receives entry chances everywhere, but the depth and early experiences are different.

In summary, a rapid statistical evaluation shows that 34.5% of the total of 84 functions gets high and very high, 19% good, 35.5% limited and 11% no support from Web-based technology.

TABLE 3.1
Support of Management Functions by Web Technology

Level of support, management processes and functions	Very high	High	Good	Low/very low	None
Client Contact Point					
• Receive problem report	x				
• Handling calls				x	
• Enquiry handling	x				
• Receive change requests	x				
• Handling orders	x				
• Make service requests			x		
• Opening and referring trouble tickets	x				
• Closing trouble tickets		x			
Reactive Fault Management (Operations Support, 2nd and 3rd Tier Support)					
• Problem isolation and determination by handling trouble tickets			x		
• Problem diagnosis				x	
• Taking corrective actions to resolve faults			x		
• Repair and replacement				x	
• Fault referring to 3rd parties				x	
• Backup and reconfiguration			x		
• Recovery				x	
• Logging events and corrective actions	x				
• Proactive problem management	x				
• Chronic trouble and fault identification				x	
• Periodic fault reporting	x				
• Vendor performance reporting		x			
• Establish thresholds and alarm rates	x				

TABLE 3.1 continued

Level of support, management processes and functions	Very high	High	Good	Low/very low	None
Proactive Fault Tracking					
• Tracking manually reported or monitored faults				x	
• Tracking the status and progress and escalating problems if necessary	x				
• Referral				x	
• Dispatch and coordinate technicians				x	
• Create and maintain a trouble ticketing database	x				
Changes Control					
• Managing moves, adds, and changes	x				
• Testing completed service orders (moves, adds, and changes)				x	
• Routing service orders				x	
• Maintaining the configuration database	x				
• Supervising the handling of changes			x		
• Equipment provisioning	x				
Planning and Design					
• Needs analysis				x	
• Projecting application load				x	
• Sizing resources				x	
• Authorizing and tracking changes			x		
• Raising purchase orders	x				
• Producing implementation plans			x		
• Establishing company standards					x
• Quality assurance					x
Implementation and Maintenance					
• Implementing change requests and work orders			x		
• Maintaining resources				x	
• Inspection				x	
• Maintaining the configuration database				x	
• Provisioning service		x			
Fault Monitoring					
• Proactively detecting problems			x		
• Opening trouble tickets		x			
• Referring trouble tickets		x			
Performance Monitoring					
• Identify monitoring needs; which data to be collected				x	
• Monitoring the systems and networks performance			x		
• Monitoring service level agreements			x		

Level of support, management processes and functions	Very high	High	Good	Low/very low	None
• Monitoring 3rd party and vendor performance			x		
• Maintaining a performance metric database				x	
• Optimization, modeling, and tuning		x			
• Reporting on usage statistics and trends to management and to users (availability, utilization, exception)	x				
• Performance thresholds and alarms	x				
• Performance analysis for managed objects				x	
• Define which data are accessible by customers				x	
Security Management					
• Threat analysis including proactive security measures				x	
• Administration (access control, passwords, partitioning, encryption, authentication)			x		
• Develop and deploy violation indicators					x
• Detection (evaluating services and solutions)				x	
• Recovery (evaluating services and solutions)				x	
• Create and maintain security logs				x	
• Security reporting	x				
• Ongoing security analysis and security plans				x	
• Protecting the management systems				x	
Systems Administration					
• Software version control				x	
• Software distribution		x			
• Systems management (upgrades, disk space management, job control)			x		
• Server administration			x		
• Administering the user definable tables (user profiles, router tables, security servers)				x	
• Local and remote configuring resources	x				
• Names and address management				x	
• Applications management		x			
Accounting and Billing					
• Asset management — create and manage the asset database				x	
• Costing services					x
• Receive and process accounting data				x	
• Billing clients and deploying the payment process				x	
• Usage and outage collection			x		
• Calculating rebates to clients					x
• Bill verification				x	
• Create and manage usage resource database				x	
• Software license control					x
• Create and deploy accounting management reports			x		

4 Web Basics and First Application

4.1 INTRODUCTION

This chapter explains a few basic terms that are required to understand how this technology may help to unify, simplify, and standardize systems and network management. The chapter offers a short introduction to Web basics. These basics are absolutely necessary to understand the applicability of this technology for managing systems and networks.

Internet service users today use a small but powerful set of applications, whether they are provided by an internet service provider (ISP), or in a corporate enterprise network (intranet). The most widely used internet applications are e-mail, World Wide Web (WWW) content browsing, and file transfer services. These services are provided by highly powered servers within the network, and the software implementing these applications (e.g., Web page hosting and mail forwarding). The definition of internet service management should include the functions required to configure these server applications to perform properly, and to monitor and measure their status and performance (e.g., application downtime, average response time, observed request/response rates, etc.). Figure 4.1 shows the typical layers.

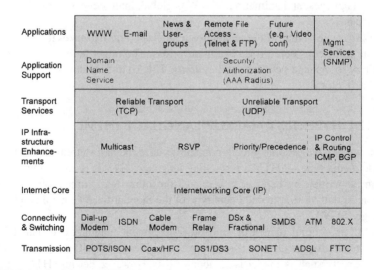

FIGURE 4.1 Positioning WWW in the layered communication architecture.

Application support services such as domain name service (DNS), which converts the widely seen host names like "www.company.com" into internet processing (IP) addresses, and authorization services provide common support across applications. These are also software applications running on network servers. Internet service management should also include the functions to configure, monitor, and measure their status and performance (e.g., DNS successful response rates, invalid request rates, wrong password attempt rates, etc.).

Transport services provide the option for reliable transport of information (error detection and retransmission), or simple unacknowledged transfer. These services may operate end-to-end (e.g., in the case of file transfers between an end user and a remote global internet server). In this case, the network does not get involved at the transport level. In other cases, when for instance the user is accessing a Web server internal to the network, the transport service — in this case TCP (transmission control protocol) — is provided by the network. As a result, internet service management should include the monitoring of TCP status and performance (e.g., number of active connections, rate of new connection requests, rate of dropped connections, etc.) at network end-points.

IP infrastructure enhancements provide differentiated service at the IP router level. These emerging capabilities of, and extensions to, the current IP features will become key to future applications on the internet, including RSVP (reserve bandwidth reservation protocol) providing reserved bandwidth to enable internet telephony and video conferencing. It is questionable whether these features should be considered as part of network or internet service management.

WWW is a graphical internet service to connect words, expressions, documents, pictures, languages, and animation. WWW is global, interactive, graphical, dynamic and associative.

WWW is one of many internet applications. Its popularity makes it an interesting candidate to be considered for use in many areas. The target here is the use of this technology to manage networks and systems. This chapter is devoted to the basics of this technology.

4.2 THE HYPERTEXT MARKUP LANGUAGE (HTML)

Web browsers have become widely popular because they all share understanding of a simple media type — HTML formatting language. HTML is easy to understand, and can be written by hand or generated from other text formats by translators. HTML is actually a simple document type of the Standardized Generalized Markup Language (SGML).

HTML is simpler than nroff and other document languages in that it is not programmable. As a result, the descriptive capabilities of HTML are limited to low-level constructs, such as emphasis or indented lists. However, because HTML parsers are rather forgiving of HTML coding violations, many Web pages contain coding mistakes used purposely to achieve particular layout effects on popular browsers.

HTML is optimized for display rather than printing or storage. HTML has no notion of pages, making formatted printing difficult.

A few examples will demonstrate the power and simplicity of this technology. Figure 4.2 shows a very simple inquiry system. It is a linear structure enabling the user to scroll down to more detailed information. There is only one linear link to the next page. This structure is very easy to maintain.

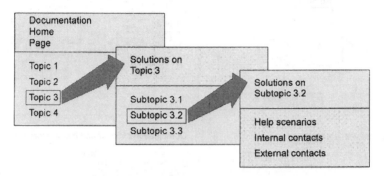

FIGURE 4.2 Example of a simple inquiry system.

The maintenance is somewhat more complicated with the inquiry system shown in Figure 4.3. The connections are not as well structured as in the previous example. Assuming that the content is well known to the user, the user can find the information more rapidly.

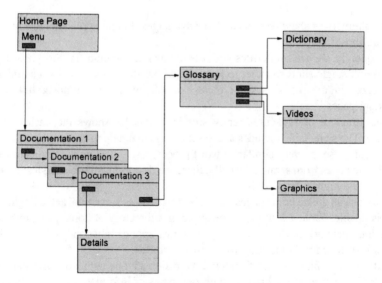

FIGURE 4.3 Example of a more complicated inquiry system.

There are a number of alternatives for organizing home pages and their links to each other. Figure 4.4 shows examples of Web structures that are hierarchical, linear,

extended linear, a combination of linear and hierarchical, and a typical Web structure.[13]

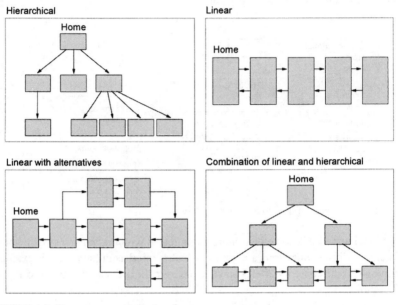

FIGURE 4.4 Home page organization form.

All alternatives show benefits and disadvantages. In real applications, combinations are most likely.

Frequently, we see similarities with the movie making industry. Storyboards are
used to link single shots together to form the whole story. It is easy to customize to
user needs. Figure 4.5 shows a typical example of a very complex linking of
individual pages.[13]

The structure of HTML is really simple. Table 4.1 shows the basics of the
structure. The same table includes a rich set of tags that help to bring in presentation
details, but those are very similar to word processors. Users are not enthusiastic to
write home pages from scratch. Usually, there are development tools requesting user
entries at the highest level, only.

But one can create home pages on one's own. It takes some time at the beginning,
but it is doable. Table 4.2 shows an example of a directory of home page addresses
for various network devices, operating systems, applications, and databases. This
page is just the entry home page for further inquiries.

After HTML files are transferred to a Web site, anyone with a browser can view
them. HTML provides the browser with two types of information:

- Mark-up information that controls the text display characteristics and
  specifies Web links to other documents.
- Content information consisting of the text, graphics, and sounds that the
  browser displays.

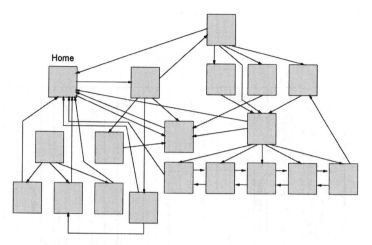

FIGURE 4.5 Storyboard example.

Documents on the Web can be interconnected by specifying links that allow the user to jump from one document to another. Links are visually displayed on the Web pages as pictures or underlined text.

4.3 WEB BASICS

The World Wide Web is an internet technology that is layered on top of basic TCP/IP services. The Web is in fact now the most popular internet application next to electronic mail. Like most successful internet technologies, the underlying central functionality of the Web is rather simple:

- File naming mechanism — the Universal Resource Locator (URL)
- A typed, stateless retrieval protocol — the HyperText Transfer Protocol (HTTP)
- A minimal formatting language with hypertext links — the HyperText Markup Language (HTML)

4.3.1 THE UNIVERSAL RESOURCE LOCATOR (URL)

The Universal Resource Locator (URL) is part of a larger family of file naming mechanisms called Universal Resource Names (URN) that are used to designate objects within the WWW. URLs name the physical location of an object; URNs name the identifier without regard to location. Uniform Resource Citations (URCs) describe properties of an object. At this time, only URLs are in widespread use.

URL is the home page address, such as: http://www.snmp.com/. A URL consists of three main parts:

1. A service identifier, such as http
2. A domain name, such as www.ups.com
3. A path name, such as www.ups.com/tracking

TABLE 4.1
Control Tags in HTML

<HTML>
<HEAD>
<TITLE> Web Tutorial
<HEAD>
<BODY>

</BODY>
</HTML>

HTML TAGS

Tag	Use
<OL>...</OL>	A ordered (numbered) list. Items in the list each begin with <LI>.
<UL>...</UL>	An unordered (bullet or otherwise marked) list. Items in the list each begin with <LI>.
<MENU>...</MENU>	A menu list (a list of short items or paragraphs).
<DIR>...</DIR>	A list of especially short (1-2 word) items. Directory lists are not often used in most HTML files.
<LI>	Individual list items in ordered, unordered, menu, or directory lists.
<DL>...</DL>	A glossary or definition list. Items in the list consist of pairs of elements: a term and its definition.
<DT>	The term part of an item in a glossary list.
<DD>	The definition part of an item in a glossary list.
<EM>...</EM>	Emphasized text.
<STRONG>...</STRONG>	Strongly emphasized text.
<CODE>...</CODE>	A code sample.
<KBD>...</KBD>	Text to be typed in by the user.
<VAR>...</VAR>	A variable name.
<SAMP>...</SAMP>	Sample text.
<DFN>...</DFN>	A definition, or a term about to be defined.
<CITE>...</CITE>	A citation.
<B>...</B>	Bold text.
<I>...</I>	Italic text.
<TT>...</TT>	Text in typewriter font (a monospaced font such as Courier).
<HR>	A horizontal rule line at the given position in the text.
 	A line break; start the next character on the next line (but do not create a new paragraph or list item.
<BLOCKQUOTE>	A quotation longer than a few words.
<ADDRESS>	A "signature" for each Web page; typically occurs near the bottom of each document and contains contact or copyright information

TABLE 4.2
HTML Program Example

```
File name:    Fault.html

<HTML>
<HEAD>
<TITLE>Fault Directory Home Page</TITLE>
</HEAD>
<BODY>
<H1>Comment: This directory serves to locate additional and in-depth information<BR>
on hardware and software components</H1>
<P>Your customer support center is located<BR>
1997 Excellence Drive<BR>
College Park, UT 12345<BR>
</P>
<HR>
<H2>Hardware Components</H2>
<OL>
<LI>Multiplexers <A HREF="http://www.nortel.com/">Nortel Home Page</A>
<LI>Routers<A HREF="http://www.cisco.com/">Cisco Home Page</A>
<LI>Switches<A HREF="http://www.bay.com/">Bay Networks Home Page</A>
</OL>
<HR>
<H2>Software Components</H2>
<OL>
<LI>Operating Systems<A HREF="http://www.novell.com/">Novell Home Page</A>
<LI>Databases<A HREF="http://www.oracle.com/">Oracle Home Page</A>
<LI>Applications<A HREF="http://www.sap.de/">SAP Home Page</A>
</OL>
<HR>
<ADDRESS>
Last updated4/17/1997<BR>
Web Master:Kornel Terplan<BR>
Copyright 1997<BR>
</ADDRESS>
</BODY>
</HTML>
```

The first part of the URL defines for the browser software which protocol to use to access the requested information. The most frequently used service identifiers are:

http://
ftp://
gopher://
telnet://

Like TCP/IP, SNMP, and other popular protocols, URLs were originally considered to be temporary solutions until more powerful mechanisms could be developed. The simplicity and intuitive nature of URLs no doubt contributed to their rapid acceptance.

4.3.2 THE HYPERTEXT TRANSFER PROTOCOL (HTTP)

HTTP is the protocol used for access and retrieval of Web pages. As such, it is widely viewed as the core Web protocol. It is an application-level protocol used almost exclusively with TCP. The client, typically a Web browser, asks the Web server for some information via a "get request". The information exchanged by HTTP can be any data type, and is not limited to HTML.

HTTP usage has already surpassed that of older internet access and retrieval mechanisms, such as file transfer protocol (FTP), telnet, and gopher. However, these older services often coexist with and are supported by HTTP-based Web browsers.

HTTP is a simple protocol; its clients and servers are said to be stateless because they do not have to remember anything beyond the transfer of a single document. However, HTTP's simplicity results in inefficiency. For a typical HTML page, the client first retrieves the HTML page itself, then discovers. There are potentially dozens of images contained within the page, and issues a separate HTTP request for each. Each HTTP request requires a separate TCP connection. HTTP pages are not real time. To retrieve new network status, the user must call up the Web page again. HTTP/Web is only good for monitoring one device at a time. This is the reason why Java is considered necessary for continuous monitoring.

To overcome this multistep process, typical Web browsers may open several TCP connections at once. However, this practice may overload slower-speed communication links. HTTP is a textual protocol — all headers are transferred as mostly ASCII text — simplifying the writing of simple browsers.

4.3.3 WEB BROWSERS

Web browsers function as clients, asking Web servers for information by using the HTTP protocol. Each request is handled by its own TCP connection and is independent of each previous request. As noted earlier, just the retrieval of one HTML page may require establishing several TCP connections. Consequently network managers need to be aware of the resource limitations of their internet or intranet infrastructure when rolling out Web applications, since Web usage is significantly resource consumptive. Examples of popular Web browsers include:

Mosaic
MS Internet Explorer
Netscape Navigator
HotJava
Webspace

These and other Web browsers are increasingly being used to support internally developed corporate Web applications ranging from company job postings and notices about benefit policy updates to supporting Lotus Notes-based groupware activities. Some of the common tasks which Netscape Navigator and Microsoft Internet Explorer support include:[20]

- Viewing documents created on a variety of platforms
- Creating and revising content
- Participating in threaded discussions and news groups
- Viewing and interacting with multimedia presentations
- Interfacing with existing legacy data, meaning non-HTML based data and applications
- Gaining seamless access to the internet

Browsers as we know them today are expected to be integrated into office application programs, such as Word and Excel.

4.3.4 WEB SERVERS

Web servers store, maintain, and distribute information to clients using the HTTP protocol. Web servers contain the Web pages that may be individually designed and maintained by the owners of the Web servers. There are numerous hardware and software platforms to support Web servers. Some examples include:

Connect Oneserver
Macintosh Web Server
MS Internet Information Server
Navisoft/AOL Naviserver
Netscape Commerce Server
Netware Web Server
Open Market Webserver
Secureware Secure Web Server
Spry Internet Office Web Server
Spyglass Server

Server software is needed to handle requests from browsers, to retrieve files and to run application programs. Web servers must usually handle large numbers of requests and must deal with difficult security issues. The performance of the Web server has a major impact on the overall performance of the intranet. Web servers are available for both UNIX and Windows NT from Microsoft, Netscape, and from others. It is expected that in the next 2 to 5 years stand-alone Web servers will be replaced by servers that are an integral part of the operating system. In addition, these Web servers will handle many tasks that require custom programming today, such as seamless connection to databases, video and audio processing, and document management.

4.4 MANAGING NETWORK AND SYSTEM COMPONENTS

The rapid deployment of the TCP/IP protocols has meant that most networking vendors feel compelled to support the TCP/IP open standards as well as proprietary protocols such as SNA, DECnet, IPX/SPX, NetBeui, and AppleTalk. As a result, the TCP/IP protocols today are the most widely used protocols on any computing platform with any operating system. Personal computers, minicomputers, mainframes, supercomputers, personal digital assistants, as well as dedicated network devices such as routers, hubs, switches, gateways, and printers all support the TCP/IP protocol suite.

One of the challenges facing a networking vendor is management of the networked device. Besides providing the device functions such as routing or printing, a vendor has to provide a method of managing the device. To date, there have been a number of approaches. The first approach used mostly in the early days of networked devices is to provide support for a "dumb" terminal such as a DEC VT100 or IBM 3270 to attach to the device through a dedicated serial port. This approach minimizes development expense, in that standard terminals or PC-based terminal emulators are used for the management application. In general, however, these text-oriented displays have not been as well received as graphical user interfaces.

This led to the second approach, which is to develop a proprietary management application. This approach generally leads to the most efficient management of the device with the strongest support for the user, since the vendor has complete control of the management application. One of the problems with this approach is the cost of development and quality assurance, especially if multiple platforms are supported. An additional problem is that of ongoing maintenance. As client computing platforms change, the networking vendor must not only develop and maintain their product capabilities, but they must also make sure their management applications continue to work.

The third approach to device management has been the use of SNMP. This protocol is part of the TCP/IP family and has been widely adopted by device manufacturers. While SNMP is heavily used in the world's largest corporations, it has not received as warm a welcome in medium-sized and small companies. One of the factors limiting appeal is the cost of dedicated SNMP management consoles. Another problem with the SNMP approach is that the presentation of the management information is often not as user-friendly as a vendor would like.

A fourth approach to device management is now being implemented by some leading edge manufacturers. Recognizing the growth of the intranet with its widespread deployment of Web browsers, these vendors have seen that the reasons for intranet growth provide an attractive solution to network management, also. By incorporating Web servers into their products, these vendors have given their customers an intuitive, user-friendly way to manage their devices using open protocols. This approach has all the benefits of the older dumb terminal approach for minimizing development costs, but provides a consistent cross-platform graphical user interface for an enhanced user experience. In addition, the Web protocols provide the ability for a vendor's customer to link back to the vendor's Web site for new product information, product documentation or customer support. These vendors and others believe that Web protocols represent a good approach to today's network management since they provide enhanced device management and reduced vendor costs.

For the future, there are additional possibilities. Using Web protocols, it will be possible to enhance the customer support process by building pages that automatically gather device configuration information when the customer fills out a trouble report. Using Java applets delivered from a built-in Web server, a device will be able to display dynamic graphs of device performance, or sound audio alarms. As the Web protocols mature and become even more widely deployed, these vendors predict they will be able to increase customer satisfaction and product sales by allowing their customers to manage their devices with Web browsers.

4.5 STANDARDS FOR WEBIFICATION

In July 1996, five major vendors announced an initiative to define *de facto* standards for Web-based Enterprise Management (WBEM). This effort, spearheaded by Microsoft, Compaq, Cisco, BMC, and Intel, was publicly endorsed by over 50 other vendors, as well. The initial announcement called for defining the following specifications:

- HyperMedia Management Schema (HMMS): an extensible data description used to represent the managed environment that was to be further defined by the Desktop Management Task Force (DMTF).
- HyperMedia Object Manager (HMOM): a data model consolidating management data from different sources; a C++ reference implementation and specification, defined by Microsoft and Compaq, to be placed in the public domain.
- HyperMedia Management Protocol (HMMP): a communication protocol embodying HMMS, running over HTTP and with interfaces to SNMP and DMI.

SunSoft has also announced a programming environment for developing Web-based network and systems management software. This environment, called Solstice Workshop, consists of a JavaManagement API, (JMAPI), a small footprint database, and a Java programming environment. Solstice Workshop's big drawing card is its extensibility and the popularity of Java's "write once run anywhere" appeal. JMAPI requires Java, whereas HMMP/HMMS/HMOM specifies HTML/HTTP, although Java is not specifically excluded. Java is a new programming language that closely resembles C++. Java is designed for creating animated Web sites. Java can be used to create small application programs, called applets, which browsers download and execute.

Prior to these announcements, three developers from Hewlett Packard produced an internet draft proposal proposing use of port 280 for exchanging HTTP management data. This same internet draft describes a very lightweight HTTP Manageable MIB as well as a tunneling facility for SNMP over HTTP.

Among these three competing efforts, the WBEM is certainly the broadest in scope, addressing not only protocol issues, but also data modeling and extensible data description as well. While JMAPI includes object class definitions, it does not go as far as data description.

The initial euphoria over WBEM and JMAPI is starting to wear off, and it is time for doing the hard work of writing specifications and, more importantly, building products. Customer demand will push Web-based management to its limits, but disillusion is sure to set in if a lack of progress becomes obvious on the standards front. However, there are several emerging products that have been developed with an eye for supporting current and future standards, that bring to market a practical approach to take advantage of Web-based management.

4.6 ACTUAL STATUS OF USING TECHNOLOGY

Independent of the standards, the early implementations have concentrated on the following areas:

- Providing actual status information for systems and network components on a Web page to be accessed by authorized clients.
- Providing actual information, e.g., reports on behalf of the management platform to distribute (to be pulled!) by management clients.

In the first case, Web software is directly put into devices, such as routers, bridges, multiplexors, and hubs. Managers can use off-the-shelf Web browsers to monitor and control individual devices remotely. This offering serves as a useful addition to existing management platforms, particularly those based on SNMP. These early implementations by a couple of vendors show the following benefits:

- Hardware and software costs are minimal. Vendors often include Web utilities in the base price of their products. For access, all managers need is a standard-issue PC running any available Web browser — even the freebies available on the internet.
- Remote access offering managers location flexibility. They do not need to work from special consoles to download Web-stored data. Any dial-up connection to the internet will suffice.
- Management platform expertise is optional. Web utilities present data in easy-to-read home pages; no need to negotiate complex management commands.

But there are drawbacks, as well. The most important are:

- Functions are limited. Although some products let net managers reconfigure devices from remote sites, Web utilities cannot match conventional platforms like SNMP for the depth and detail of management information. Also, some Web-based products are proprietary.
- Real-time reporting is not an option. Today's products require managers to download data. They do not deliver information as it is collected.
- Security can be a problem. Unless Web utilities are placed behind firewalls on internal networks, they are prone to invasion by anyone with a Web browser.

In the second case, the report generator can co-reside with a Web server. Managers can call up the Web server and get statistical information about faults and performance. The only requirement is to convert from the report generator into a format that can be read by Web servers using the graphics interchange format (GIF) standard defined in HTML. In this case, the managers have to build their own Web page interface using HTML text editors before they can read the reports.

With Web-based tools, data are stored in a familiar format and retrieved using a straightforward interface — the Web browser. In contrast, conventional platforms usually require a high degree of familiarity with the inner workings of the management system. With SNMP, for instance, network troubleshooters need a thorough understanding of the agents, protocols, and console commands used to extract information from the system.

The simplicity of Web-based management tools translates directly to lower costs. Because Web-based products work with client and server software that has already been developed, vendors do not have to spend a lot on research and development. That means they can turn out Web-based utilities faster and, more importantly, for less. Companies building their own Web-based management platforms can also keep hardware and software costs low. Commercial Web server software costs as little as $200. Developers can put their Web utilities on off-the-shelf PCs. Depending on the application, a Web-based management tool could run on a 486 PC with 8 MBytes of RAM, a configuration that costs about $1,200.

Of course, the cost of building a Web application could add considerably to the overall cost of home-grown Web-based management. Developers need to be proficient in Web protocols like HTML and HTTP. They also need to be fluent in device management programming.

Web-based tools are less expensive compared with SNMP-products. Internetworking vendors typically bundle an SNMP agent in their products for free, but then companies usually have to invest up to $10,000 or more for an SNMP management console. Then they have to buy vendor-specific management applications to run on the platform. One such management application, CiscoWorks from Cisco, costs around $10,000. When remote management is factored in things get even more expensive. The most efficient way to manage remote equipment is via RMON1 or RMON2. These agents cost about $1,000 per remote LAN segment.

The ability of Web-based products to deliver remote management can help cut management costs on two levels. First, Web tools can help reduce the need for network technicians to be deployed to remote sites. Second, because Web management packages work with intuitive browsers, rather than comparatively cryptic SNMP consoles, they can help cut the cost of staff training.

For all their usefulness, Web-based management systems do have some distinct limitations. While Web-based tools can be used to enable and disable device operations and generate reports that give basic topological statistics, they cannot supply more granular details about network or systems activity, such as when nodes are communicating with each other and what types of protocols are being used. For those features, network managers still need a full-blown platform like any of the SNMP products.

Security of Web-based tools is another key concern. Unlike SNMP consoles, which reside on private networks, Web management tools can be set up to be accessed from anywhere on the internet. Theoretically, anyone with access to the internet has the ability to call up a site's manager page.

To prevent unauthorized access, vendors have equipped their offerings with password protection. Usually, two levels are offered, including authentication. With the basic level of security, the manager simply dials in from a remote PC and sends a password to the IP router. This is risky because the password is sent in clear, non-encrypted text, which can be intercepted by eavesdropping devices. The second level of security encrypts the password. It is altogether a very promising basis for simplifying systems and network management. In particular, this new technology would integrate many functions from both areas. Thus, education and training for the managing teams can be unified and standardized.

4.7   ANALYZING WEB TRAFFIC

Observations in the transmission channel give enough information about the communication. Logs provide all the necessary information for analyzers. Each user inquiry contains the following information that may be used for further analysis:

- Internet address of the sender
- Date and local time
- Type of inquiry
    Get
    Head
    Link
    Post
    Put
    Unlink
    Textsearch
- Identification of documents
- Versions number of the HTTP protocol
- Results of the dialog
- Length of the required document

Most of the tools referenced in subsequent chapters use this basic information.

4.8   DYNAMIC HTML

HTML has serious limitations. HTML does not provide the flexibility Web publishers need to create home pages. HTML pages are static, and dynamic updates are not really supported. Both attributes, flexibility and dynamics, are absolutely necessary when Web technology is to be successfully implemented for network and systems management. Most technologies used to add interactivity to pages by using server-based CGI programs, Java applets, browser plug-ins, ActiveX controls and scripting languages, which had little to do with HTML. But now with dynamic HTML (DHTML), new client-side technologies, combined with scripting languages like JavaScript, may solve many of the problems with HTML.

DHTML extends the current set of HTML elements, and a few other elements such as style sheet properties, by allowing them to be accessed and modified by scripting languages. Dynamic features, making pages come alive with movement and interactivity, can be added by exposing tags to scripts written in a language like JavaScript or VBScript.[16]

The tags are accessed through the document object model (DOM). The DOM describes each document as a collection of individual objects, such as images, paragraphs, and forms down to individual characters. The DOM of DHTML can be complex, but does not always require a lot of work.[16] Developers may use the object model to find an image on a page and replace it with another when a user rolls a cursor over it. Such rollovers, or animated buttons, are common. DHTML also can animate a page by moving objects around, build an expanding three structure to navigate a site or create a complex application like a database front end.

The common denominator is expected to be the DOM. DOM is the basis for DHTML. It is a platform- and language-neutral interface that will allow programs and scripts to dynamically access and update the content, structure, and style of documents.

DOM has been accepted by both of the leading suppliers, Microsoft and Netscape. Their DOM implementation is very similar, differences are coming with other features, like positioning, dynamic fonts, and multimedia controls, as shown in Table 4.3.

Beyond the extras like dynamic fonts and multimedia controls, the core ideas of Netscape and Microsoft are similar. With support for CSS (cascading style sheet) and absolute positioning, advanced layout can be made to work under each browser. With DHTML and absolute positioning, it is possible to create sophisticated multi-media applications that can avoid frequent dialogs with the Web server. But building DHTML-based pages is still programming. Including dynamic elements in a page is a major step away from a static page paradigm and into the idea of Web pages as programs.

The DOM sets out the methods by which Web developers can access elements of HTML and XML (Extensible Markup Language) documents to manipulate page elements and create dynamic effects, and serves as the key enabling technology for dynamic HTML. There are three principal areas of XML applications:

- High-end publishing, which views XML and SGML (Standard General-ized Markup Language) as highly structured document language.
- Use of the extensible nature of XML by Web developers to create application specific markup tags.
- Use of XML as a data exchange format for distributed Web applications.

With XML and DHTML, it is relatively easy to share the user interface and information on the Web.

TABLE 4.3
DHTML Approaches by Microsoft and Netscape

Netscape	Microsoft
Document object model	Document object model
Many HTML objects scriptable	All HTML objects scriptable
Event capturing	Event bubbling
Some elements modifiable after page load	All elements and style modifiable after page load
Page text not modifiable — only replaceable after page load	Text fully modifiable after page load
Absolute positioning	Absolute positioning
CSS positioning	CSS positioning
Layers	
Dynamic fonts	Dynamic fonts
TrueDoc	Open type
Multimedia controls	Multimedia plug-ins
LiveAudio	Transitions, filters, and animation
LiveVideo	
	Data binding
	TDC, remote data services

4.9   EXTENSIBLE MARKUP LANGUAGE (XML)

XML can help to eliminate the major limitations of HTML, with features that include Web searches, inter-industry communication, and enabling a new form of distributed Web-based application. But XML does not solve everything, and it does not make HTML obsolete.

Both HTML and XML are subsets of SGML, but XML can define HTML as a document type definition (DTD) of its own. They meet again only with regards to DHTML, in which both require the use of DOM. Figure 4.6 shows the relationship of HTML and XML.[17]

While the core syntax of XML is fairly well defined, there are many other areas that need addressing. XML provides no presentation services. Another technology must be deployed to present XML data within a Web browser. Eventual use of a style sheet language like CSS, or the Extensible Style Language (XSL) seems likely. Many users implement HTML as the presentation language for XML. To support presentation, Java applets may be downloaded to present even complex data forms. XML mirrors SGML in that it lacks linking capabilities. In order to eliminate this weakness, the Extensible Linking Language (XLL) is added to XML. In addition, in order to support scripting capabilities, there is also a need to connect XML with DOM.

Without presentation, scripting, and linking, XML is limited to just being a data format. However, there are applications defined as vertical for supporting specific industries or horizontal for generic use. Microsoft has defined CDF (Channel Def-

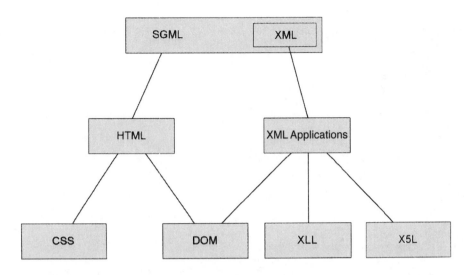

FiGURE 4.6 The relationship of HTML and XML.

inition Format) to push content to selected targets. Open Software Description (OSD) has been defined in XML to support software installation procedures. Synchronized Multimedia Integration Language (SMIL) is used to define multimedia presentations for Web delivery. Also meta languages, such as Resource Definition Framework (RDF), will be defined in the future.

The challenges facing XML are significant. The specifications of associated technologies such as style sheets and linking are not yet complete. XML style sheets which are based on DSSSL (Document Style and Semantics Specification Language) will most likely compete against CSS. The linking model of XML is more advanced than HTML, but it is incomplete and too complex. The interaction between XML and DOM needs further clarification.

Industry analysts assume that XML will be used together with HTML. HTML is widely used, and getting more powerful with CSS and DOM. XML may add formality and extensibility. Formality allows for guaranteed structure, exchange and machine readability, which is difficult though not impossible with HTML. Extensibility means the opportunity to create specialized languages for specific applications. Such languages may have significant power within particular intranets or in the area of managing networks and systems.

4.10 SUMMARY

HTML and its extensions may become the common denominator of future management applications. In order to go beyond presentation and information distribution, dynamic home page updates are absolutely necessary. Under XLM, with additional language units, requirements for flexibility and dynamics can be met.

5 Directions of Web-Based Management Standards

5.1 INTRODUCTION

If there are delays in implementing standards, or when there is a disagreement among standards bodies, vendors and users go ahead on their own. If this happens, multiple directions may be represented that may or may not comply with future standards. The losers are the users who cannot convert their investments into the standardized solutions.

In order to offer a more complete platform, the new standards, individually or in combination, should be implemented. The leading providers of management platforms, such as Cabletron, Computer Associates, IBM/Tivoli, Hewlett-Packard, Microsoft, and Sun do not wait for complete standards, but equip their products with Web-extensions. Those extensions are considered tactical solutions. They may give way to more stable standards, such as CIM (Common Information Model), presently in the works.

This chapter addresses the three principal directions, IETF, Java, and WBEM, in some depth. Also third-party middleware solutions are discussed. They can be used stand-alone or in combination with existing management platforms.

5.2 WEB-BASED MANAGEMENT FROM IETF

Web-based management is the application of World Wide Web (WWW) tools for the management of systems and networks. This includes using hypertext transfer protocol (HTTP) servers and browsers for providing static, dynamic, and interactive content of management information. An HTTP server acting in a management role can provide information in a variety of forms, including HyperText Markup Language (HTML), graphics, executable code and binary encoded information. Together, this capability allows HTTP to function as a powerful protocol for the management of systems and networks. For HTTP servers acting in a management role, the HTTP server may also be providing non-management content. It is therefore necessary to provide a mechanism for a WWW browser or network management application to have direct access to the management information.

HTTP is not meant to replace simple network management protocol (SNMP). HTTP is expected to work together with SNMP. This combination can provide many benefits, including ease of use, low client-side installation needs, and security. SNMP is required for the instrumentation of systems and networks.

The standardized TCP port for HTTP is port 80. An HTTP server listening on this port may provide content spanning a wide information base, including non-management related content. For management usage, this requires that the management content be intermixed with non-management content. A WWW browser or network management application must therefore have Java knowledge or the ability to determine where the management content resides on an HTTP server. A well-known HTTP management TCP port solves this problem by allowing only management content through the HTTP management interface. This allows a browser or network management application to easily use or discover an HTTP server acting in a management role. The proposed HTTP management TCP port is port 280 to be used for management. In cases where this port is not available, port 80 may be used. An alternative to a standardized HTTP management port, a standardized Universal Request Indicator (URI), was considered. Although this mechanism could work, it was decided that the problem of attempting to standardize on a character sequence would prove to be too difficult.

An HTTP server operating in a management mode on port 280 may also be using port 80 for non-management content. This allows for the clean separation of management and non-management content. A TCP port 280 interface should only supply management content. An HTTP server that does not utilize TCP port 280 for management content may intermix management and non-management content on port 80. In this case, a browser or network management application must determine the HTTP management capability through other means, e.g., via the HTTP Manageable MIB (management information base).

An SNMP agent in operation with an HTTP server allows management information to be accessed using either the SNMP protocol or using HTTP. In order to determine if an SNMP agent also supports HTTP, an SNMP MIB is utilized. The HTTP Manageable MIB provides SNMP objects that advertise an agent's HTTP capabilities. This allows a network management application using SNMP to query the HTTP Manageable MIB to determine its HTTP management capabilities and interfaces. The presence of this MIB in an agent implies that an HTTP server is operational in a management context. In order to determine the exact interface for HTTP access, the HTTP Manageable MIB provides an MIB object, "httpMgDefaultURL". This object represents the complete Universal Request Locator (URL) for management access to the agent via HTTP. The value of this URL will reflect port 280 usage when applicable.

A second MIB object defines an agent's capability to perform SNMP over HTTP. The "httpMgSNMPEnabled" object represents a truth value indicating if the HTTP server can perform SNMP over HTTP. If set true, the HTTP server supports the SNMP over HTTP tunneling protocol.

5.3 JAVA MANAGEMENT API FROM SUNSOFT

The Java computing environment provides the base capabilities to deliver solutions across a number of operating systems and network protocols. To fully exploit the power of the Java computing environment for solving management problems, Sun has developed extensions to the Java base classes that specifically address management problems. These classes are collectively known as the *Java Management API* (JMAPI).

5.3.1 JAVA MANAGEMENT API (JMAPI)

The Java Management API from SunSoft is a rich set of extensible objects and methods for the development of seamless system and network service management solutions for heterogeneous networks. This core set of application programming interfaces (API) can be used across a diverse array of computing environments involving numerous operating systems, architectures, and network protocols, enabling the development of low-maintenance, heterogeneous software from a single source.

The Java Management API of Solstice WorkShop is written purely in Java and is portable to any Java-enabled platform. Users can write their own Java classes once, and then run it on the operating system of their choice — Solaris, Windows NT, Windows 95, OS/2 — anywhere Java can run, the software can run also.

The software investment in SNMP and other network management protocols is protected. The Java Management API is protocol-independent and works with native libraries to access event monitoring and activity reporting data provided by standard system and network management protocols.

An easy-to-use, low-cost, Open Database Connectivity (ODBC)/Java Database Connectivity (JDBC)-compliant relational database is provided with Solstice Work-Shop to store network and system management information. The database runs in the SunSoft Solaris or higher operating environment for Sparc, and a version for the Windows NT environment is also available. Having true database capabilities available for application development solves many traditional system management problems. The benefits of the database include:

- Centralization — a single, logical view of all administration configuration information is centrally maintained.
- Performance and distributed optimization — the database and infrastructure can encapsulate the caching and replication of data.
- Data security — the database can be a secure name space for storing authorization information.
- Transaction management and integrated concurrency control — introducing transaction management and concurrency control greatly heightens the reliability and consistency of the overall system.
- Communication structure for a distributed commit protocol - to maintain consistency in a distributed environment, transactions must have the properties of atomicity, consistency, insulation, and durability. Concurrency control and distributed commit protocols are necessary to implement these properties.
- Localized failures — if a node fails or the administration data becomes inaccessible at one node, the other nodes in the network can continue to operate through copies found in the name services.
- Extensibility — the data can be extended beyond traditional system administration data.

Java WorkShop includes capabilities to visually assemble and publish portable Java-based system and network administration applications:

- A Web-centric development tool that has an intelligent graphical user interface.
- An integrated tool set that works together to speed up development.
- Publication tools for organizing Java projects and publishing them on the internet.
- Multiplatform support for developing and delivering Java projects on popular computing environments. Java WorkShop combines true Java with proven, easy-to-use Web-centric development tools for developing individual projects in popular operating environments.

5.3.1.1   Java Management API Features

The Java Management API provides the user interface guidelines, Java classes, and specifications for developing seamless integrated system and network service management applications. It includes the following features:

- Java Management API User Interface Style Guide — the style guide interaction model is constructed to address the configuration and troubleshooting tasks of administrators in networking environments. The basic user interface metaphor is a page: the majority of the user's interaction is with a page presented in a Web browser, and navigation is primarily conducted in a page-to-page manner. The pages can be displayed on and interacted with, any Java-enabled Web browser.
- Admin View Module — this module is an extension of the Java Abstract Window Toolkit that is specially designed for developing user interfaces for distributed management applications. The Admin View Module offers a base set of user interface components, such as tool bars and state buttons, and a set of power components, including a help subsystem, hierarchy browser, property book, and configuration viewer.
- Base Object Interfaces — the base object interfaces support constructing objects that represent distributed resources and services that comprise the enterprise computing environment. These interfaces allow developers to define abstractions that contain distributed attributes and methods and persistent attributes.
- Managed Container Interfaces — these interfaces allow management applications to perform actions on a single group of managed objects, instead of each instance. This permits management applications to scale upwards by allowing for multiple instances to be treated as one.
- Managed Notification Interfaces — these provide the basic foundation from which more complex event management services can be easily built. Asynchronous event notification between managed objects or management applications is supported.

- Managed Data Interfaces — these support mapping classes and instances of base objects to a relational database. Managed data interfaces are implemented on the appropriate subset of the Java Database Connectivity (JDBC) specification and support a number of commercially available relational database engines.
- Managed Protocol Interfaces — the classes implemented by the managed protocol interfaces provide the infrastructure to perform distributed operations securely. These interfaces are built on existing Java interfaces for both security and distribution.
- SNMP Interfaces — the SNMP interfaces extend the managed protocol interfaces to allow extensions of the base objects to contain information obtained from existing SNMP agents. SNMP is the most prevalent management protocol — the Java Management API is immediately useful by supporting SNMP agents.
- Managed Framework Interfaces — the classes implemented by managed framework interfaces provide the mechanism to perform distributed operations securely. These interfaces will be built on existing Java interfaces for both security and distribution as they become available.
- Applet Integration Interfaces — these interfaces allow software developers to seamlessly integrate their Java applets into the Java Management API. Different levels of integration are available, including registered applets, registered management pages, and registered links.

The Java Management API is a collection of Java classes that allow developers to more easily build tools to provide integrated management solutions by taking advantage of the Java computing environment. By combining Java and the Java Management API, developers wanting to develop integrated management solutions gain the benefits described below.

The Java Management API further enhances the platform independence provided by Java, by allowing secure downloading of libraries that implement native methods.

Integration is the key — the classes provided by the Java Management API allow for easy integration from the user interface components to the object definitions. By registering the pages and object definitions, navigation throughout the management information space is seamless.

Eliminates agent versioning and distribution problems — management in the enterprise environment is inherently distributed. This requires administrators to perform operations on resources that are located throughout the network. All distributed management products refer to the software component that implements these remote operations as agents. Agents are very specific to the version of software or hardware for which they provide the management interface, which creates a problem. If a new capability is added, an agent typically has to be replaced. Unfortunately, agents suffer from the software distribution problems that are prevalent in the enterprise environment. The Java Management API solves the agent versioning and distribution problem by securely downloading the appropriate classes and native libraries on demand. It also ensures the correct version of classes and libraries are downloaded for a particular management operation. Clients download the software from a central location, avoiding the agent distribution problem.

A model for representing distributed resources — the resources that must be managed in the enterprise environment are distributed across a number of systems. For example, a host has configuration information stored in DNS (domain name service), connectivity information stored in network services, and the operating system running on that host provides interfaces to query the active state of the host. Management application developers think about managing the host resource, not how the resource is implemented. Java Management API classes provide the ability for developers to produce managed object abstractions that are useful for describing managed resources, without having application developers worry about the implementation of those abstractions.

Secure, distributed management operations — Java Management API allows for secure, distributed management operations. It safeguards remote management operations from unauthorized accessing and spoofing by ensuring only trusted Java code runs on a client. Java Management API authorizes and authenticates all remote invocations of Java classes and native methods.

Protocol independence — using the downloading capabilities of Java, it is possible to develop an intelligent agent to accept different legacy protocols, like SNMP, and still take advantage of the Java Management API. This allows existing resources that use standard or priority protocols the ability to start using the Java Management API immediately.

Tailored for distributed system, network, and service management applications — the Java Management API not only provides useful custom UI components, but these are specially designed for distributed system, network, and service management applications.

Promotes code reusability — provided custom user interfaces and service components offer templates for development methods and promote code reusability.

Provides a model for representing distributed resources — the Java classes provided enables developers to think about managing networked resources rather than how those resources are implemented.

Promotes application consistency and integration — the Java Management API provides consistency to application developers in the areas of style, interface, and functionality, as well as specifying a high degree of integration and a common look and feel across distributed applications.

In order for JMAPI to be successful the following goals must be fulfilled.

- Leverage existing technologies. The JMAPI cannot implement all of the necessary functionality from scratch. Rather the user must rely on other existing technologies for the basis of implementation.
- Minimize dependencies. The users must attempt to eliminate dependencies on technologies that are not considered commodities.
- Bridge the reality of today with the future. A large installed base of nonintegrated management applications exist today. Migration issues must be addressed in order to ensure the future implementation of integrated applications.

5.3.2 ARCHITECTURE OVERVIEW

The architecture builds on existing technologies, which minimizes the amount of infrastructure that must be implemented. This strategy also allows focus on solving the customer's distributed system management problems.

It is crucial that the architecture scales to a number of different environments. It does this in two ways. First, the component that allows a machine to be managed is small. Agent objects for management operations are securely downloaded and executed. This minimizes the distribution and versioning problem for management operations and easily allows for modification and extension of the management operations. Second, the Java Virtual Machine resides on the key platforms that need to be managed. At the highest level, the architecture consists of the following components:

Browser user interface — the browser user interface is the mechanism from which an administrator issues management operations. These operations may be invoked either interactively through a web browser or stand-alone application. A stand-alone application can have either a graphic or command-line user interface style.

Admin runtime module — the admin runtime module is the mechanism that provides active instantiated management objects to applications. It includes the agent object interfaces, notification interfaces, and managed data interfaces. Within the JDBC-compliant managed data interfaces, security and data access provisions exist to ensure data security. For example, the database can perform data authorization and authentication.

Appliances — these are simply the networked devices to be managed. The strategy is to push management close to managed devices with dynamic downloading of agents. A Java terminal can be thought of as an Appliance as well as a DNS server. Though these machines perform radically different functions, they are managed through the admin runtime module and are required to have "agent" software installed.

Figure 5.1 shows a configuration that has two admin runtime modules. Note that these admin runtime modules communicate with the browser user interface and the appliances. The admin view module directly contacts the admin runtime module it wishes to have perform the management operation. Figure 5.1 also shows that a number of different types of networked devices can be appliances. For example, a name service server can be thought of as an appliance. The services it provides may be completely controlled by the admin runtime module. Personal computers can also be managed directly from the admin runtime module. Figure 5.1 shows a configuration that has one browser user interface and two admin runtime modules.

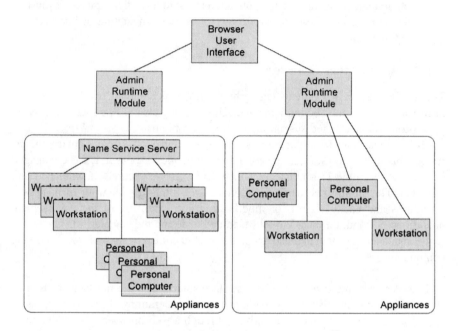

FIGURE 5.1 High-level architectural components.

Figure 5.2 shows a configuration of the three primary components (BUI, AVM, and appliance) that illustrates the distributed nature of JMAPI and is the most common configuration. The architecture of JMAPI does not prevent any combination of these components from residing on a single computer.

The components use the Remote Method Invocation (RMI) system for communication across machine boundaries. The components require that computations running in different address spaces, potentially on different hosts, be able to communicate. For a basic communication mechanism, the Java language supports sockets, which are flexible and sufficient for general communication. However, sockets require the client and server to engage in applications-level protocols to encode and decode messages for exchange, and the design of such protocols is cumbersome and can be error-prone.

The Java remote method invocation system has been specifically designed to operate in the Java environment. The Java language RMI system assumes the homogeneous environment of the Java Virtual Machine, and the system can therefore follow the Java object model whenever possible. Though not shown on Figure 5.2 the Java runtime system must be present in every component.

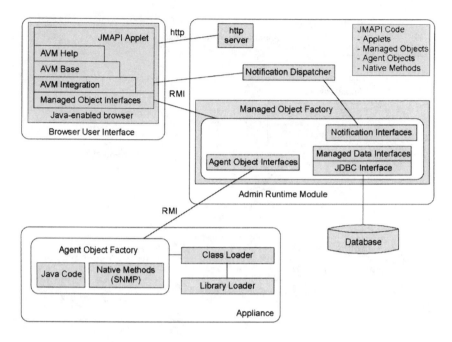

FIGURE 5.2 Component decomposition.

5.3.2.1 Browser User Interface

The BUI is the component where the system administrator performs tasks across various resources. The BUI consists of the following elements.

Admin view module (AVM)

The AVM is comprised of key client side classes for developers of JMAPI-based applets. The primary role of these classes is to provide user interface and application-level functionality. The AVM is built completely on top of Java's Abstract Window Toolkit (AWT). By taking this approach the AVM is completely portable and window system independent. Figure 5.3 shows the overall architecture of the AVM and how it is used to construct a JMAPI-based applet.

The AVM classes are broken into three packages: AVM help, AVM base, and AVM integration. This allows a developer to best decide what level of functionality and integration to introduce into an applet.

The primary objective of AVM help is to provide a general purpose help environment. General purpose means it is intended that JMAPI application developers and independent software vendors (ISVs) can use the help system in a range of ways to provide application online help. As an example, applications that comply with JMAPI standards for conformity could have help files that integrate seamlessly into one common help system shared by multiple applications. This means that multiple applications would share one common index, glossary, table of contents/navigator, and so on. Applications that do not comply with JMAPI standards for conformity

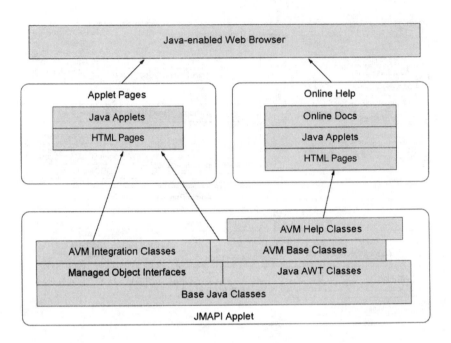

FIGURE 5.3 Admin view module architecture.

could have help files activated and displayed within AVM help, but those help files are not integrated into one common help information space. Help for a nonconforming application simply has use of the help system, but does not offer benefits of integration such as consistency and related ease of use.

In keeping with the goal of a general-purpose help system, AVM help does not require any proprietary tools, scripts, or programs to produce or generate help files. While tools may come along to facilitate authoring of AVM help, they are not required. The only requirement is that help files be in HTML format and include a set of JMAPI help authoring tags that can be parsed during installation time to produce an index, glossary, and table of contents/navigator.

The AVM Help includes the following:

- TOC/Navigator — displays a hierarchy of topics available in application help.
- Doc Generator — the `jmapidoc` program is available for generating index, glossary, or TOC/Navigator files for an application. This doc generator can also be used by help authors to prototype and test their work.
- Standard Help Files — these are help files that application developers and ISVs can pass to their end users. These primarily include information such as Help on AVM help, and Help on basic user interface components.
- Help Templates — these are HTML template files, including AVM help keywords and examples of their use.

The AVM help classes depend only on the AVM base classes, the Java Abstract Window Toolkit (AWT) and the Java base classes. This allows AVM help to be used without any dependencies on the underlying managed objects.

The AVM base classes are an extension of Java's AWT that are specifically designed for developers creating integrated management solutions. These classes are used to implement a user model that builds on the Web browser hypertext style of navigation. The links used in navigation are between the services and resources that comprise the enterprise computing environment.

The AVM base is further divided into three packages that reflect common functionality. The base user interface classes naturally extend the AWT to provide a set of components necessary to build a rich user interface. These interfaces define the following classes:

- Image button
- Scrolling windows and panels
- Toolbar
- Image canvas
- Convenience dialogs
- Busy tool

The power user interface classes enable developers to use more graphic and eloquent components in constructing their solutions. These interfaces define the following classes:

- Table
- Hierarchy browser
- Charts and meters

The management user interface classes support the user interface style and interaction model described in the Java Management API User Interface Style Guide. These interfaces define the following classes:

- Property book
- Page header
- Link label
- View configuration

The AVM base classes depend only on the Java AWT and the Java base classes.

The primary role of the AVM Integration classes is to provide integration between the AVM base classes and the managed object interfaces. By using these classes, an application developer constructs a management solution that is tightly integrated with all other JMAPI-based solutions. Probably, the most effective usage of these classes is to generate property books directly from a managed object.

The AVM integration classes also allow for management applications to register their components, so when new solutions are provided, the integrity of the Web of management information can be maintained. These interfaces provide the following functionality:

- Register/unregister management applets
- Register/unregister management pages
- Register/unregister management links
- Register/unregister new extensions to the managed object interfaces. This includes the Java class definitions, the implementation of the discover interfaces, and if necessary, default property books and class browsers. If the object simply extends existing object types, links must be applied to the existing object's property book

The AVM integration classes depend on the managed object interfaces, AVM base classes, Java AWT, and the Java base classes.

Managed object interfaces

The managed object interfaces use RMI to perform remote management methods. Managed objects are used to provide abstractions of resources in the enterprise and are derived from the class ManagedObject.

Java-enabled Web browser

The Java-enabled Web browser is a commercial Web browser. The applets that run inside the Web browser will use the AVM classes and managed object interfaces to perform management operations.

5.3.2.2   Admin Runtime Module

The admin runtime module (ARM) is the mechanism that provides active instantiated management objects for a number of appliances and is the focal point of administration. The ARM consists of the following elements.

HTTP Server

An HTTP server is necessary to use a Web browser and provide some bootstrap capabilities for Java elements. An HTML file allows loading of initial Java applets and JMAPI objects. After the applets take control, it uses the managed object interfaces to communicate with the ARM.

Managed object factory

The managed object factory is accessible through the managed object interfaces from a JMAPI applet. An application developer calls MOFactory.initialize() to establish a connection to a managed object factory. To get a list of instances of a particular class of managed objects the method MOFactory.listMOClass() is invoked. This method uses the managed data interfaces to retrieve the list of classes from the database. To create a new instance of a particular class of managed objects the method MOFactory.newObj() is invoked. This method causes the managed object factory to create a "shell" of the object which can be manipulated by the applet.

Only one instance of each object is created in the managed object factory. The managed object factory returns unique handles to each client. This means that multiple clients could potentially be updating the same managed object. JMAPI applets can register for notifications on changes to an instance of a managed object via the ManagedObject.addObserver() method.

The managed object factory implements actual management operations through interactions with agent objects interfaces and managed data interfaces. Though key, the managed data interfaces are largely hidden by the managed object interfaces.

JMAPI applets access the managed object factory through three primary interfaces, as well as the getters and setters for the managed object attributes. These interfaces are ManagedObject.addObject(), ManagedObject.deleteObject(), and ManagedObject.modifyObject(). These methods all perform the same basic operations:

1. Establishes a transaction context to perform the operation.
2. Prepares the database for any updates.
3. Invokes perform(Add/Delete/Modify)Actions(). This method invokes Agent Object Factory to perform operations on the appliances. The performActions method must be implemented by a developer of a JMAPI managed object. If there are no actions, the developer can inherit an "empty" performActions method from the ManagedObject class.
4. Commits any database updates.
5. Closes the transaction context.

The performActions method takes a CommitAndRollback object as an argument. This object tracks what has been performed so that if any exceptions occur during the execution of a performActions method, the appropriate rollback operations can be performed. Likewise, when a performActions method completes successfully, any commit operations will be performed. This model enables developers of management operations to have a single way to perform clean-up when there is a failure.

Managed data interfaces

The managed data interfaces support mapping attributes of extensions to the base object interfaces to a relational database. These interfaces are implemented on the appropriate subset of the Java Database Connectivity (JDBC). These interfaces support a number of commercially available relational database engines.

One of the largest administration problems today is maintaining an accurate, consistent, and reliable repository for persistent management information. This information is as crucial as any information to an enterprise, but it is not treated as carefully as corporate data. This practice not only effects the reliability of systems, but also is a potential security risk. By integrating database technology, the following problems that plague traditional mechanisms used for persistent storage of management information are solved:

1. Location transparency for distributed access — the characteristics of location transparency include
   - A single, logical view of all administration data
   - The ability to retrieve or modify administration data from any workstation in the network
   - The ability to move from one workstation to another without resetting access paths for administration data.
2. Performance and distributed optimization — the database can encapsulate the caching and replication of data.
3. Data security — the database can perform data authorization and authentication.
4. Transaction management and integrated concurrency control — introducing transaction management and concurrency control greatly heightens the reliability and consistency of the overall system.
5. Communication structure for a distributed commit protocol — to maintain consistency in a distributed environment, transactions must have the properties of atomicity, consistency, insulation, and durability. Concurrency control and distributed commit protocols are necessary to implement these properties.
6. Localized failures — if a node fails or the administration data become inaccessible at one node, other nodes in the network can continue to operate through copies found in the name services or management components.

The current files and name service tables that contain administration data are inadequate for enterprise-wide distributed management. The reliability and integrity of these mechanisms can be easily compromised. Also, standard administration files and name service tables only provide a small amount of the information needed to manage the enterprise. For example, the definition of a user that is maintained in a network name service is generally focused on the user identity. When defining a user in the scope of the enterprise, additional information, such as where their mail file resides, the set of software and data to which they need access, and their mail stop must be maintained. By using commercial databases, the user is not constrained by existing definitions of resources in files and network name services. Definition of resources can be developed, and extended by administrators, that more closely match the distributed computing model found in today's enterprises.

Deploying database technology enables scaling of enterprise management data not possible using files or name services. Commercial databases are engineered to handle tens of thousands of entries. Using database technology and name services together avoids having to administer every system in the enterprise.

There are many varieties of network name services and a heterogeneous collection of systems using those services in an enterprise environment. Having a database maintain the real enterprise management data allows for a consistent view regardless of system or name service type. This strategy assists in effectively managing a heterogeneous environment.

Agent object interfaces

The agent object interfaces are the interface to agent objects residing on the appliances. Since agent objects are really RMI objects, invocation of their methods look just like invocations on local Java instances. Agent objects are typically invoked in one of the performActions methods, though this is not required.

Notification dispatcher

The Notification dispatcher performs filtering and forwarding of events from all the appliances managed by the ARM.

5.3.2.3 Appliance

The appliance simply represents the system to be managed. Most, if not all, of the management of an appliance, occurs on the ARM. The elements of an appliance are as follows.

Agent object factory

The agent object factory creates and maintains instances of agent objects. This is expected to be running on every machine that wishes to be managed via JMAPI.

Requests to create agent object instances are made from managed object instances by AgentFactory.newAgentObj().

Agent object instance

Agent object instances are in fact RMI remote objects. When these objects are invoked they call Java code or Native Methods to implement the management operation. If necessary, the Class Loader will download the Java Code and the Library Loader will download the Native Methods.

5.3.3 SNMP INTEGRATION

SNMP is the most prevalent management protocol and in order for the Java Management APIs to be valuable immediately, the support of existing SNMP agents is absolutely necessary. By allowing SNMP information to be available for managed object developers, richer managed object definitions can be implemented.

Specifically, JMAPI provides the following for integration with existing SNMP agents.

- A set of Java classes that implements the SNMP protocol and interfaces to use the protocol.
- A set of JMAPI managed objects to more easily use the Java classes that implement the SNMP protocol.
- A JMAPI managed object that acts as an SNMP trap handler that receives all SNMP traps and converts them into instances of JMAPI events.

5.3.4 EVENT NOTIFICATION

The Java Management API notification interfaces provide the event management mechanism foundation that allows building of complex event management. The model features asynchronous event notification between managed objects and management applications. This eliminates the need for management applications to poll at regular intervals to check for state changes.

The notification interfaces facilitate the building of hierarchical event management services. This allows the event management services to be configured in a number of different ways. Different notification interfaces are used to register interest in each other's events. This allows each level of the hierarchy to isolate the event to the domain that it has control over.

Implementation of the notification interface is an efficient lightweight mechanism that can and should be used liberally. Any host in the enterprise can be designated as providing an event management notification. All JMAPI infrastructure events are sent to this branch of the tree. Applications can register with this branch to receive all JMAPI events.

5.3.4.1   Event Notification Tree

The basic component is the event tree. The event tree is a hierarchical, ordered tree of period separated strings or words. Each of these words represents a branch or level of the tree. Applications can register interest in a specific branch of the tree. When an event is received, by the notification dispatcher, the event tree is traversed until the branch is found.

Once the branch is found all registered consumer's Filter objects are called. If the Filter evaluates true then the Action class for that consumer is executed. Once all of the registered consumers of this branch have been found, the notification dispatcher then works its way back up the tree searching for additional registrations. All of the found registrations are then processed just like the initial branch. The further down the tree hierarchy the more specific the event registration becomes. The opposite is true the higher up the tree the registration. Consumers registered at the tree root are considered for all events to the tree. For instance the tree shown in Figure 5.4 could be constructed to monitor financial markets.

In the example shown in Figure 5.4, the user could register with the branch:

"*.markets.stocks.NASDAQ.SUNW"

to be notified of events to the NASDAQ stock SUNW. To be notified of all events posted for NASDAQ stocks one could register with the "*.branch markets.stocks.NASDAQ" branch. To receive events for all market events one would register with the "*.markets" branch.

5.3.4.2   Event Generation

Events can originate from within the JMAPI framework or come from an outside source. The event has associated with it a set of attribute name and value pairs. These data are opaque to the event dispatching mechanism and is passed directly to the registered consumer's filter and action objects.

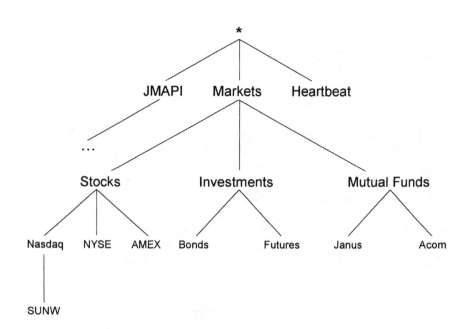

FIGURE 5.4 Event notification example.

5.3.4.3   Registration

To receive notification that an event has occurred the application must register interest in the event. To register for event notification the application must provide two classes, the filter and the action. These classes are the basis for filtering and performing an action based on the event.

5.3.4.4   Unregistration

Once an application no longer is interested in receiving events it can unregister with the event handler.

5.3.4.5   Filter and Actions

When an application registers with the notification dispatcher it must supply a filter and an action class. These classes control the behavior of the registry when an event is triggered. The filter and action classes that are registered must implement the filter and action interfaces.

5.3.4.6   Heartbeat

The notification dispatcher generates a heartbeat event every 60 seconds. Applications can register with this branch and be delivered heartbeat events.

5.3.5 OBJECT MODEL

JMAPI is a lightweight management infrastructure, but without classes that implement abstractions for the resources and services to be managed in the enterprise, it is of little value. JMAPI provides a base-level set of classes that developers will be able to extend for their specific implementation needs. However, by providing these base-level classes integration and consistency for the most common management classes can be assured.

The object model is largely decomposed around physical and logical boundaries. Physical elements are truly physical entities. This means little real management can be performed on these entities. Monitoring some of their physical characteristics (like temperature) is the primary "management" function that can be performed. Logical elements are typically realized in terms of physical elements. Logical elements typically implement complete management functionality. This means that users are able to control as well as monitor resources abstracted through logical elements. Figure 5.5 shows the class hierarchy for the JMAPI base-level classes. Also, in order to keep the diagrams readable, no associations or attributes are shown.

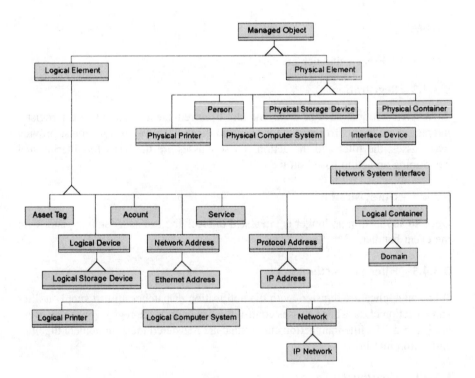

FIGURE 5.5 JMAPI base-level object class hierarchy.

Figure 5.6 shows the references between the fundamental classes of physical and logical elements and containers. This diagram also shows that every type of object can be tracked as an asset and through asset tag have a primary contact for that element. This relationship is not only for management, but can be used for service contacts where appropriate.

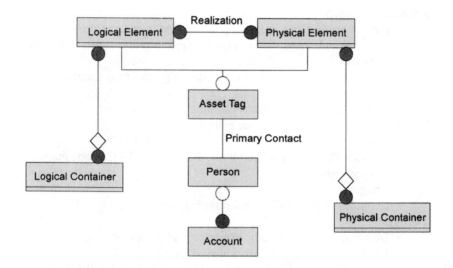

FIGURE 5.6 JMAPI base-level object references.

Management of distributed systems is inherently comprised of the relationship between computers, the network, and the services provided and consumed by resources on the network. Figure 5.7 shows these relationships.

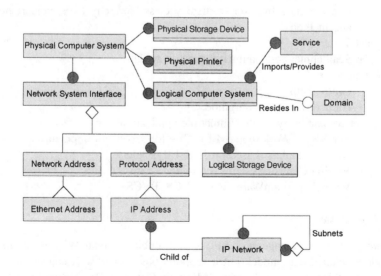

FIGURE 5.7 JMAPI computer and network references.

5.3.6 JAVA WORKSHOP COMPONENTS

Java WorkShop is a Web-centric development tool with an intelligent graphical user interface. It offers an integrated tool set that works together. Its components are:

Portfolio manager
- Publication tools for organizing application integration projects.
- Promotes code reuse via creation and customization of personal applet portfolios.
- Share portfolios internally or commercially with final applications.

Visual Java
- Automates creation of the application's user interfaces.
- Automated Java source code generation.

Source editor
- Works with WorkShop/TeamWare, SCCS, RCS, PVCS code management systems.

Build manager
- Compiles only files that need updating, saving time.

Debugger
- Debug applications locally or remotely across the network.
- Integrated with the Java WorkShop Applet Tester.
- Debug applets on HTML pages or in a stand-alone Java application.
- Step into, over, and out of code and set break points graphically.
- Evaluate and change data values.
- Navigate the call stack.
- Suspend and examine individual or groups of threads.

Source browser
- Automatically creates HyperText link to source code.
- Use the class browser to display class hierarchy trees, constructors, and methods.

Applet Tester
- Scan applet code, animate, and run applets.

Documentation
- Online help.
- Hardcopy installation guide.

Product compatibility — its compatible applications are
- Sun Visual WorkShopTM for C++ for server development.
- All Java applets (based on JDK 1.0 or later).
- Version Control Systems Supported.
- WorkShop/TeamWare, SCCS, RCS, PVCS.

5.3.7 SUMMARY

In summary, Java Management API is less ambitious than WBEM. It does not provide a detailed data model, but it supports object classes. It enjoys the support of powerful third parties, including IBM/Tivoli, Platinum, Bay Networks and 3Com.

5.4 WEB-BASED ENTERPRISE MANAGEMENT

The Web-based Enterprise Management (WBEM) initiative establishes an architecture that supports the management of the enterprise across a network. The architecture defines the structures and conventions necessary to access information about the objects being managed, centralizes the information for cross client analysis, and supports location transparent access to managed objects for both analysis and manipulation. WBEM has been designed in such a way that it is compatible with all the major existing management protocols, including SNMP, DMI, and CMIP.

One of the key components of this initiative is the definition of a standard protocol to access management information, allowing management solutions to be platform independent and physically distributed across the enterprise. This protocol is known as the HyperMedia Management Protocol (HMMP).

HMMP is based on modeling the management environment as a collection of cooperating management entities. Each entity can take on one or more of four roles within the management environment: client, server, producer, and consumer.

An entity acting in the role of a client will request management information from an entity acting in the role of a server. An entity acting in the role of a producer will send event or indication information to an entity acting in the role of a consumer.

Entities in the managed environment communicate using a common protocol, called HMMP. The information content of the managed objects is modeled using the meta-schema defined by the Common Information Model (CIM). The medium for describing the schema is through Managed Object Format (MOF). MOF is based on a formal syntax, and serves the purpose of providing a human-readable description of managed objects as well as a machine possible way of introducing managed objects to HMMP server implementations.

This framework is built on widely adopted internet technologies and protocols. As such it represents work-in-progress and does not represent current products of either of the providers.

Specifically, customers have the following management requirements:

- A scalable management framework that addresses management requirements for both small and large systems
- Contain costs for systems and network administration and operation
- Rich, highly functional management applications that make network and systems management proactive and automated
- Reduce the network complexity of multiple, redundant functions of management platforms, applications, and agents
- Integrate elements of management solution seamlessly and consistently, allowing management applications to share information with other applications
- Have lower costs for management environments, including hardware, software, and training

In short, customers are looking to lower costs, increase flexibility, and reduce the complexity involved in managing their networks and systems.

The initiative defines standards for WBEM that elegantly remove several hurdles to distributed systems management. The strength of the proposal lies in its simplicity. It draws on ubiquitous internet technology to provide a common base for systems and network management, using the Web browser as the primary user interface. WBEM provides an easy-to-use, cost-effective, proactive, automated way of accessing consistent management data. The viability of Web technology is evidenced by the way business users have embraced the internet, the only true distributed architecture to boast such broad acceptance.

None of the companies sponsoring the proposal owns the standard. The initial sponsors are inviting wide industry participation to promote broad acceptance of the proposed standards and thus accelerate the development and deployment of innovative applications for systems and network management.

Based on a very popular, easy-to-use Web-based interface, the proposed management standards identify a consistent way of working with a wide range of management information.

Applications and devices that embrace these standards will be accessible and controllable from any client system equipped with a Web browser. As a result, network and system management will benefit from the richness of the internet, which affords abundant, easily accessible content and is incorporating innovative technologies at a rapid rate.

The standards effort directly addresses these key issues, providing three key advantages:

- Scalability. With a simple Web browser as the management interface, organizations can cost-effectively take advantage of networking technology they already have in place to manage a wide range of network resources, such as routers, hubs, PCs, workstations, distributed applications, and databases. When the same technologies used for building networks are used to create management applications, the scalability of the applications can match that of the network. The proposed standards provide such scalability by allowing a system administrator to learn and implement just one interface to monitor and maintain low-end devices and systems as well as mainframes and everything in between. The standards will support a broad range of management solutions and will build on internet innovations to meet the demanding requirements of the most complex heterogeneous computing environments.
- Increased choice in applications, greater functionality. The proposed open standards offer a single foundation on which to build management applications, obviating the need to design different versions for different management platforms and making applications more efficient and cost effective. They therefore free developers to concentrate on innovative functionality rather than system differences and allow them to bring applications to market more quickly. A major benefit for users will be signif-

icant: a greater selection of management applications and added functionality that takes advantage of rapidly evolving Web technology.
- Lowered costs for set up and operation. A single interface for managing all networks, systems, and applications will greatly reduce the complexity that currently frustrates system administrators. The proposed management standards will free them from having to access management applications from specially outfitted consoles. Instead, they will work at any Web-enabled client systems distributed throughout an organization to access distributed management applications. Access is controlled by the security measures implemented within HTTP. A management system based on a Web browser interface that eases access to management data for networks of UNIX, Windows NT, MVS, VMS, and Netware platforms will be less costly to learn, set up, operate, and support. Likewise, as easier application development is enabled, management solutions will proliferate and competition will impact prices. Today thousands of developers are creating open internet solutions. The Web-based technology will enable them to apply this innovation to distributed management applications.

The key elements are as follows:

- Management information made available in HTML for access by Web browsers
- Scalable architecture that supports small to large systems and networks
- An object oriented management schema and management protocol that allows management application software to view the system in a systematic manner
- Use of widely deployed internet and Web protocols

The management framework leverages existing management infrastructures such as SNMP and the rapidly developing internet application framework based on the WWW. It specifies the basic notion of managed objects (MO) and how management value is delivered through standard browser platforms. Any resource on the network, such as routers, PCs, printers, operating systems, software applications, etc. can be an MO. In their simplest form, MOs do no more than identify themselves by providing static information such as product descriptions, manufacturer name, model number, serial number, etc. To implement such an object, a manufacturer or network administrator needs only provide a static HTML file with the desired information on the target system. More sophisticated MOs provide configuration and control services to surface instrumentation capable of controlling resource specific options. These operations can be performed in a secure environment by leveraging readily available security services in the internet arena. In addition, the management framework makes available a management schema that allows viewing the managed system as a collection of objects.

The user interface to the managed system is provided through standard off-the-shelf internet browsers. The ubiquity of internet browsers makes almost every computer a potential management console. All that is needed to access and manage an

MO is access to a browser, knowledge of the URL by which the MO is addressable, and proper security/validation for access to manageable information.

The management framework also includes an element that is known as a management application (MA). The MA is application functionality that is usually located in the network. The MA is used to provide management functionality of all types. A specific example of the MA is the object manager (OM) that is used in conjunction with the management schema and the management protocol to provide an object oriented information model view of the managed system. Additionally, MAs can be used to support other management protocols such as SNMP and DMI on a proxy basis.

The management framework can provide rich information formats for presentation and display since it uses HTML and other Web technologies. It opens up the management applications arena to the enormous network-based applications development thrust around the internet.

MOs are constructed with HTTP/HTML technologies. MOs are systems components that provide information required for management purposes. MOs are addressable via URLs. A single MO can provide two views of its management information. All MOs provide an HTML view of their management information. Additionally, MOs can provide an object oriented management schema view of their management information.

It is important to emphasize that MOs represent an application of existing internet technologies to accomplish the management function. No modifications to existing fundamental technologies and standards are implicit in their definition. The management framework's use of existing open technology standards has the benefit of providing opportunities to build value added management applications that leverage these open standards.

MOs provide the ability to read management information, change management information to control purposes, and to report the occurrence of asynchronous events. Their functionality is similar to that performed today in traditional management systems by special purpose management agents, such as SNMP or DMI. However, the management framework differs from traditional management agents in that it does not require a special purpose console to view the information available from the management agent. The management framework enables the use of standard, open HTML/HTTP browsers to access system and network management information and to exercise control functionality. Other software may also be used in combination. That is, software other than the browser can communicate with an MO as long as it makes use of the HTML/HTTP protocols. Thus, MOs can be openly used as a foundation for extensions.

The use of HTML/HTTP technology for management information allows the integration of management information with other information sources that utilize these technologies. This capitalizes on the trend in which business organizations are making greater amounts of business operational information available via HTML/HTTP. For example, it would be possible for the network manager who is using an HTML/HTTP browser to view network management information to use that same browser to look at operational schedules and to make decisions about scheduling network maintenance. Figure 5.8 shows the browser–MO relationship.

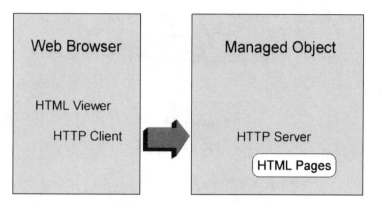

FIGURE 5.8 Relationship between managed objects and browsers.

The management schema is used to model management information in a structured, object-oriented manner. Use of the management schema enables management applications to access and manipulate management information systematically using an object oriented data model. A key element in the use of the management schema is the management protocol that is used to propagate the management schema data in a distributed system. The management protocol makes use of HTTP as its transport protocol.

Management applications (MAs) play a key role in providing multiple management functions. They can serve as proxy to access management information in SNMP, DMI, and CMIP. This information is being made available in a browsable HTML form. Additionally, it is accessing managed objects (MOs) and returning its URL as a hyperlink to the browser. Figure 5.9 shows this hierarchy.

A Management Application (MA) can function as both HTTP server and client. This dual functionality allows for discovering connected MO resources and may serve as a vehicle for delivering unsolicited event information to the browsing client. The MA can log event information for later forwarding, if no administrator is currently active. Additionally, the MA can use other means of reporting events such as by pagers and e-mail.

The management framework does not require a central console, opting to distribute the console anywhere on the network via HTML connections. In the event that no console is currently active (e.g., no active HTTP session), the MA may provide store and forward capabilities to guarantee receipt of unsolicited events. The MA is the site of a wide range of functionality. An MA can provide discovery, proxy, cataloging, and other services. The scope of discovery services is implementation specific and no single discovery technique is specified by the management framework. Discovery of nodes in non-HTTP managed systems such as SNMP should follow present discovery methods specific to the network transport employed. This preserves code investments made to date by enterprise management platform software. Once nodes are identified, the MA may systematically attempt management transactions via each back end protocol it supports. The MA then adds value by

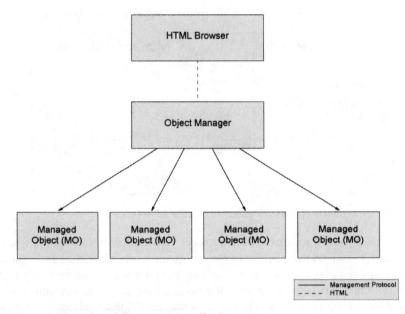

FIGURE 5.9 Hierarchy of management applications.

creating and exposing an HTML view of manageable systems, perhaps sorted by
their respective protocols (SNMP, DMI, etc.).

MAs may employ established Web catalog technologies (e.g., spiders, crawlers)
for MO URL discovery. A Web spider, or crawler, refers to software that locates
documents published on Web sites, brings them back to be indexed, then builds and
constantly updates a searchable database of all Web sites visited. Given an initial
URL, the crawler/spider software can follow the hyperlinks of HTML documents
to find and index all the documents linked through that first page. Each subsequent
document is searched for further links, until all links are traversed. The end result
of the Web "crawling" is an indexed, multiple keyed database of all Web sites known
to the spider/crawler. MAs can also make use of directory services such as those
provided by LDAP (Lightweight Directory Access Protocol) to organize MO information such as URLs.

When the management schema and the management protocol are used, the MA
provides a specific functionality. In this role, it is called the object manager. It has
an integral role in implementing the management schema. The object manager
provides management applications with an object oriented view of the managed
system. The object manager uses the management protocol to communicate with
MOs that support the schema. Figure 5.10 illustrates the overall organization of a
system that is using the object manager.

The benefits can be summarized as follows:

- The management framework leverages widely used internet protocols. It
  makes use of the Web browser as a ubiquitous network management

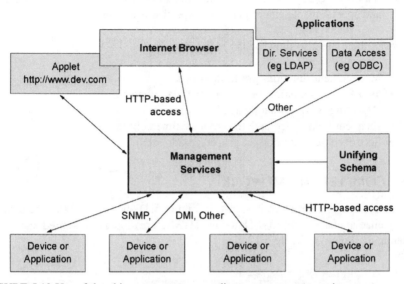

FIGURE 5.10 Use of the object manager to coordinate management services.

console. A Web browser running on a variety of platforms can be operated from anywhere in the network hierarchy to manage any MO. No longer is it required to maintain a single centralized, specialized management console. It makes use of the fact that knowledge of using Web browsers is widespread.

- The management framework provides an extensible object oriented management schema and management protocol to enable creation of management applications that can view the managed system as a collection of objects. This schema provides for modeling all elements of a system — both hardware and software.
- Under the management framework architecture, each managed object is self contained. It presents its own rich-content view to a Web browser. Each vendor can create a custom, branded, graphical view without the need to become experts in the specifics of management system console. The development to support this view need only be done once and the support is easily distributed. Most importantly, the development of these views (HTML pages) can be done easily using a variety of easy to use tools that are widely available.
- As businesses make use of Web technologies to provide access to business information, management information will be in the same form as other business process information. The network manager can use the same Web browser that he or she used to look at management information in a server to look at operational schedules to see when to take the server down for maintenance.
- Distributed management is supported by placing management information on various distributed Web servers. Location flexibility is guaranteed by

remote access by the browsers. Hardware and software are less expensive, and special management platform expertise is optional.

However, there are also drawbacks:

- Management functions are limited.
- Two-way communication is not yet fully supported.
- Reporting is somewhat delayed.
- Frequent home page updates are very time consuming.
- Security issues are not yet properly addressed.

5.5   COMPLETE FRAMEWORK

The more complete structure is shown in Figure 5.11, which indicates the schema to organize managed objects. Dynamic HTML creation is supported using the schema, as shown in Figure 5.12.

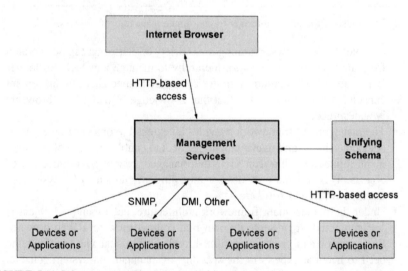

FIGURE 5.11 Schema to organize managed objects.

Besides management services, additional applications, such as directory services and data access to databases, can be integrated. Also, applets may be connected to the management framework, as shown in Figure 5.13. Thus, the two initiatives, JMAPI and WBEM, can be unified.

The reasoning for new management protocol under HTTP is:

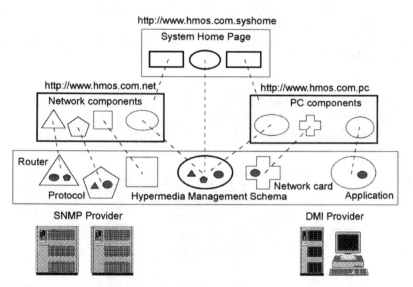

FIGURE 5.12 The process of dynamic HTML creation.

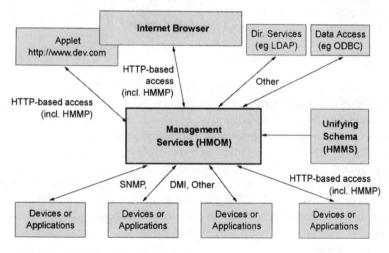

FIGURE 5.13 Installation of Java applets.

- There is a need to model the entire managed environment; the HyperMedia Management Protocol (HMMP) carries data represented by self-describing, extensible schema.
- It facilitates secure, remote management by taking advantage of existing security work on HTTP.

- HTTP is universally supported and, as a result, API wars and ownership issues can be avoided.
- There is a need to integrate existing management protocols, such as SNMP and DMI.

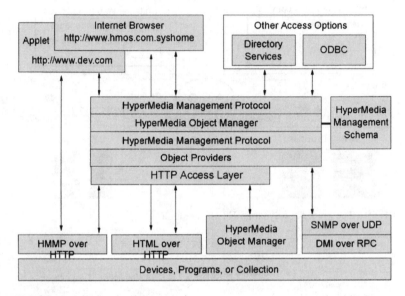

FIGURE 5.14 Detailed technology overview.

The detailed technology overview is shown in Figure 5.14.

The Desktop Management Task Force (DMTF) has developed a Common Information Model (CIM) to take advantage of object-based management tools and provide a common way to describe and share management information enterprise-wide. Using HyperMedia Management Schema (HMMS) as an input, the new model can be populated by DMI 2.0 and other management data suppliers, including SNMP and CMIP, and implemented in multiple object-based execution models such as JMAPI, CORBA and HMMS. CIM will enable applications from different developers on different platforms to describe and share management data, so users have interoperable management tools that span applications, systems, and networks, including the internet.

CIM is a conceptual information model for describing management that is not bound to a particular implementation. This allows for the interchange of management information between management systems and applications. This can be either "agent to manager" or "manager to manager" communications which provides for distributed systems and network management.

In a fully CIM compliant world, it should be possible to build applications such as Service Level Agreement tracking applications using management data from a variety of sources and different management systems such as TME, OpenView, ManageWise, SMS, etc. The management data would be collected, stored, and analyzed using a common format (CIM) while allowing property extensions providing "value add".

There are two parts to CIM, the CIM Specification and the CIM Schema. The CIM Specification describes the language, naming, meta schema, and mapping techniques to other management models such as SNMP MIBs, and DMTF MIFs, etc. The meta schema is a formal definition of the model. It defines the terms used to express the model and their usage and semantics. The elements of the meta schema are classes, properties, and methods. The meta schema also supports indications and associations as types of classes and references as types of properties.

The CIM Schema provides the actual model descriptions. The CIM Schema supplies a set of classes with properties and associations that provide a well-understood conceptual framework within which it is possible to organize the available information about the managed environment. The CIM Schema itself is structured into three distinct layers:

- Core schema — an information model that captures notions that are applicable to all areas of management.
- Common schema — an information model that captures notions that are common to particular management areas but independent of a particular technology or implementation. The common areas are systems, applications, databases, networks, and devices. The information model is specific enough to provide a basis for the development of management applications. This schema provides a set of base classes for extension into the area of technology specific schemas. There are currently four common schemas:
    1. Systems
    2. Applications
    3. Networks (LAN)
    4. Devices
- Extension schemas — represent technology-specific extensions of the common schema. These schemas are specific to environments, such as operating systems (for example, UNIX or Microsoft Windows).

More schemas are planned for definition in the areas of directory enabled networks (DEN), service level agreements, and distributed application transaction measurement (DATM). Others will follow.

The formal definition of the CIM Schema is expressed in a managed object file (MOF) which is an ASCII file that can be used as input into an MOF editor or compiler for use in an application. The Unified Modeling Language (UML) is used to portray the structure of the schemas. Techniques to develop UML (VISIO) files from MOF files are being developed.

This is the first time in this industry that a common method of describing management information has been agreed and followed through with implementation. Other efforts have failed because of the lack of industry support. Because the model is implementation independent, it does not provide sufficient information for product development. It is the specific product areas — applications, system, network, database, and devices — and their product specific extensions that produce workable solutions.

The current status of CIM-related projects is that CIM defines rules and categories for an information model that provides a common way to describe and share management information enterprise-wide. The group will define a meta schema or basic modeling language; a core schema, the base set of classes specific to systems, networks, and applications; and a common schema, a base set of platform-neutral, domain-specific extensions of core schema.

CIM will take advantage of emerging object-based management technologies and ensure that the new model can be populated by DMI and other management data suppliers, including SNMP and CMIP. The CIM is being designed to enable implementations in multiple, object-based execution models such as CORBA (Common Object Request Broker Architecture) and COM (Common Objects Model), and object-based management technologies such as JMAPI (Java Management API).

5.6   ENABLING TECHNOLOGIES FOR PLATFORM AND DEVICE LEVEL MANAGEMENT

The implementation of the standards may take many forms. Basically, there are two models to implement: the two-tier model implements the Web server directly into the managed objects; the three-tier model implements the Web server into the management station or management platform.

In a two-tier model, the management software is integrated with the rest of the network or systems device firmware. Users point their browsers at the home page residing within the device. In such a model, the management software may not need to perform any translation. It may convey all management information using the HTTP protocol alone.

In the two-tier model users simply need to point their browser at the home page contained within the device to manage it. Network device vendors can equip managed objects without any installation disk. However, this model requires users to open separate URLs to each managed object. If there are many Web-manageable devices that are typical for large systems and networks, the user will have to open a browser window for each manageable device. This model also tends to be device-centric and may not be able to provide database storage and other processing capabilities. Figure 5.15 shows the structure of the two-tier model.

In summary, in a two-tier model:

- The management software is integrated with the rest of the network or systems device firmware.
- This may be in an embedded form.
- Users point their browser at the home page residing within the device.
- The management software may not need to perform any translation.
- It may convey all management information using the HTTP protocol alone.

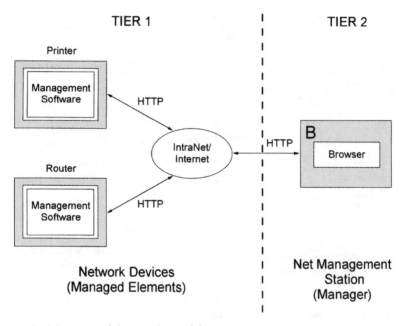

FIGURE 5.15 Structure of the two-tier model.

In a three-tier model, the management software runs as an application over the operating system and collects and disseminates the information gathered from network and systems devices to the browser. When a user points his or her browser at the management software's home page, the management software relays aggregated management information to the browser. In doing so, the management software may translate traditional management protocols, such as SNMP, to Web protocols, such as HTTP. Figure 5.16 shows the structure of the three-tier model.

In summary, in a three-tier model:

- The management software runs as an application over an operating system.
- The software resides between the browser and network or systems devices.
- Users merely point their browsers at the management software's home page.
- The management software relays aggregated management information from the management software to the browser.
- Management software may translate traditional management protocols into Web protocols.
- Three-tier models may not require any change to the managed objects.

Selecting the appropriate model depends on many factors. The three-tier model definitely offers greater capabilities. Here, the management software can leverage the capabilities provided by the host operating system, such as increased memory,

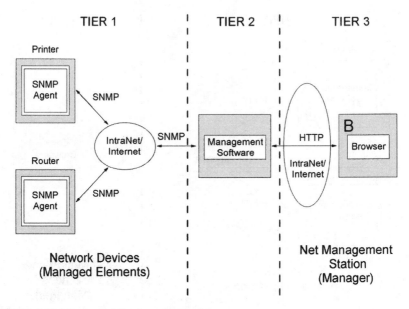

FIGURE 5.16 Structure of the three-tier model.

processing power, and storage space. Additionally, a three-tier model provides a network-centric view to the browser. The user needs to know only the URL of the management software to manage all devices. All network management information can be aggregated, processed, and conveyed over a single connection between the browser and the management software.

There are several points to be considered before deciding which model may be the right choice. Table 5.1 compares both models. These differences are a result of different integration mechanisms of the two models. In the three-tier model, the management software resides external to the managed object and provides a network-centric view to browsers. In the two-tier model, the management software is embedded into the device firmware, and tends to offer only device-centric information to the browser.

A hybrid model combines the advantages of both models. Using the two-tier model, management software can be integrated within the device firmware. This provides device-centric Web-based management capabilities to all users. Users can, for instance, check the status of a printer by pointing the browser at the printer home page.

By incorporating a management protocol agent such as SNMP, the device is adaptable to a three-tier model as well. Network-centric information such as topology information, fault information, and management information processing capabilities can be made available to external management software. Additionally, the device may also be managed using traditional SNMP managers as platforms. There are a few products supporting the models.

TABLE 5.1
Comparison of the Models

Feature	Three-Tier Model	Two-Tier Model
Function	Device management using HTML pages, Java applets.	Device management using HTML pages, Java applets.
Installation	External to device, on a hardware platform such as Windows 95/NT; needs an installation disk to be shipped with device.	On device, requires change to device firmware. Does not need any shipment of installation disk.
Primary requirement	Device should support a management protocol agent such as SNMP.	No management protocol agent required. Needs to be ported on target hardware.
Features	Can support features other than basic device management to offer a network-centric view. Management information can be aggregated, processed, stored and delivered on a single stream between the browser and the management software. Can leverage on host operating system to perform capabilities such as logging, storage and delayed analysis.	Features restricted to device management. Management information typically cannot be stored or processed as limited by device memory and processor bandwidth constraint, and is delivered on.
Development time	Rapid, as can leverage on host operating system capabilities.	Longer as needs to be ported onto device. The development time really depends on the functionality of the embedded environment and the degree of features desired.
Remote management	Firewall needs to enable remote access to only the single hardware platform that has management software installed.	Firewall needs to enable access to each device that needs to be managed on the network.
TCP connections	Only one TCP connection — from browser to management sofware.	Separate TCP connection from browser to management software on each device.

Cyberware and CyberManage from Wipro: Wipro offers solutions for both two- and three-tier models. One of them is CyberManage, with the following attributes:

- HTTP front end, SNMP back end, and CyberCore.
- Protocol conversion and security features are embedded.
- CyberApplets and CyberDaemons implement generic network management functions.
- CyberKit allows creation of HTML pages for device management.

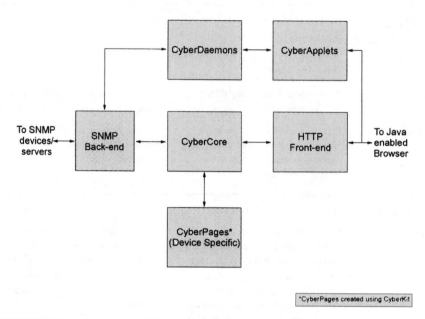

FIGURE 5.17 Architecture of CyberManage.

Figure 5.17 shows the structure of this solution.

The other product is CyberWare, with the following attributes:

- HTTP front end and CyberCore.
- Protocol conversion and security features are embedded.
- CyberApplets and CyberDaemons implement generic network management functions.
- CyberKit allows creation of HTML pages for device management.
- CyberPages are compressed and dynamic.

Figure 5.18 shows the structure of this solution.

EmWeb from Agranat Incorporated: The portable Web server and development architecture of EmWeb are the basis for developing and deploying Web-based management capabilities into systems and network equipment. C source code can be incorporated into HTML documents. This makes it easy to process and serve dynamic information. Embedded Web technology is getting popular with manufacturers. With the rapid expansion of the Web and growing demand for Web-based management capabilities, more and more companies are planning to embed Web servers into their products.

By eliminating the need for applications developers to use CGI or other raw interfaces to process HTML forms and provide dynamic document content, the EmWeb architecture speeds up development, prototyping, and implementation and reduces time-to-market for Web-based products. In addition, the system requires little memory, significantly less than conventional approaches. In addition to the

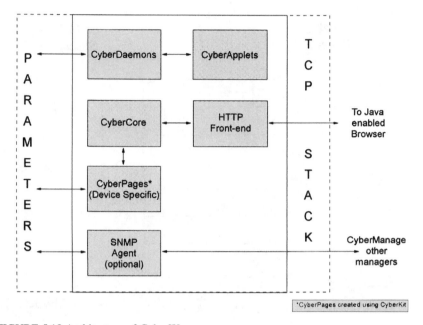

FIGURE 5.18 Architecture of CyberWare.

unique HTML-to-C integration, dynamic document capabilities, and small footprint, the EmWeb architecture also features a number of innovative run-time capabilities: run-time assembly of documents from multiple components, run-time creation of new elements in the URL tree, and run-time, on-demand downloading of document archives. Other features include both basic and digest authentication and support for proxy management applications.

EmWeb consists of a compiler and a server. The EmWeb-Compiler runs on an engineering development workstation under UNIX or Windows and is used to compile directories of HTML, Java, test, or graphic files into a compressed run-time database represented by generated C code. The database is then compiled and linked with the EmWeb-Server and the developer's embedded software.

Dr. Web from SNMP Research: The Dr. Web product family tries to combine the benefits of both SNMP- and HTML-based technologies. This product provides a straightforward mapping between HTML constructs and SNMP data. It supports standards-based transition to a Web-based management environment. Customers and vendors may retain their investments in SNMP-instrumented devices and systems by combining them with low-cost universal browsers. Figure 5.19 shows the single stack solution, supporting both SNMP managers and Web servers.

N-Vision from Edge Technologies: N-Vision is a Java front-end for the HP OpenView network management platform. Using N-Vision and a Web browser, network managers can access OpenView-related information across the intranet or via remote dial-in, without the cost, overhead, or resource consumption of supporting multiple X-Windows sessions. The N-Vision component set includes a Graphical

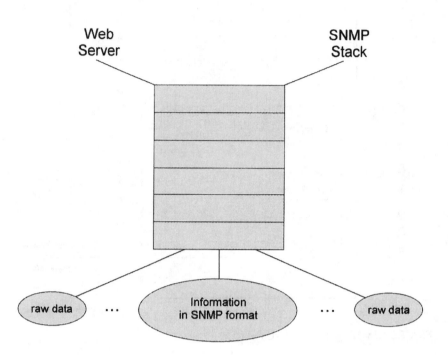

FIGURE 5.19 Single stack support by SNMP Research.

Topology Display, SNMP MIB Browser, OpenView Event Browser, and Administration Utilities.

Orbit family from Gecko: The Orbit family is a Java-based application to help access management related information in management platforms. The first version of the product family has been implemented for Spectrum from Cabletron.

The Orbit product family comprises (Figure 5.20) a free API toolkit, the Orbit Planet; an application server, the Orbit Star; and free access to a library of public domain Java applets.

Orbit Star is a server application that coexists with the management application, or remote from the management application where supported by the API or command line interface (CLI). Orbit Star accepts API or CLI calls from one or more Orbit Planet via Orbit Shadow. Orbit Star plays the role of an object request broker. These calls are passed to the management application by Orbit Star and the results passed back to the relevant Orbit Planet. One Orbit Star can control up to three Orbit Planets. When used with Spectrum, it plugs into the Spectroserver via a proprietary interface called the Spectrum Synchronous API. If used with other platforms, additional Orbit Stars should be developed and implemented.

Orbit Planet is a public domain Java package, consisting of class, method, and interface definitions that implement the API or CLI of a management application.

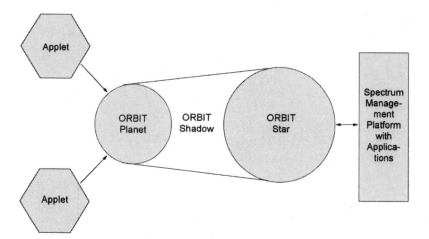

FIGURE 5.20 Orbit solution by Gecko Software.

Communication with a management application is through Orbit Shadow to an Orbit Star. It runs on user workstations and handles thin client applications.

Orbit Shadow is an application layer protocol, implemented using TCP/IP sockets, that controls data requests and responses between Orbit Stars and Orbit Planets.

Benefits of using the Orbit family include:

Easy access to remote management platforms

Access to Spectrum via any HTML browser application that supports Java

Access to Spectrum from all operating systems and hardware that support Java or HTML with Java support

Use of existing Java applets

Orbit Shadow is a public domain middleware

5.7   SUMMARY

This chapter has summarized the major directions of industry standards. Actually, Java-based solutions are competing with Web-based enterprise management. But it is not real competition because hybrid solutions are also in sight. It is up to device and platform vendors to implement existing *de facto* industry standards. Web server functions, including Java applets, can be implemented into both managed objects and management platforms. Both alternatives show benefits and disadvantages. In most cases, a hybrid model also works best.

Standardization is extremely important for the Web-based technology. The CIM (Common Information Model) initiative led by the DMTF may be the foundation for joint use of the schema, Java applets, and existing links to management applications in use.

6 Management Platforms and the Web

6.1 INTRODUCTION

Management platforms have been the most important tools to integrate management applications over the last decade. They have helped to streamline management by offering application programming interfaces (APIs). They are typically client/server structures requiring powerful thick client workstations. Web based solutions represent just the opposite — thin clients are implemented into Web browsers. This chapter outlines how management platforms can be altered and extended to accommodate Web technology.

Management platforms, alone or in combination with other existing management structures, seem to take the lead. Management platforms of today are the result of many small evolutionary steps over the last 20 years. The central manager topology (Figure 6.1) has only one management system that concentrates and processes information collected in managed objects, such as modems, multiplexers, switches, hubs, routers, etc. The central manager includes all the applications needed to perform the management functions and all the databases required to maintain management information. For the communication between the central manager and the agents, standard protocols, such as common management information protocol (CMIP) and telecommunications management network (TMN), *de facto* protocols, such as SNMP in most commercial enterprise implementations, and proprietary protocols, such as NMVT in still operational SNA networks, can be implemented. But the high degree of centralization in one location and the practical limitation in terms of managed devices presents a serious scalability problem. This structure is used for relatively small networks, only.

More distribution is supported with the manager of managers (MoM) approach (Figure 6.2). The element management systems (EMS) are actually the central managers of Figure 6.1. They can be designed around homogeneous groups of devices, specific management functions, or other groupings. The MoM acts as a single integration focal point for distributed EMSs. The protocols used are determined by the MoM, and by the EMSs, respectively. This structure may be used for medium and large networks. MoMs may even be networked with each other, providing cooperative management between peer MoMs.

Management platforms do not require a new topological framework, but can be used with any of the central managers, MoM, or networked MoMs.[7] The emphasis in management platforms is on the development, installation, and operation of portable management applications that can provide management of heterogeneous systems and networks. The solution is not limited to any particular topology. The basic idea is the separation between application platform and management applica-

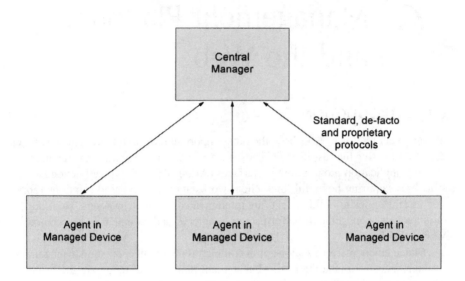

FIGURE 6.1 Central manager.

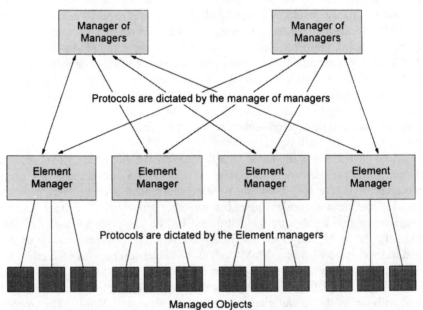

FIGURE 6.2 Manager of managers.

tions by using APIs. Management platforms employ core management services and
a set of interfaces that allow the platform to coordinate and integrate various device-

dependent and device-independent management applications. The structure of the management platform is shown in Figure 6.3.

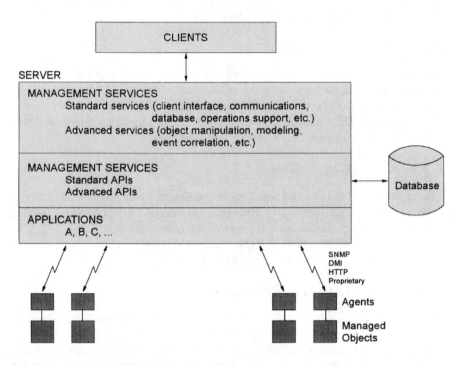

FIGURE 6.3 A distributed management platform.

The management platform is usually based on a client/server architecture. Management applications, databases, and core services can be distributed among several computing platforms.[7] The most common client/server relationship can be created between platform services acting as the server and the graphical user interfaces acting as clients. Multiple management platforms can communicate with each other in order to manage larger administrative domains or to provide support for various management applications. This client/server paradigm is the target for change by Web-based systems and network management.

6.2 MANAGEMENT PLATFORM ATTRIBUTES

Actually, there is no scientific definition of a management platform. In order to decide whether certain products qualify as a platform, an elaborated list of attributes is going to be addressed first. When products are able to support the basic platform attributes, they are qualified as platforms. The advanced attributes may serve then as differentiators among platforms.

The basic platform attributes are described below.

6.2.1   HARDWARE PLATFORM

One observes here a wide variety of hardware, including Intel 386/486, Pentium, HP 9000, RS/6000, Sun Sparc, Tandem, Alpha, Syste/88, and eventually others. Backup support should be addressed, here, as well.

6.2.2   OPERATING SYSTEMS

The industry expects a certain streamlining or, in other words, a shakeout in respect of operating systems, supporting the management platform. At the present, the operating systems to be considered include AIX, DOS/Windows, OS/2, SunOS, Ultrix, Sinix, UNIX, Windows, Windows NT, and eventually others. Future solutions will concentrate around a UNIX version and Windows NT.

6.2.3   NETWORK ARCHITECTURES

The targeted networks to be managed are very different. Many products are expected to manage legacy networks and more open networks at the same time. The most widely used protocols supporting network architectures include DECnet, IPX/SPX, OSI, SNA, DSA, APPN, TCP/IP; Guardian, and eventually others. Capabilities of managing SNA and TCP/IP are the highest priority.

6.2.4   NETWORK MANAGEMENT PROTOCOLS

The products are expected to support at least SNMP. It is an additional advantage when they can do more. SNMP support may include the capabilities of working with proxy agents, with the capability of converting non-SNMP into SNMP. Protocols to be supported include CMIP, CMOT, LNMP, NMVT, RMON1, RMON2, SNMPv1, SNMPv2, SNMPv3, and eventually DMI to manage desktops.

The management platform provides SNMP support in several ways. First and foremost is the ability to poll SNMP devices and receive SNMP traps, as described previously. However, in order to configure polls on management information base (MIB) variables of various devices, one must first know what those variables are. Management platforms provide MIB "browsers" for this purpose. An MIB browser queries user-selected SNMP network devices and displays their MIB values. In addition, most platforms can display line or bar graphs of those MIB values, provided they are in numeric form (counters, etc.).

MIB browsers are crude tools, at best, displaying raw and often cryptic, low-level device information. For this reason, platforms also provide MIB application builders that allow users to quickly create applications for displaying information on MIB objects in a more meaningful way. MIB applications may include graphing real-time information on selected network nodes. However, even MIB applications builders are limited in supporting high-level analysis, which is more often provided by third-party applications.

MIB compilers allow users to bring in third-party, device-specific MIBs (also called "private" MIBs or "extended" MIBs) and register them with the management platform. While most platforms ship with a number of third-party MIBs, they do not include all possible MIBs from all vendors. An MIB compiler is necessary for adding support for third parties whose MIBs are not shipped as part of the standard platform.

Some MIB compilers are more robust than others. Some MIB compilers will fail or abort processing if there is an error in the MIB being compiled. Unfortunately, errors in third-party MIBs are not rare. Therefore, it is desirable to have an MIB compiler that can flag errors and recover, rather than stop dead.

6.2.5 GRAPHICAL USER INTERFACE

The basic job of a graphical user interface (GUI) is to provide color-coded display of management information, multiple windows into different core or management applications, and an iconic or menu-driven user interface. By providing a standardized interface between the user and the underlying tools, the GUI simplifies what a user needs to learn and provides a standard tool for application developers.

Most management operations are available from a menu bar; others from context menus. Point-and-click operations are standard features, as is context-sensitive help. Most platforms allow some degree of customization of maps and icons.

While most platform GUIs are the same, there can be a few subtle differences. Some GUIs have larger icons than others. While this makes it easier to read information on the icon and distinguish status changes more quickly, a screen can quickly become cluttered with just a few large icons. Icon size is strictly a matter of user preference. The most widely used GUIs are Motif, OpenLook, OS/2 Presentation Manager, and Windows.

6.2.6 DATABASE SUPPORT

The database is the focal point for key data created and used by the management applications. They include MIB data, inventories, trouble tickets, configuration files, and performance data.

Most platforms maintain event logs in flat-file ASCII format for performance reasons. However, this format limits the network manager's ability to search for information and manipulate the data. Therefore, links to relational database management systems (RDBMSs) are now important aspects of platform architectures. Examples of databases supported include Ingres, Sybase, Informix, and Oracle.

An RDBMS is essential for manipulating raw data and turning it into useful information. Users can obtain information from an RDBMS by writing requests, or queries, in Structured Query Language (SQL), a universally standard language for relational database communication.

Integral RDBMSs are also appearing in high-end applications, such as Cisco's CiscoWorks and Cambio's Command.

While most management platforms also supply report writer facilities, these tools are generally not top-notch. However, most higher quality third-party reporting applications can extract data from an RDBMS using SQL.

6.2.7 Core management Applications

The management platform is expected to offer core services and interfaces to other applications. The basic management applications to be provided are discovery/mapping, alarm management and platform protection.

6.2.7.1 Discovery and Mapping

Device Discovery/Network Mapping Discovery refers to the ability of the network management system to automatically learn the identity and type of devices currently active on the network. At minimum, a management platform should be capable of discovering active IP devices by retrieving data from a router's IP tables and address resolution protocol (ARP) tables.

However, even this capability does not guarantee that all IP devices on a given network will be detected. For example, relying solely on routing tables is inadequate in purely bridged networks where there are no routers. Thus, a more comprehensive discovery facility should also include other mechanisms such as broadcast messages (PING and others) that can reach out to any IP device and retrieve its address and other identifying information.

On the other hand, discovery mechanisms that rely completely on broadcasting (e.g., PING) will incur a tremendous amount of overhead in finding devices out on the network. Ideally, a management platform should support a combination of ARP data retrieval and broadcasting.

Furthermore, a complete network discovery facility should be capable of detecting legacy system nodes, such as DECnet and SNA. Currently, most platforms rely on third-party applications or traffic monitoring applications to supply discovery data on non-TCP/IP devices.

Another desirable feature is the ability to run automatic or scheduled "dynamic discovery" processes after the initial discovery, to discern any changes made to the network after the initial discovery took place. In large networks especially, overhead and consumed bandwidth for running a dynamic discovery process continually in background mode may be too great; therefore, the ability to schedule discovery at off-peak hours is important.

It is also important for the user to have the ability to set limits on the initial network discovery. Many corporate networks are now linked to the internet, and without predefined limits, a discovery application may cross corporate boundaries and begin discovering everything on the global internet. Some management platforms allow users to run discovery on a segment-by-segment basis. This can help the discovery process from getting out of hand too fast.

Many management platforms are capable of automatically producing a topological map from the data collected during device discovery. However, these automatically generated maps rarely result in a graphical representation that is useful for humans. Particularly when there are hundreds of devices, the resulting map can look very cluttered — enough to be of little use.

Even when the discovery process operates on a limited or segment-by-segment basis, there is eventually going to come a time when the operator must edit the automatically generated network map to create a visual picture that is easier for human beings to relate to. Therefore, the ability to group objects on the map, and move them around in groups or perform other types of collective actions, can be a real time-saving feature.

6.2.7.2 Alarm Capabilities

Management platforms act as a clearinghouse for critical status messages obtained from various devices and applications across the network. Messages arrive in the form of SNMP traps, alerts, or event reports when polling results indicate that thresholds have been exceeded.

The management platform supports setting of thresholds on any SNMP MIB variable. Typically, management platforms poll for device status by sending SNMP requests to devices with SNMP agents, or Internet Control Message Protocol (ICMP) echo requests ("pings") to any TCP/IP device.

The process of setting thresholds may be supported by third-party applications or by the management platform. Some platforms allow operators to configure polls on classes of devices; most require operators to configure a poll for each device individually.

Most platforms support some degree of alarm filtering. Rudimentary filtering allows operators to assign classifications to individual alarms triggered when thresholds are exceeded: such as "informational," "warning," or "critical." Once classifications are assigned, the user can specify that only critical alarms are displayed on the screen, while all other alarms are logged, for example.

More sophisticated alarm facilities support conditional alarms. An example of a conditional threshold may be "errors on incoming packets from device B > 800 for more than 5 times in 25 minutes." Conditional alarms can account for periodic spikes in traffic or daily busy periods, for example.

Finally, the platform should support the ability to automatically trigger scripts when specific alarms are received.

6.2.7.3 Platform Protection

The platform is expected to offer security features that go beyond the attribute of the operating system. Feasible choices include password, standard and user-definable privileges, encryption, and access control.

6.2.8 APPLICATION PROGRAMMING INTERFACES (APIs) AND DEVELOPMENT TOOLKITS

APIs and developer's toolkits platform vendors encourage third-party applications by providing published APIs, toolkits that include libraries of software routines, and documentation to assist applications developers. Another aspect to this effort is the "partners programs" — the marketing angle of encouraging third-party applications development.

An API shields applications developers from the details of the management platform's underlying data implementation and functional architecture. Management platform vendors generally include in their developer's kits several coded examples of how APIs can be used, as well as the APIs themselves.

In most cases, when an application takes advantage of platform APIs, it must be recompiled with the platform code resulting in a tightly integrated end product. Many independent software vendors (ISVs) and other third-party developers lack resources necessary to pursue this level of integration. Or, perhaps a more accurate way of stating this is that ISVs aren't convinced that putting out the extra effort to fully integrate their applications with all leading management platforms will result in a proportionally larger revenue stream. ISVs and other third-party developers face a choice: tightly integrate their products with one management platform vendor, or loosely integrate them with all leading platform providers. Most third parties have chosen the latter route, as they are unwilling to turn off prospective customers who may have chosen a different platform vendor as their strategic management provider.

As a result, at least 80% of the third-party applications available today are only loosely integrated with the underlying management platform — at the menu bar — and completely ignoring APIs and other environment libraries. This is expected to change as the market matures, and as platform vendors begin to offer high-level APIs which make porting applications from one management platform to another into an almost trivial exercise.

In summary, published APIs and libraries make it possible for ISVs and other third parties to write applications that take advantage of other basic services provided by the management platform. To date, few third parties have taken full advantage of platform APIs, although this is expected to change over the next few years.

6.2.9 DISTRIBUTION CAPABILITIES

Depending on the geographical locations of local area networks (LANs), some companies prefer to control entire networks from a centralized workstation. Others want to distribute some function and still others want individual departments or business units to manage their departmental resources independently. Management platforms can be configured in different ways, including client/server, peer-to-peer, or management domain. If multiple managers are in use, manager-to-manager communication is essential. This item is a real differentiator between platform products.

6.2.10 NETWORK MODELING

Network modeling is an artificial intelligence capability that can assist in automated fault isolation and diagnosis as well as performance and configuration management. Modeling allows a management system to infer the status of one object from the status of other objects.

Network modeling is facilitated by object-oriented programming techniques and languages such as C++. The goal of modeling is to simplify the representation of complex networks, creating a layer of abstraction that shields management applications from underlying details.

The building block of this technology is the "model" which describes a network element, such as a router. A model consists of data (attributes) describing the element as well as its relationships with other elements. Abstract elements such as organizations and protocols can also be modeled, as can nonintelligent devices such as cables. A model may use information from other models to determine its own state; modeling can reduce the complexity of management data and highlight the most important information. In this way, fault isolation and diagnosis can be automated. In addition, models can be used to depict traffic patterns, trends, topologies or distributions to assist in performance and configuration management.

6.2.11 SUPPORT OF FRAMEWORKS

Standardization committees have been trying to streamline integration efforts. They offer recommendations for platforms including the communication between managers and agents, more core applications and for the depth of application integration.

6.2.12 OBJECT ORIENTATION

Object-oriented and objects-based technologies are helpful in relation to user interfaces, protocols, and databases. The use of object request brokers (ORB) and CORBA provides a glue needed to accomplish interoperability between heterogeneous systems.

Table 6.1 summarizes these principal platform attributes.

TABLE 6.1
List of Platform Attributes

Hardware platform of the product
Operating systems
Network architectures
Management protocols
Graphical user interfaces
Database support
Core management applications
Application programming interfaces
Distribution capabilities
Network modeling
Support of frameworks
Object orientation

6.3 PLATFORM SUPPLIERS AND THEIR WEB-BASED SOLUTIONS

Practically all platform providers emphasize their capabilities to extend their platforms by using the Web technology. A couple of management platforms are going to be introduced in alphabetic order.

Table 6.2 lists some of the principal suppliers of management platforms.

6.3.1 INTRASPECTION FROM ASANTE TECHNOLOGIES

IntraSpection is the first SNMP management platform based entirely on Web technologies. It is an open, standards-based SNMP management platform that runs on

TABLE 6.2
Suppliers of Management Platforms

Supplier	Platform
AT&T	BaseWorx
Bull	ISM/Open Master
Cabletron	Spectrum
Compaq/Digital	TeMIP
Computer Associates	Unicenter TNG
Hewlett Packard	OpenView
IBM/Tivoli	TME 10
Micromuse	NetCool
Microsoft	SMS
Novell	ManageWise
Objective Systems Integrators	NetExpert
Platinum	Poems
SunSoft	Solstice Enterprise Manager
TCSI	Object Services Package
Ungermann Bass	NetDirector

a Windows NT server and delivers standard SNMP protocol data units (PDUs) graphically to any Java-enabled Web browser. Thus, IntraSpection provides network management capabilities for the entire network anytime, anywhere with a universal Web browser.

IntraSpection includes true multiple platforms support as network managers can manage the entire network with one Java-enabled browser instead of various Macintosh, UNIX, or NT workstations. It provides the same GUI, operating procedures, and functionality across all platforms. Java technologies enable IntraSpection to deliver real-time network status monitoring, statistics graphs, network discoveries, and problem reports. All of this information is constantly updated and delivered to the client browser automatically.

In addition, the product speeds up problem identification, isolation, and resolution. Network managers have the flexibility to identify, isolate, resolve, and monitor the entire network from any place with a Web access. There is no need to physically be present at the management station. IntraSpection also simplifies the implementation of SNMP by providing multi-vendor hardware support in a single unified platform. Both Asante and third-party hardware devices may be managed down to the port level.

Figure 6.4 shows the architecture of IntraSpection. It is comprised of five software modules. The Map Manager builds a topology diagram of the network. The Device Manager graphically represents each network element. The Trap Manager gathers device statistics, and also stores that information on a third-party database that is running on the same server. The MIB Manager allows the network manager to search the public MIBs, special repeater, Ethernet and bridge MIBs, plus the RMON MIB. Finally, the Common Gateway Interface (CGI) module translates HTML to/from SNMP commands and responses.

IntraSpection also provides a powerful development platform. Unlike the traditional network management software platform which requires special programming, IntraSpection gives users the ability to develop a complete device management

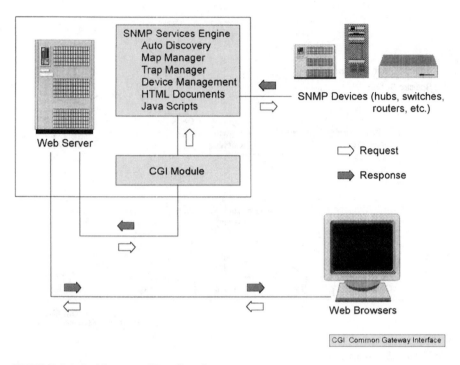

FIGURE 6.4 Architecture of IntraSpection.

system with one HTML page. It is completely modifiable and can be customized to meet specific user needs.

6.3.2 SPECTRUM FROM CABLETRON SYSTEMS

Spectrum Enterprise Manager is designed as an open management platform, to be implemented in multi-vendor environments. The architecture is based upon a client/server paradigm, with various interfaces to other systems. It consists of two principal elements:

- A graphical user interface, called the SpectroGRAPH, that provides a motif-based interface for the end-user.
- The management server that consists of two components: the Virtual Network Machine (VNM) creates models of the various network entities, such as cables or network devices. The Device Communication Manager (DCM) is a multi-protocol communications engine, with protocol support for SNMP, CMIP, IEEE 802.1 and ICMP/PING command, as well as extensions for any proprietary protocols. Figure 6.5 shows the architecture of Spectrum.

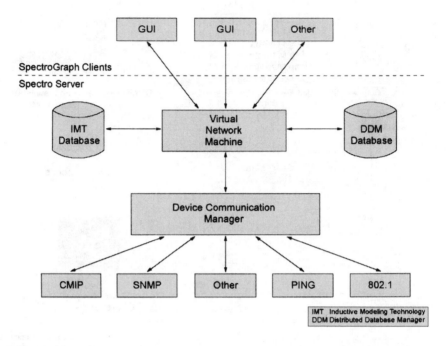

FIGURE 6.5 Architecture of Spectrum.

In a typical implementation, the SpectroGRAPH and SpectroSERVER run on different hosts on the network. The two systems are typically connected via a UNIX socket. Spectrum is highly scalable with many hundreds of SpectroSERVERS working in parallel.

Spectrum Enterprise Manager can support both UNIX and NT workstations. Both types of workstations can interoperate.

Spectrum utilizes two databases. The Distributed Database Manager (DDM) contains an archive of network events and statistics. The Inductive Modeling Technology (IMT) database models network relationships from a variety of perspectives, such as topology, alarms, hierarchies, and even organizations. Both databases are resident with the SpectroSERVER, but can provide integrated, enterprise-wide reports, alarm views, automated application notification, and other enterprise-wide features. Many applications use IMT to build higher levels of automation. For instance, Spectrum Resolution Expert provides customers with automated fault resolution using an AI technology called case-based reasoning. It helps to diagnose network and systems problems drawing on past case histories.

All existing management applications running on Spectrum can be accessed by universal browsers. In addition, there are three extensions that are using Web-based technology: Web AlarmView, Web-based Reporting, and Web-based Resolution Expert.

Web AlarmView is a sophisticated fault isolation application. Using IMT, Web AlarmView centralizes the results of fault isolation data from anywhere in a network and across multiple managed domains, using a universal Web browser. It helps to continuously supervise networks without physical presence. After operators are paged about problems on the network, they can pull up the Web AlarmView application on a laptop, and the application will pinpoint exactly where the problem is occurring.

Web-based Reporting brings pertinent Spectrum-related reports to the desktop, permitting network operators, administrators, CIOs, and other IS professionals to easily obtain vital reports on the state of the corporate network. These Web-based reports can be automatically scheduled to cover everything from router or server failures to intranet usage, to global status of network health. Web-based reports provide a familiar, easy-to-use application interface, while facilitating remote and home access.

Web-based Resolution Expert uses case-based reasoning that provides users with automated fault resolution. Basing corrective recommendations on knowledge gathered from previous problems, it recommends a prioritized set of solutions for systems and network problems. This application is accessible by a universal Web browser. SpectroRx has been adapted to the Web using Java. In this application, a Web server accesses the remote SpectroGRAPH where SpectroRx resides. When invoked, SpectroRx provides the remote user with a list of faulty device or software attributes, as well as suggestions to correct the problem based on past experience.

6.3.3 TNG FROM COMPUTER ASSOCIATES

TNG features, as an absolute novelty for a management platform, a three-dimensional, animated, graphical user interface, called the Real World Interface. The core platform is bundled under the Common Object Repository component which hides the object manipulation and object storage processes. Objects representing the abstraction of actual managed resources and objects created by the platform services are stored in the platform object database. Query and search capabilities allow core management functions and applications to access the management information. Figure 6.6 shows the simplified view of the TNG architecture.

The availability of a Java browser, based on either a two-dimensional or virtual reality three-dimensional interface, provides an alternative graphic environment. This Web interface, in particular, delivers on the framework's promise of managing everything from anywhere. The Java browser interface allows users to manage a Web site with Unicenter TNG from virtually any internet browser. The attributes are:

- It uses ordinary HTML to present static information.
- It uses Java to build the more advanced user interfaces required to deal with all the complex information that Unicenter owns.
- It uses VRML (Virtual Reality Modeling Language), the internet standard for 3D information, to present 3D views.

However, the Web browser does not connect directly to Unicenter TNG. The user needs the Web browser plug to connect into a socket. A Java server provides the socket.

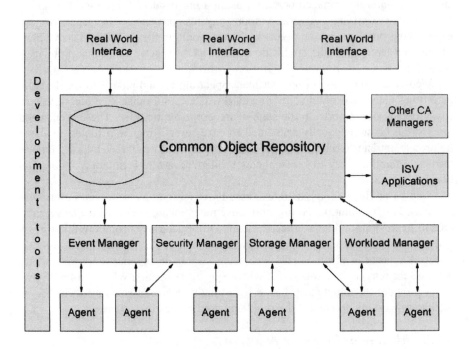

FIGURE 6.6 Simplified view of the TNG architecture.

This server provides many valuable services. It presents the information that the browser needs. It formats reports and other information as HTML, it feeds the data to the Java interface, and it renders the network description from the repository into VRML files. It also acts as the initial launching point, delivering the Java applet down to the client. To get its information, the server connects to all the services within the Unicenter architecture. Naturally, it gets the bulk of its information from the repository. Unicenter TNG does not send all detail information from the agents up to a centralized repository, however. Indeed, that much management traffic might well overload the network.

The agents and managers keep most detail information locally, sending only essential information, such as location, identification, object class, and status, up to the repository. The server needs to talk directly to managers spread across the network because Unicenter has a distributed architecture. Still, for monitoring and managing a specific system, the browser can talk to the agent directly.

The browser interface requires very little in the workstation. It needs connectivity to the network, a Web browser, a Java engine, and a VRML browser. These components are available with practically any browser.

The look and feel of the browser interface is modeled on the standard Unicenter TNG interface. This user interface builds on the previous paradigm because it is well understood by thousands of users. However, the structure of the interface has been consolidated to bring together GUI elements that better fit the browser. In particular, the system tries to present most information in a single window, which is the common approach in browsers.

The browser interface included with the Real World Interface provides a 3D view of the world, the network, and the resources in it. The browser version of this 3D view is also quite similar to the classical version. In the browser interface, the Real World Interface is built using VRML, which is an emerging standard for 3D content on the Web. The user can navigate through the world, either manually or in autopilot mode, by clicking on objects. The status of objects is displayed with the familiar red color. The 2D map navigation works identically, meaning that double-clicking on icons enters them and opens up details.

The tree browser lists the objects in the containment hierarchy, from countries, cities, and buildings, through networks and subnetworks, down to computers, disk drives, databases, and processes. The right pane can take various appearances, just like the Windows Explorer: detailed list, icon list, and small and large icons. In addition, the Unicenter Explorer-style interface provides a 2D map in the right pane as another arrangement of the contents of the tree. The Property notebook works in the Explorer-style browser as well; the detailed properties and status of any object in the tree are displayed in the right pane.

The tree browser, 2D map, 3D map, and notebooks represent information in the repository, which knows which objects exist and their main properties, including their status.

At times, users need to view detailed, real-time data. This information is not resident in the central repository. The Explorer-style browser allows users to get at such data using the tree structure by drilling down into the system. By opening up the target computer's Unispace, the managers that are controlling the machine or the agents that are monitoring it become accessible. All the managed objects in the system, the file systems, memory, CPUs, and active processes, appear in the tree, seamlessly integrated with the larger objects such as computers, networks, and building.

Thus, the browser hides the data source from the user. A network is simply viewed as a containment hierarchy, and the browser provides nearly infinite drill-down, regardless of the management component actually providing the data.

In order to get real-time data on what is happening in the managed objects, such as CPU, disks, etc., the Explorer needs to talk to the agent that is actually monitoring the systems. The browser offers an Agent View that displays dynamic metrics sent by the agent. The Agent View provides a number of pages, each with a number of controls. The actual configuration can be tailored depending on the situation. Each agent monitors different data and provides an appropriate representation updating its measurements. Agent View also allows management of the agent. For example, the user can alter alarm thresholds, the poll interval, and other agent policy speci-fications.

The browser can also monitor performance data coming back from the Perfor-mance Agent. For each object selected in the tree browser, the performance monitor shows an appropriate metric. It also permits explicit selection of which metric to monitor. The performance scope shows the real-time metric, continually updated, compared with the historical data for the same parameter in the left pane of the chart.

Inside Unispace, each system presents its management and administration functions: event management, storage management, workload management, software distribution, and so on. Most management disciplines display data in some form of familiar notebook. For example, under Event Management is the message record, which displays a list of message records in the right pane of the Explorer. Opening a message record shows a notebook with the various categories of properties of that record.

The Report Browser shows the various categories of reports available. The report is displayed in the Web browser in the form of HTML text. The Web browser displays product help files and online documentation. The help system uses a similar split screen with a table of contents in the left pane, allowing users to select a chapter while presenting the detailed information in the frame of the bottom.

TNG includes many functional modules, which provide event management, security management, storage management, workload and performance management, as well as backup and recovery functions. Management of distributed resources is based on a manager-agent infrastructure which relies on a mix of proprietary and standard agents. TNG allows scalable, multilevel, hierarchical build-up of manager-agent structures as required for managing large enterprise networks.

The following application packages run on top of the TNG platform:

- Software delivery
- Advanced help desk
- Open Storage Manager
- Single sign on
- Internet Commerce Enabler

The company is acquiring products, but more than in the past, pays a lot of attention to integration.

6.3.4   TME 10/NETVIEW FROM IBM/TIVOLI

TME 10 integrates systems and network management. Systems management is provided by Tivoli, and network management is supplied by IBM. TME 10 NetView enables users to discover TCP/IP networks, display network topologies, correlate and manage events and SNMP traps, monitor network health, and gather performance data. The Tivoli part is known for the ability to easily effect changes on many devices, distribute software very effectively, and support inventory and asset management. Figure 6.7 shows the architecture of TME 10, with emphasis on systems management functions.

The net.TME initiative is targeted primarily at corporate customers using internet services for internal or intranet communications. The net.TME is a four-pronged strategy, including new Tivoli products, new interfaces supporting third-party internet management applications, new internet management spearheaded by Tivoli, and Web-enabling enhancements to Tivoli's existing product line.

The first product announced is Tivoli/net.Commander, a specialized, bundled version of TME 10 Distributed Monitoring, TME 10 Software Distribution, and the

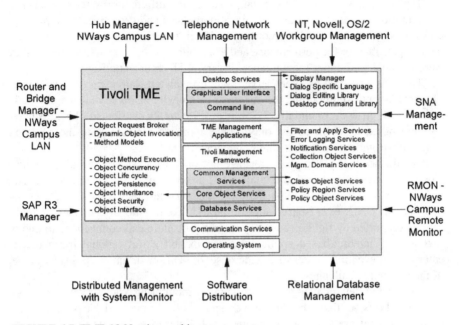

FIGURE 6.7 TME 10 Netview architecture.

Tivoli Management Environment (TME) framework, all optimized for managing aspects of the internet environment. The first release concentrates on deployment and configuration as well as availability and performance management for Netscape on Solaris and Microsoft Information Server on NT. Subsequent releases add support for user access control, including mail alias management and enterprise user console integration. That release will also support additional Web servers, including Open Market, Spyglass on UNIX, Lotus InterNotes, and IBM ICS on UNIX and NT.

Tivoli/net.Commander autodiscovers all internet servers and services, creating icons for each on the management console. The product then establishes dialogues for configuration and deployment, enabling administrators to more easily set up parameters for new servers. The Tivoli/Sentry component provides a scrolling list of monitors including, for example, one that monitors the size of Web server log files to ensure that they do not grow large enough to impact performance. It also makes it easier to configure load balancing via DNS round-robin management. DNS round-robin is a widely used algorithm that automatically connects those attempting to access a Web site to the next available web server.

The initial version of net.Commander also supports out-of-the-box browser deployment for Netscape on Solaris and Microsoft Info Server for NT. This capability, supported by Tivoli/Courier, allows IT administrators to push client browsers down to remote desktops. The benefit to this approach is a greater degree of centralized control over browser deployment, as well as embedded helper applications provided by net.Commander, and a standard set of bookmarks available to all users across the enterprise.

Typically, most end-user organizations today use different browser versions and configurations across the enterprise, since individuals and departments simply FTP down off the internet at will. According to Tivoli, however, central IT staff are still held responsible for the performance and availability of these browsers, even if they were not deployed under the guidance of central IT organizations.

Tivoli believes that as client/server systems evolve toward even greater degrees of network-centric computing, the degree of complexity involved in managing these systems will grow exponentially. Tivoli is positioning its distributed object technology, embodied in TME, as the only viable approach for managing the network-centric environment through a single, integrated interface.

Tivoli's net.TME attempts to manage not only Web servers, but also the new cloud of internet services that include mail, proxy, news, gopher, directories, and FTP. When organizations deploy these internet services, they also enable a whole new class of UNIX or NT-based applications. Unlike traditional client/server applications supported by rigid, proprietary remote procedure call connections to one or two servers, internet-based applications can exhibit a truly global reach that is enterprise or even inter-enterprise-wide in scope. This environment poses a new set of management challenges.

One of the new challenges in particular is monitoring Web server activity — tracking who is "hitting" the Web server, and where. To this end, Tivoli also offers a Tivoli/Plus integration module linking Tivoli Enterprise Console to a third-party application called Net.Analysis from NetGenesis Corporation. Net.Analysis is designed to track and display real-time Web content usage. The product parses Web server log files and stores them in a relational database, allowing administrators to run reports showing who is hitting the Web site and which pages they are hitting.

The final plank of the net.TME platform is the introduction of Web-enabling technology to existing Tivoli products, including Web browser interfaces. This allows administrators as well as end-users to access selected TME functions using a Web browser interface.

For example, laptop users will go through the Web browser to access Tivoli/Courier for the purpose of pulling down software distributions. The Web interface also provides an easier way for senior level managers to obtain accurate real-time data on TME-managed resources, such as summarized reports tracking the number of software distributions completed of the problems detected and corrected automatically via TME.

Tivoli is certainly correct in claiming that the scale of the computing environment has grown due to the proliferation of Web technology. Not only must network and systems administrators manage applications spanning multiple sites, but also now face the possibility of inter-enterprise applications.

According to Tivoli, successful management of internet environments requires an open, standards-based approach embracing a mastery of distributed object technology and integrating management of the existing client/server environment. Rather than managing individual servers, or just using the Web with existing tools, Tivoli is seeking to promote use of an Internet Management Standard (IMS) as well as to offer Web technology integrated into TME.

The new Java-based Web interface of TME 10 NetView, compatible with both Netscape and Microsoft browsers, makes it simple for administrators and their teams to view network information from a dynamically updated display. With URL and password, administrators and operators can remotely diagnose problems, having easy access to information such as topology maps, SNMP events, node status, dynamic object collections, object information, and the status of NetView itself. This Java interface enables users to access a complete range of management information using a universal browser.

There is a three-tiered architecture, made up of TME 10 NetView for OS/390, a Central NetView Server, as well as Attended and Unattended Regional NetView Servers, which provides flexibility in managing dispersed network environments. The Central NetView Server features event correlation and filtering, as well as integration with the TME 10 Enterprise Console and TME 10 Framework, making it possible to install, configure and administer TME NetView servers from one central point, across multiple distributed platforms. Regional NetView servers feature attended or unattended management of remote offices, the ability to offload work from the central NetView Server, the ability to locally manage a remote network during a wide area network (WAN) outage and reduction in event traffic over the network. The Regional NetView capability delivers all the core functionality of TME 10 NetView to either attended or unattended remote offices, while addressing concerns over limited bandwidth and memory capabilities in these remote offices. TME 10 NetView also offers event filtering to offload processing from the central NetView console.

Basically, all members of TME are accessible by Web browsers. Users can view network and systems information from any universal Web browser. The result is that the management products make information available to a much broader range of users and allows easy access from remote locations. Tivoli is supporting the Web-based Enterprise Management (WBEM) initiative by allowing customers to display and report data for use in trouble-shooting and performing inventory operations, using WBEM-based data.

The Distributed Monitoring tool includes Inspector, which is a powerful graphical trend analysis tool accessible via a Web browser. It allows one to remotely access and troubleshoot distributed systems and provides a graphical representation of multiple metrics for one or multiple distributed devices. This visualization quickly leads to understanding of the nature of the problems and helps to find corrective actions.

Application Policy Manager (APM) is the final component of TME 10, the company's solution for managing distributed applications from the desktop to the host. It features a 100% Java-based graphical user interface (GUI), which allows administrators to conduct management operations from any platform supporting the Java Virtual Machine or any Java-enabled Web browser. This power to manage from anywhere provides administrators with unmatched flexibility, resulting in greater productivity.

6.3.5 OpenView from Hewlett Packard

The OpenView family provides an integrated network and systems management solution. It consists of a number of products from Hewlett Packard (HP) and also from Solution Partners. The most important components of the OpenView family are

- Network Node Manager — it meets the requirements for a powerful SNMP core solution.
- IT/Operations — it represents an advanced integrated operations and problem management solution for networks and systems.
- IT/Administration — it represents an integrated solution for change management. It also includes inventory, asset, software and user management.
- PerfView, NetMetrix and MeasureWare — they represent performance management solutions for networks and systems, and may be considered as the foundation for service level management.
- OmniBack and OmniStorage — they are typical systems management solutions for powerful backup and storage management.

Figure 6.8 shows OpenView with its principal components.

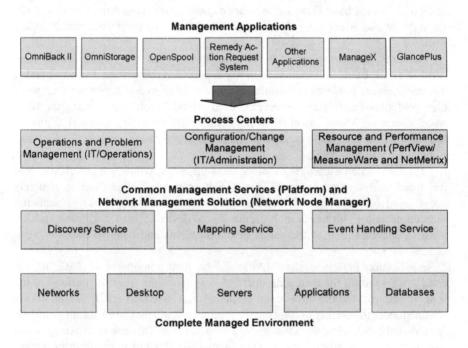

FIGURE 6.8 Principal components of OpenView.

HP is targeting OpenView Network Node Manager at managing the internet/intranet infrastructure rather than Web servers and services. HP promotes a three-tier OpenView strategy for managing and leveraging the internet:

- Manage the corporate intranet infrastructure, including network infrastructure, servers and internet applications, and security
- Manage the infrastructure of internet service providers
- Leverage internet technologies in OpenView solutions

The enhancements in Network Node Manager (NNM) have significantly increased the product's scalability, making OpenView-based management of corporate internet/intranet infrastructures possible. Management of Web servers and applications is largely provided by the generic server and application management capabilities of IT/Operations. HP is targeting management of internet service providers' infrastructure through its HP OpenView DM offering, and HP OpenView Event Correlation Services. Internet service providers may include carriers, cable companies, value added networks, and others. Finally, HP is exploring and prototyping Web technology extensions to OpenView products, including the following:

- Web access to OpenView event repositories for problem management support
- Web access to the OpenView map
- Internet as a software transport vehicle

6.3.5.1 Using IT/Operations for Internet Management

IT/Operations is capable of managing processes and applications running on any computer for which HP provides an IT/Operations agent. Supported systems include HP-UX, Solaris, AIX, SCO, Windows NT, among others. IT/Operations agents are capable of intercepting SNMP traps, UNIX logfile messages, and events generated when IT/Operations agents detect threshold crossings. Using these attributes, Netscape Commerce Servers can also be managed. They can run under HP/UX and support secure electronic commerce and communications on the internet and TCP/IP intranets. The server permits corporations to publish HTML-formatted documents (Web pages) and deliver them using HTTP. To ensure data security, the Netscape Commerce Server provides server authentication, data encryption, and user authorization. Communications support also includes the Common Gateway Interface (CGI) and the Secure Socket Layer (SSL) protocol.

To support manageability, the Netscape Commerce Server records several kinds of errors, all of which can be collected by an IT/Operations agent reading the logfile of the server. These errors include the following:

- Unauthorized — occurs when users attempt to access protected server documents without proper permission.
- Forbidden — occurs when the server lacks file system permissions needed to execute a read or to follow symbolic links.

- Not found — occurs when the server cannot find a document or has been instructed to deny a document's existence.
- Server error — occurs when the server has been misconfigured or affected by a core dump, out of memory, or other catastrophic error.

HP provides an IT/Operations template for handling these errors. Users can derive proper responses, including forwarding events to the appropriate IT/Operations or database operators, or triggering a script for deleting hypertext links to documents that no longer exist.

Each error type described above can be associated with error codes.

IT/Operations agents are capable of collecting these error messages and forwarding user-specified events to the IT/Operations console for operator attention and problem resolution. For example, in the case of server error, possible causes of the problem may include the following:

- CGI is not enabled on the Web server — preventing electronic commerce application from running
- Permissions have not been specified properly
- CGI script is not specifying a shell or other program to be run
- Syntax error in the script

Syntax errors are typically resolved by tweaking application scripts, which may be written in CGI, Practical Extraction and Report Language (PERL), or Tool Command Language (TCL). Many Web server applications for electronic commerce are written in C language and implemented with CGI, PERL, or TCL scripts.

6.3.5.2   Monitoring Web Page Availability with IT/Operations

IT/Operations can be deployed to monitor Web page status as well as Web Server status. Specific functions supported include:

- Monitoring Web access logfiles and error logfiles
- Monitoring the HTTP deamon
- Viewing server access statistics
- Integrating the native Netscape administration and configuration tools into IT/Operations
- Starting up and shutting down the Web server and administrative interface
- Modifying access configuration

HP has developed a script that can be used by the IT/Operations agent monitor to check the availability of the Web server system, the HTTP port, and the Web page. The script uses the Korn shell, one of four major UNIX command and script interpreters in use today. This script, designed primarily for Netscape Commerce Server, can theoretically be modified and extended to monitor other Web servers as well.

In order to meet the needs of today's IT organizations, a new Java-based user interface has been added to IT/Operations. The features and benefits of such an interface can be summarized as follows:

Ease of use

- The Java-based interface combines the familiar concepts of IT/Operations with Windows-like concepts (similar to ExplorerView), to minimize training time and reduce the operator's learning curve.
- Most functions available in the IT/Operations Motif Operator user interface are supported in the Java version. The characteristics of Java also add functionality that is not available in the standard user interface, such as sorting and shifting columns in the IT/Operations' message browsers.
- It is available on the Windows NT operating system. The Java user interface allows the management of large heterogeneous environments from PCs running the Windows NT operating system.
- Through a special application-bank entry, local Windows NT applications can be tightly integrated with the Java user interface, resulting in a more powerful, integrated Windows NT operator workstation.

Scalability and distribution

- The number of operators that can concurrently access IT/Operations from a Java user interface is greatly increased.
- This addresses the needs of customers with large environments. The size of environments is continually increasing.
- The Java user interface minimizes network traffic, enabling it to work over low-bandwidth lines.
- It is not common to have a LAN connection for example at home or in a remote office, yet management is available whether at home or on the road.
- The Java user interface runs on any machine with a Java compliant browser or as a stand-alone application on HP-UX or the Windows NT operating system.

Lower total cost

- Previously the operators had to have a UNIX workstation or special tools on NT PCs to obtain the same functionality.
- No additional IT/Operations software or hardware needs to be installed and maintained on the client systems, other than a Web browser.
- The Java-based interface is designed to take up minimal resources on the client.

6.3.6   SYSTEM MANAGEMENT SERVER FROM MICROSOFT

SMS (System Management Server) is a centralized, scalable management system for heterogeneous, distributed PC and server computing environments. It is entirely developed by Microsoft as part of its strategy to provide comprehensive management capabilities for Microsoft solutions. The main functions provided by SMS are systems administration, software management, and diagnostics. The platform design has been extended to include network management capabilities. It is based on the client/server architecture. A distributed management example is shown in Figure 6.9.

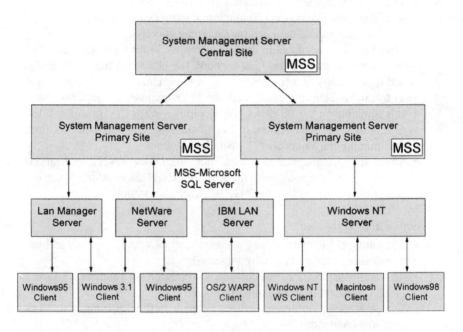

FIGURE 6.9 System Management Server (SMS) distributed management.

The SMS-based management structure assumes logical grouping of servers and their domain into sites. The sites can be arranged into hierarchical structures. One can have a central site SMS, which centrally manages the whole network. The central site has its own database that stores information pertinent to the whole network. Remote consoles are available for the central sites to distribute the workload of operations. At the next level of hierarchy, multiple SMS primary sites can be deployed. The primary site has databases, Microsoft SQL Servers to store management information limited to that site. The database can be installed on the SMS servers or can be separated from them. The primary sites control the secondary servers which do not have a database. The management information pertinent to each secondary site is stored at the primary site.

SMS provides three principal management applications:

- System administration (desktop PC/server administration, security, configuration, inventory. and queries)
- Software distribution (packages, jobs, and network applications)
- Diagnostics and remote troubleshooting (events, alerts, and network monitoring)

Microsoft is very much interested in extending the capabilities of SMS to incorporate more network management functions.

SMS 2.0 agents with Windows NT 5.0 server and workstation are using WBEM to deliver enterprise-scalable configuration and change management solution for MS Windows operating system based desktops and servers.

Windows Management Instrumentation (WMI) provides the basis for instrumentation in future Windows environments. Close coupling of WMI with services developed to conform to the WBEM initiative will allow Microsoft to simplify instrumentation and provide consistent, open access to management data. Future Windows NT operating systems include a structured set of instrumentation services within the operating system. A key component of these services is WMI. WMI is a set of extensions to the Windows Driver Model (WDM). WMI provides an operating system interface through which instrumented components can provide information and notification. It provides a bi-directional instrumentation access mechanism. It brings together the management data from the hardware platform, drivers, and applications and passes the consolidated data into a consistent management information store. This store, developed to conform to the requirements of WBEM, uses CIM as the basis for exposing and interacting with this information. CIM and WMI are core enabling technologies. Together these core technologies provide a powerful and consistent mechanism enabling management applications, platforms, and consoles to perform the following types of management tasks on Windows-based hardware and software:

- Monitoring and reconciliation of hardware/software faults and alerts
- Pre-emotive maintenance
- Upgrade management and version control
- Capacity planning and performance management
- Enhanced security and asset management
- Operations management
- Automated management

Figure 6.10 shows the architecture overview of WMI.

Access between WMI and hardware devices is via an important low-level component, known as the Windows Driver Model. Each instrumented hardware device (e.g., disk drive, network interface card, etc.) provides device-specific management access to WDM via its own, WDM mini driver. The WDM mini driver that is provided by the hardware vendor passes specific information to standard interfaces in the WDM class driver which is provided by Microsoft. The WDM class driver passes the device information to the WMI kernel mode subsystem.

Most high-level applications execute exclusively in user mode; they have no direct interaction with the kernel. All such applications can integrate directly with the WBEM agent. Interface usage and guidelines will be made available in the WBEM SDK. WDI provides the communication between the management information store and the instrumented device drivers. WMI is also responsible for negotiating and delivering events (e.g., device status, application performance metrics, device errors) from devices and software to the management information store.

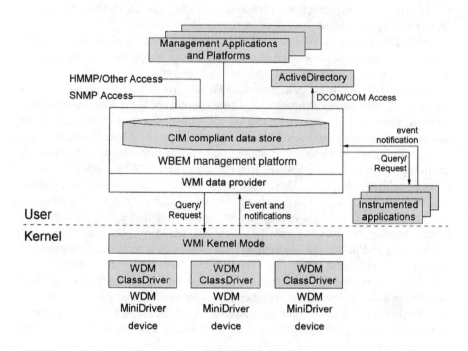

FIGURE 6.10 Windows Management Instrumentation (WMI) architecture overview.

The WBEM management agent, comprising the management schema, object information store, and access mechanisms, provides a universally accessible, device/application extensible storage mechanism for statically and dynamically instrumented data. The schema is implemented according to the guidelines provided by the DMTF CIM to maximize interoperability between systems and network management systems. Through the WBEM agent it is possible to integrate and unify existing instrumentation mechanisms, including SNMP, DMI, CMIP, and proprietary technologies. WBEM allows administrators to consolidate information from these many different instrumentation mechanisms, while leveraging the benefits of the coherent and extensible instrumentation of the Windows environment through WMI.

6.3.7 SOLSTICE MANAGEMENT FROM SUN MICROSYSTEMS

The network management product family includes Solstice Site Manager (SM), Solstice Domain Manager (DM), and Solstice Enterprise Manager (EM). Solstice SunNet Manager (SNM) is one of the most widely used management platforms. It has been extended by Cooperative Consoles, and became the basis of Site and Domain Managers.

Site Manager is designed to meet the requirements of smaller sites, managing up to approximately 100 nodes. It includes SNM plus the sender portion of Cooperative Consoles which allows management data, including topological information, events, and traps, to be forwarded to the Domain Manager. Site Manager can also work together with ManageWise.

The Domain Manager is designed to meet the requirements of larger or multisite environments. This product includes SNM, the sender and receiver portion of Cooperate Consoles, and an advanced layout tool. It may be used in one of three configurations:

- Stand-alone platform for large sites
- Central manager connecting multiple Site and Domain Managers
- Peer-to-peer with other Domain Managers

Key features of the Domain Manager include:

- Event management, including event-based actions
- Scheduled requests and alarm reports
- User tools, including the console, topological map, link management, discover, layout, browser, and grapher tools

Distributed network management is the foundation for the Solstice Site and Domain Managers. Multiple Site Managers can be deployed, and be connected to a Domain Manager. Multiple Domain Managers are also possible. In addition, the management of larger networks can be simplified by spreading the management load across two different types of agents: device-based agents and proxy agents that act as middle managers. The middle managers localize network management polling to minimize network management traffic. Both the Site and Domain Managers include a number of integrated SNMP features, including the Proxy Agent, Trap Daemon to translate and forward traps, the MIB2-schema utility for MIB translations, and support for the protocol operations enhancements for SNMPv2.

Figure 6.11 shows the architecture of Solstice management. It represents the next-generation network management platform. It is based on a distributed, object-oriented, client/server architecture that allows it to scale to manage large, distributed, or mission critical networks. The client/server architecture provides true multiuser support. Security is based on defined users and groups. Access controls can be specified on a platform, on applications, or application-features.

In order to increase scalability, multiple management information servers (MIS) can be deployed. They can communicate with each other and present a consistent view of the network.

The new Java Management Interface (JMI) in Solstice Enterprise Manager provides the high-level Java APIs and associated infrastructure to develop low-cost, multi-platform Java applications. These applications take full advantage of the powerful, distributed management services of the management platform. Users now have:

- Greater flexibility in how client applications are developed
- A wider range of platforms and devices for client application deployment
- A new set of options for how networks can be monitored and managed

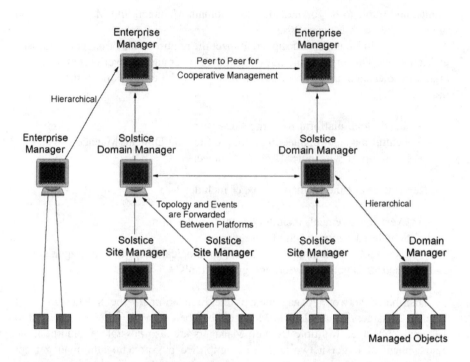

FIGURE 6.11 Architecture of Solstice management.

This new Java Management Console (JMC) enables network operators and administrators to browse network topology, view fault data, and gather device details — all from one integrated, easy-to-use, thin-client Java application. A configuration wizard enables operators to dynamically create a customized view of the network to filter out the noise of extraneous equipment or network domains, which allows them to focus only on their specific management responsibilities. The application integration utility allows additional browser-based applications from other management vendors to be integrated into JMC, allowing central console for launching required management functions. JMC is a technology release, not yet a supported product.

Because of its capability, capacity, reliability, high availability, and performance, Solstice Enterprise Manager is best suited for managing large networks. Its adherence to many telecommunications and internet standards makes it highly suited to the network management needs of telecommunications carriers and internet service providers. Access control can also be configured down to the individual managed object level. It has a rich development environment which enables customers, ISVs and original equipment manufacturers to build solutions on top of the platform that best suits their own needs.

6.4   WEB INNOVATIONS

Intelligent agents play a key role in advanced management structures. Web-based systems and network management relies heavily on agents in both WBEM and Java concepts. Java applets may even be considered as mobile agents. An agent is a self-contained software element responsible for performing part of a programmatic process. Therefore, it contains some level of intelligence, ranging from simple predefined rules to self-learning artificial intelligence interference machines. It acts typically on behalf of a user or a process enabling task automation. Agents operate rather autonomously — they are often event or time triggered — and may communicate with the user, system resources, and other agents as required to perform their task. Moreover, more advanced agents may cooperate with other agents to carry out tasks beyond the capability of a single agent. Finally, as transportable or even active objects, they may move from one system to another to access remote resources or to meet or cooperate with other agents. Agents may be characterized by intelligence, communications, operations, cooperations, and mobility.

Intelligent agents may be classified as follows:[14]

1. Single-agent systems
   - Local Agents (personal assistant, advisory assistant)
   - Networked Agents (personal assistant, smart mailboxes, retrieval agents, process automation)
2. Multi-Agent Systems
   - Distributed artificial intelligence-based agents (distributed problem solving)
   - Mobile agents (telecommunications, network management, electronic markets)

In single-agent systems, an agent performs a task on behalf of a user or some process. While performing its task, the agent may communicate with the user as well as with local or remote system resources, but it will never communicate with other agents. In contrast, the agents in a multi-agent system may cooperate extensively with each other to achieve their individual goals. Of course, in those systems, agents may also interact with users and system resources.

Mobile agents are primarily for large networks with many intelligent systems. Agents may get different policy-driven tasks from the management platform or from users. The same platform may incorporate a Web server. Agents asynchronously perform tasks in different components. Performance can be good because agents are tuned to the tasks. But mobility causes communication overhead. The final decision depends on the interaction patterns and the size of the agent.

The following deployment alternatives may be considered for mobile agents:[4]

- Asynchronous and cooperative processing of tasks: the possibility of delegating specific tasks by means of mobile agents to one specific or even multiple nodes allows for highly dynamic and parallel computations.

Particularly this supports disconnected operation of tasks and weak client computers.

- Customization and configuration of services: in the light of an electronic marketplace, agent technology allows instant provision of new services either by customization or (re)configuration of existing services. In this case, agents act as service adaptors and can be easily installed.
- Instant service usage and active trading: mobile agents realizing service clients travel to potential customers providing spontaneous access to new services. This feature enabling easy distribution of service clients can be exploited to perform active trading.
- Decentralization of management: mobile agents allow decreased pressure on centralized network management if necessary. Also network bandwidth needs can be reduced by delegating specific management tasks from the central operation to dispersed management agents. Mobile agents representing management scripts enable both temporal distribution (over time) and spatial distribution (over different network nodes) of management activities.
- Intelligent communications: agents provide the basis for advanced communications. They support the configuration of a user's communications environment, where they perform control of incoming and outgoing communications on behalf of the end user. This includes communications screening, intelligent adaptation of services to network access arrangements and end user devices, as well as advanced service inter-networking and integration.
- Information retrieval and support of dynamic information types: mobile agents provide an effective means for retrieving information and services within a distributed environment and support for dynamic information types within electronic mail and advanced networked information systems.

The manager-agent relationship is significant in managing systems and networks. The manager can delegate certain management tasks to agents. That happens actually with element management systems, manager of managers, and with platform-driven solutions. Delegation means that the manager downloads/pushes scripts to the agents. It could be Java scripts. The distribution software in use can be different. Distribution protocols are not relevant in this respect. The tasks remain the same for the agents until the next version is downloaded. The execution of operations follows prescheduled or delayed decision rules set by the manager. Mobile management applications represent an extension of the above scenario. In this case, the manager generates a mobile agent that performs specific management tasks autonomously and purposefully at specific agents in order to collect status information, deploy changes, download scripts, etc. in a coordinated way. The visiting sequence of mobile agents can be set up by their managers.

The use of mobile agents is not in contradiction to Web-based management. Mobile agents execute tasks in management agents that can be accessed by universal

Web browsers. In another approach, it can be said that mobile agents collect, process, and prepare information to be distributed by Web tools.

Traditionally, the Web-based management model uses the "pull" technique to view, review, select, and download information. It requests that members of the management team periodically use their browser to access Web servers. The result is that important events and status changes may remain unobserved. Other Web-based management activities, such as configuration management, distribution of reports, preventive maintenance are not impacted because people initiate these activities. Selected or "smart" push may help to distribute high-priority messages to selected users. The prerequisite is that events, alarms, and status changes are detected, interpreted, correlated, and, depending on their impacts, sent or referred to the right persons. Code books or expert rules can help with the first steps, push-products with the second. Figure 6.12 shows the basic ideas of this push solution. If the selection criteria are carefully chosen, and message lengths are kept short, Web-pushing will not cause any serious bottlenecks in the access networks.

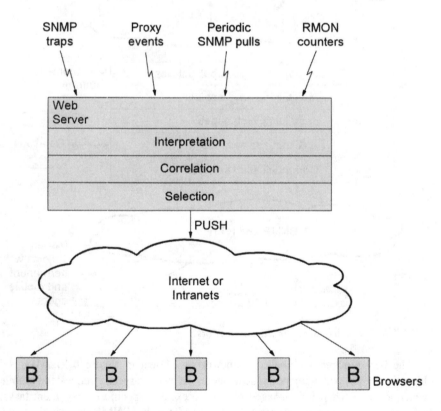

FIGURE 6.12 Web-based push.

6.5   WEB-BASED FRAMEWORK OF THE FUTURE

Web-based technology for systems and network management has already made the breakthrough with different practical solutions. Those solutions are fragmented, and concentrate on viewing and information distribution capabilities. Platform vendors, as seen earlier in this chapter, extend their platform by Java applets, and improve access to information from universal browsers. Using pushing technology for Web browsers is just in its beginning steps. More experience has been available with intelligent agent technologies. Both permanent and mobile agents are in use in telecommunications and enterprise networks.

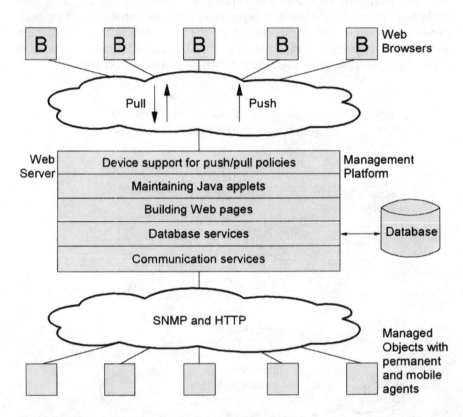

FIGURE 6.13 Web-based best practice framework.

The best practice Web-based framework is shown in Figure 6.13. Managed objects are equipped with permanent agents. If necessary and requested, mobile agents are dispatched for managed objects to execute specific management tasks. Data collection remains in most cases supported by SNMP, but dual stacks (SNMP/HTTP) may get more attention at the managed objects level. Data transfer may use both SNMP and HTTP. The framework offers various services, such as:

- Communication services: managing the communications with managed objects, and dispatching and supervising permanent and mobile agents.
- Database services: maintaining the internal communication interface to the database that may be relational or object oriented.
- Building Web pages: CGI type of conversion is supported here by converting DB queries/answers and raw SNMP/RMON-PDUs into HTML. If HTML is used, some editing might be required prior to presentation.
- Maintaining Java applets: in order to execute certain tasks, mainly supporting presentation services, applets are developed and maintained. If requested, they are dispatched to the Web browsers.
- Decision support for push/pull-policies: on the basis of interpreted and correlated data, decisions are made if and whom to notify. Smart push will carry the information to the right target address.

Web browsers are universal and expected to support all the features of a thin client. Differentiators are the quality of presentation, search capabilities, and the power of the local periphery.

6.6 SUMMARY

Enriching current management platforms with Web technologies will take some time. Step-by-step, browser access, Java applets, and CIM-based resource data will be integrated into management platforms of today. With the exception of isolated cases, the three-tier architecture: agent, platform with built-in Web server, and browser will dominate. In isolated cases, such as small systems and networks, also two tiers: agent with built-in Web server and browser will be implemented. In the estimation of the author, the principal management platform players will remain the same.

7 Web-Based Management Application Examples

7.1 INTRODUCTION

Platforms and webified platforms accommodate management applications for systems and networks. Webifying applications may happen two different ways: the webified management platform plays the role of the universal front end by embedding Web-server-code, or the application is webified by embedding Web-server-code into the application itself. In both cases, the access is provided by universal Web browsers.

There are two major classes of management applications. Device-dependent applications are provided as add-ons to the managed device. Device-independent applications may be implemented for many different managed devices. This chapter introduces practical examples for both areas. But this chapter goes beyond device-related management applications and also addresses Web-based storage management, analysis and reporting, software distribution, server management, and Web-based legacy management. As can be observed throughout this chapter, information publishing and distribution are very powerful and popular Web-based applications.

7.2 DEVICE-DEPENDENT MANAGEMENT APPLICATIONS

Web-based network and systems management are very popular with device vendors. They hope to standardize application programming interfaces on Web technologies. In this case, the vendors must provide one single transformation into Web format, instead of supporting multiple management platforms. As an example, hub, router and switch vendors are introduced with their Web-based management solutions.

7.2.1 OPTIVITY FROM BAY NETWORKS

Offering the Optivity network management system in combination with Web-based technology, Bay has tried to shape the future of network management. There are three fundamental applications for which Web-based tools can provide a significant benefit: individual device configuration and management, browser access to sophisticated management applications, and corporate IS access to network status data.

Web-based configuration and management of individual devices: this capability is aimed at managers of small networks who may not have their own network management system. These users want to configure and monitor the devices in their networks as easily as possible, and perhaps even gain some remote device management capabilities. What these users need is out-of-the-box device configuration tools using a Web browser. This is accomplished by providing the equipment to be configured with an agent that includes a native HTML interface. The manager then enters basic configuration parameters for each device by completing a simple online electronic form. Remote monitoring of simple device statistics will also be possible via the browser, using tabular and later graphical displays of basic device information and performance.

Web-based access from any desktop to advanced, network-wide management capabilities: this application is targeted at enterprise network support staff who currently use network management solutions such as Optivity Enterprise. Their goal is to monitor the network, understand potential faults and alarms, and provide their users with continuous network availability. Network management solutions such as Optivity, working in conjunction with management platforms, such as OpenView from Hewlett Packard or TME 10 from IBM/Tivoli, provide the foundation for these networks. Building on this foundation, Web browsers provide a number of low-cost options for easily accessing important information. For example, a staff member out on the floor troubleshooting the network may need to access an Optivity application. Through a Web browser running on any PC or laptop in the organization, the user could access the necessary application and continue the troubleshooting process, regardless of location — reducing the time and effort required to do the job.

Web reporting of network status information for browsing by IS management and others via the organization's intranet: users for this application are Information Systems group managers who do not necessarily operate the network or get involved in extremely technical details. Instead, their goal is to quickly obtain information about the state of the network, about trends over time, and notification of any potential hot spots. The Web is an excellent tool for distributing this type of information. Various people within an organization have different needs for different types of information. Members of the finance group, for instance, may need usage accounting information, while database users may need to determine system status or submit an online trouble ticket and follow it through to resolution. The corporate intranet offers a simple yet effective method for distributing this type of information to people who do not have ready access to traditional management systems. This requirement is met by NetReporter from Bay Networks. It produces a wide variety of network usage information that can be automatically exported to a corporate Web server and viewed as needed, giving users access to the important data they need.

Figure 7.1 shows the architectural framework for delivering Web-based network management solutions. The framework features three distinct elements: the nearly universal Web server itself, Web-enabled management applications, and HTTP-enabled devices.

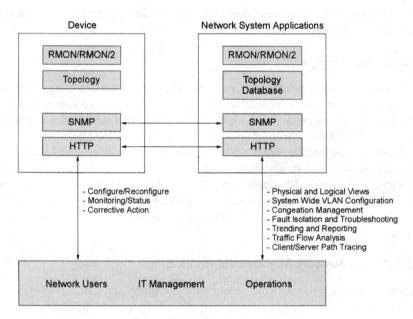

FIGURE 7.1 The Optivity architectural framework.

As Figure 7.1 illustrates, Bay Networks is currently implementing a solution that provides network managers with direct access to individual devices and to Optivity capabilities via a Web browser. While this solution will greatly simplify overall management and make information more universally available, several key points emerge from this framework that demand consideration:

- Network management application processing must still be provided, although the location of the processing will evolve over time.
- Devices must continue to become more intelligent to support functions like multilayer topology and RMON2, regardless of the shift to Web-based management tools and access.
- Management will continue to use SNMP, in addition to HTTP and any other management protocols that may become standardized, until SNMP access to legacy equipment is no longer an issue.

7.2.1.1 The Web Server

The Web server acts as the universal access tool. In the Bay Networks product road map, the browser immediately becomes a single, low-cost viewer for network data. Using the Web browser for network management will partially address one of the challenges facing both vendors and users today: the constant churn caused by evolving operating systems and SNMP platform versions.

In the future, the browser — with its user interface and overall capabilities extended by Java, AvtiveX, and other technologies — will become an increasingly strategic partner in the distributed processing of network management information.

Bay Networks will pursue these developments to deliver quality network management to the enterprise customer.

7.2.1.2   The Devices

A Web browser can communicate directly with networked devices using HTTP. The
most common reasons for connecting directly to individual network devices include
configuration and reconfiguration, simple status monitoring, and implementing specific corrective actions. For small networks, this approach alone might be a sufficient
management solution. For larger networks, this approach will typically supplement
more global tools in a variety of possible circumstances, including the final stages
of problem resolution. To support large-scale management, however, devices will
have to continue collecting and providing RMON1/RMON2 and multilayer topology
data. Critical network devices will need these capabilities to support network systems
applications.

7.2.1.3   The Network Management Application

Managing an enterprise network requires the collection and correlation of a large
amount of data. This type of processing — which is the core of the Optivity product
family — is still required in order to understand and manage the network.

As the era of Web-based management unfolds, more and more of this processing
can be distributed through Java or some other means. Optivity is the ideal vehicle
for supporting this distributed processing by its agents residing in networking
devices.

This network processing must include such functions as correlation and presentation of network statistics (offered by Optivity-OmniView), automatic baselining
capabilities (available with Optivity Analysis), and a single common point for
launching all network management activities (provided through Optivity Enterprise
Command Center). In addition, Network Atlas and LANarchitect provide a simple
interface to complex, multidevice functions like VLAN configuration and logical-
to-physical network mapping.

The technological foundation for these advanced management functions is the
intelligent agent — software embedded on network devices that collects both
RMON1 and RMON2 data and multilayer topology information. RMON1 and
RMON2 data provide a detailed view of the characteristics of traffic flowing through
the network, while multilayer topology information provides the management application with detailed knowledge of the physical and logical relationships between
networked devices. The multilayer topology capability is critical to managing a
switched network, while RMON is critical to the monitoring and troubleshooting of
client/server traffic.

As these capabilities move to the Web, the need for intelligent agents and
sophisticated processing of network-wide data will not diminish. On the contrary, a
new class of network system applications must be supported to deliver true enterprise
management. As the list above suggests, these include global configuration of mul-

tiple devices, VLAN configuration, fault correlation, threshold and alarm management, trending and reporting, and design and policy-based management.

In addition, Bay is offering a Web-based Optivity Service Level Manager, an application that borrows technology from Vital Signs for tracking application service levels.

In summary, Web-based products are

Enterprise Command Center
OmniView
Enterprise Health Advisor
BayStack 100Base-T with Web-agent

7.2.2 WEB ALARM VIEW FROM CABLETRON

WebView provides many advantages over traditional text-based interfaces, allowing network managers to configure and monitor SmartSwitches from Cabletron through standard Web browser software, while providing access to online documentation and context-sensitive help. It allows network managers to access a wide range of functions. It provides graphical displays of SmartSwitch module configurations, including MAC addresses, interface link states, full/half duplex mode, SNMP configuration, and per port RMON statistics.

WebView users have access to a comprehensive set of online help and technical documentation, including release notes, installation guides, user manuals, firmware upgrades via internet on Cabletron's Web site or a local Web server. It also lets managers set IP addresses, activate broadcast thresholding, and check power supply and fan status information. It became a standard feature of SmartSwitches.

There are five informational sections:

- An alarm table which displays information for all alarms in a table format. Information is given for each alarm regarding its alarm condition, date/time, model type name, model name, landscape, and assignments. There are also probable cause and status buttons, which give detailed information regarding the probable cause or status of the alarm.
- Alarm counts, which display the total count of alarms for each condition not filtered, as well as a cumulative total of all conditions not filtered. If any alarm conditions are being filtered out, a label will be displayed in this area stating which conditions are being filtered out. If Web Alarm View was run with a maximum number of alarms to display, this maximum value will also be displayed in this area. The alarm totals will reflect the count of all alarms in the contacted landscapes, regardless of the maximum alarm display value: the maximum alarm display value only affects the number of alarms that are displayed in the alarm table.
- Detailed alarm information, which displays either the probable cause or status of the selected alarm, depending on which button was pressed in the alarm table.

- A color definition page, which displays the colors used in Web Alarm View and their corresponding alarm condition meaning.
- An about Web Alarm View page, which displays general information about Web Alarm View.

Usually, the main page consists of five frames, if the browser is supporting frames:

1. Title of the application
2. Alarm table as described above
3. Alarm counts, filter label, and maximum display value label
4. Detailed alarm information
5. Other information about copyright, colors

If the browser does not support frames, the main page has four hypertext links:

1. Alarm table: the alarm table is displayed. Clicking on the probable cause or status button brings up a new page with the corresponding information supporting troubleshooting.
2. Alarm totals: clicking on this link brings up a page with the alarm count information, filter label, and maximum display value label.
3. Web Alarm View color definition: clicking on this link brings up a page showing the color meanings.
4. About Web Alarm View: clicking on this link brings up a page giving general information about Web Alarm View.

This product is an excellent example of how networking devices can be equipped with good Web access capability.

7.2.3   CISCOWORKS FROM CISCO

Cisco believes that it is important to the industry that they provide a common model describing the managed environment regardless of the implementation of that model. Besides supporting WBEM, Cisco hopes to integrate Java Management APIs into a future integrated solution.

Most of Cisco commands can be issued using a Web browser. This Cisco feature is accessed by using the Cisco Web browser interface. This interface is accessed by the routers home page. All Cisco routers and access servers loaded with the latest version of software have a home page, which is password protected.

From the home page, the user clicks on a hypertext link titled monitor the router. This link takes the user to a Web page which has a command field. The user can type commands into this field as if they were entering commands at a terminal connected to the router. The page also displays a list of commands. Commands can be selected by clicking on them, as if users were clicking on hypertext links.

The first phase of Cisco's initiative involves developing Web-based tools that complement its existing CiscoWorks and CiscoView applications. These tools would handle installation and configuration, including software updates, of Cisco devices. The second phase will comprise a new series of stand-alone, Web-based applications for change management, network optimization, and performance monitoring. The complementary tools and new applications will require Cisco devices to be configured as Web servers. Many Web-based tools and applications have been rolled out during the last couple of months.

CiscoWorks 2000 is a new family of Web-based and management platform-independent products for managing Cisco enterprise networks and devices. Based on internet technology and standards, current offerings include Resource Manager Essentials and CWSI Campus.

Resource Manager Essentials is a powerful suite of Web-based applications offering network management solutions for Cisco switches, access servers, and routers. Its browser interface allows easy access to information critical to network uptime and simplifies time-consuming administrative tasks. The Management Connection feature in Response Management essentials adds Web-level integration of other management tools from Cisco and partner companies, thereby enabling utilization of these tools and applications to create a seamless, central point of network administration. Comprised of six applications and optional add-on packages, it includes:

- Inventory Manager
- Change Audit
- Device Configuration Manager
- Software Image Manager
- Availability Manager
- Syslog Analyzer
- Cisco Management Connection

CWSI Campus is a comprehensive management solution for Cisco Catalyst and LightStream switches within the CiscoWorks 2000 family. A companion product to Resource Manager Essentials, it offers extensive network discovery and display, ATM and LANE configuration, user tracking, LAN/WAN traffic, and performance management capabilities on a device and network-wide basis.

This coupling of Cisco device management with Web-based technologies, internet information, and extensive third-party partnering allows the CiscoWorks 2000 family of products to deliver on Cisco's vision of a comprehensive management intranet.

In summary, users can expect from Cisco the following:

- Web-based tools for existing CiscoWorks applications or device installation and configuration, and software updates.
- Web agents for routers, switches, and other devices to build a loosely coupled Web management framework.
- Longer term, create stand-alone applications for change management and network optimization.

7.2.4 NetDirector@Web from UB Networks

NetDirector@Web delivers low-cost, graphical, platform-independent applications that provide comprehensive management of an intranet infrastructure based on the GeoLAN family of products and other Web server equipped devices. Whether at work, from home, or on the road, network administrators can securely configure, monitor, troubleshoot, or perform management tasks from any computer attached to the network. It increases network uptime, decreases administrative and training costs, simplifies remote management, and frees up the network administrator's time to focus on high impact tasks such as performance optimization, network evolution, and technology migration.

The main features of the product are:

- It provides secure anytime, anywhere management using a standard Web browser.
- It provides Java-based applications for real-time management that surpasses static HTML-based management.
- It includes NetDirectory@Web directory services and applications for policy-based management, such as software distribution or firmware downloads.
- It integrates EMPower embedded applications for automatically detecting, isolating, and fixing network problems.
- It integrates applications for automated remote monitoring and technical support from a Web browser.

The solution from UB Networks targets real-time Web-based management, integration with management platforms, and Web-based automated device management.

7.2.4.1 Real-Time Web-Based Management

NetDirector@Web includes a familiar Web browser graphical user interface and hyperlinked home pages to ease network navigation and launch Java-based applications to configure, monitor, and troubleshoot networks in real-time. Applications that provide trend analysis and network reports, access to UB Networks Technical Support and online documentation are also integrated through the Web browser so that configuration changes and network planning can be accomplished using real-data, and eliminating guess work.

7.2.4.2 Integration with Management Platforms

The NetDirector@Web Server integrates core services, such as discovery, topology, and event management, offered by open management platforms, such as OpenView, TME, Solstice, and TNG, and provides distributed network directory services that can be exploited by applications for policy-based management.

The NetDirector@Web Home Page provides a directory for the network, hyperlinking all of the GeoLAN family devices to simplify network navigation. The home page reflects the status of all discovered GeoLAN devices to show the momentary health of the devices and other useful information such as firmware version and events. The network manager can manage the network from home or on the road by linking to the devices. The home page also provides a method for the administrator to specify management policies, such as updating firmware and software across multiple devices throughout the network, or defining network behavior in the event of a broadcast storm. The home page applications are bundled with NetDirector Enterprise that integrates with OpenView on Solaris, HP-UX, Windows NT, and TME 10. Figure 7.2 shows the NetDirector@Web framework.

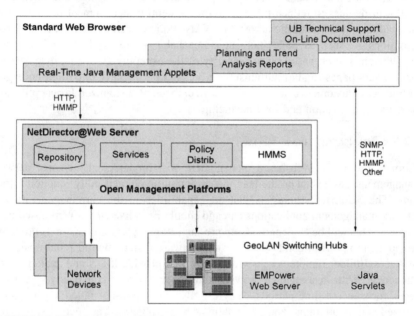

FIGURE 7.2 The NetDirector@Web framework.

7.2.4.3 Automated Device Management

EMPower is a powerful embedded management platform for the GeoLAN family of switching hubs. It enables intelligent applications to optimize network performance and automated routine tasks. It also serves as a Web server for Java applets that can be accessed either through the NetDirector@Web Server or directly from a Java-enabled Web browser. Network managers can configure policies that reflect network behavior and, when exceptions occur, obtain real-time statistics from a remote location. The EMPower Java applets provide real-time, graphical management for configuring, monitoring, and troubleshooting GeoLAN switching hubs through a Web browser. Because of Java's real-time capabilities, changes in the network status are reflected immediately, without requiring the network manager to reload Web pages. Additionally, Java applets are loaded dynamically from NetDirector@Web and EMPower Web servers so that the user does not have to pre-install network management software on the system being used to manage the network. Planned enhancements for EMPower include a Java virtual machine to allow native

Java applications to be deployed to create self-healing networks with GeoLAN switching hubs.

It further leverages the EMPower technology with automated, embedded Java applications. Based on policies determined by the network administrator, these embedded applications correct faults and optimize network performance without user intervention. For example, the Critical Node Monitor application monitors critical nodes such as routers, switches, and servers within a domain. It periodically verifies reachability and status for each node and generates an SNMP trap if a critical node becomes unreachable. Polling responsibilities can be distributed to multiple EMPower devices to reduce the burden on the central management platform, save bandwidth, and lower traffic across the WAN. Policies can be defined to distribute exceptions — such as nodes become unreachable — to the local and/or central management station based on the severity of the exception. Critical Node Monitor also triggers pages to alert administrators when a particularly important node goes off line. Also customers can create their own embedded customized Java applications for network utilization and load balancing.

7.2.5 TRANSCEND FROM 3COM

3Com believes that Web-based management will fundamentally change network management and has taken the lead in developing integrated, fully functional solutions. The 3Com experience is that all capabilities in the current generation of network management applications can and should be delivered via Web-based management. This will be evident in 3Com products moving forward. 3Com is providing two applications. Transcend Access Watch software system monitors dial-up activity for AccessBuilder remote access products, which provide ISDN and analog remote dial access. With Java-enabled browsers, administrators can graphically view usage trends for selected time periods. They can also see reports of failed log-ins, unauthorized access attempts, and systematic access problems. The second application is the dRMON Edge Monitoring System. This Transcend system is part of an overall strategy by 3Com to provide distributed RMON remote monitoring, a scalable, cost-effective means of distributing the collection of RMON data over multiple network devices. This monitoring system consolidates RMON data from 3Com network interface cards enhanced with RMON capabilities and provides full RMON coverage, especially vital to switched and high-speed network environments. Though users can still point traditional RMON clients at the dRMON Edge Monitoring System, they can also use browsers to directly access RMON data. This application manages collection, filtering, and polling for administrators to optimize LAN performance and reduce the time required for network management. Figure 7.3 shows the architecture of the Transcend dRMON Edge Monitor System.

3Com is developing additional Transcend Web-based applications as part of its efforts to provide customers with fully functional, Web-accessible network management following the proxy model. Future releases will have comprehensive Web-based capabilities with read and write functionalities. These powerful tools will enable operators to troubleshoot 3Com networks from any network browser and flexibly share operational data about them.

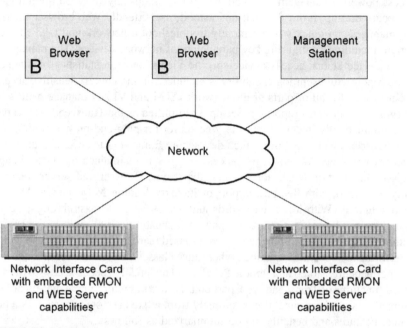

FIGURE 7.3 Architecture of the Transcend dRMON Edge Monitor System.

Utilizing the applications, network administrators are able to perform management functions, including configuring 3Com network systems, monitoring, creating intuitive reports, and viewing network statistics from anywhere, regardless of their location. The applications will provide both tabular and graphic representation of management data, including the ability to drill down into graphics for more details. Web-based solutions are designed for two market areas:

- The enterprise — applications complement and augment 3Com's existing network management applications, Transcend Enterprise Manager and Transcend Traffic Manager. The applications enable distributed access to business and operations management information more efficiently than telnet, which is command line driven. For this environment, 3Com offers a server that will enable Web-based access to network devices.
- Small office — devices are supposed to be self-configuring, but will still require a certain amount of monitoring and managing, which will be provided by an embedded Web server and the Web-based management application.

Transcend Central lets users navigate through their networks in a single view, enabling them to make quick evaluations and assessments of any network problem. Details of each device in the 3Com network can be surveyed, including firmware revisions, model numbers, reporting and status for complete information gathering and evaluation. With Transcend Web capabilities, authorized network managers can access powerful management functions from desktops anywhere on the intranet or on secure dial-up. From the well-understood, user-friendly Web browser interface, the manager can quickly and remotely troubleshoot a network and take corrective action, including configuring key parameters of network devices. The manager can check device status, access device-specific views, and run statistics or diagnostic tests. A powerful event log capability is included, giving context-sensitive access to event history for all or parts of the network. ATM and VLAN management is fully integrated, as is status reporting. Set-up is simplified as the Transcend Web capabilities automatically integrate into the Web server for plug-and-play operation.

Transcend Web capabilities include a secure framework to access security, a key concern with network managers. Access security is maintained down to the application and function level, not just into the server. Browser and server security is fully leveraged, with flexible support of industry leading Netscape and Microsoft Web solutions. With log-in passwords and access levels to pass through, network managers can be assured that these powerful capabilities will only be accessed by authorized users. This comprehensive Web-based management solution also includes a performance boosting capability, where Java classes can be downloaded on request and permanently stored at a remote PC client. This greatly speeds access to the Java-based functions of Transcend Web, particularly important for remote dial-up or ISDN users accessing these capabilities routinely from a fixed remote site, such as a home office. Features and benefits can be summarized as follows:

Features	Benefits
Provides powerful set of Web-based applications	Network administrators can perform complete management functions, including monitoring, configuration, status, and reporting
Enables geographically dispersed access to network management functions and monitoring data through Web browser	Network administrators will be able to perform operations as well as retrieve and review network data regardless of their location (work, home, remote office)
Provides shared access to monitoring data	End users can access network status, data, reducing the number of calls to the help desk
Based on 3Com's Transcend Enterprise Manager with WWW interface	Provides a single look and feel for all 3Com systems, helping make network management easier
Scalable end-to-end management for NT environments	Delivers the choice of managing one's sophisticated network from a scalable PC platform
Advanced Web-management functions including status reporting, device-specific views, statistics, diagnostics, configuration, and reporting capabilities	Enables fast corrective evaluation and action almost anywhere, at anytime, from one's desktop/laptop browser
Security framework for Web access down to the function-level	Advanced capabilities are restricted to known, trained users while other Web-management features can be accessed by a broader community; provides security from threats by outside or unknown users

Features	Benefits
Transcend Central	Provides an intuitive single view of all 3Com equipment for quick, easy navigation and evaluation
Single management application for all 3Com networking systems	Minimizes learning curve with consistent, integrated, management capabilities
Industry standard RMON with 3Com SmartAgent enhancements	Increases network management staff productivity with proactive management, autocalibration of alarm thresholds, and advanced action on events functions
Analyze and troubleshoot network problems	Helps simplify management of complex networks
Online documentation and easy-to-access bulletin board	Provides instant access to the complete hardware and software documentation; bulletin board offers easy-to-use access to receive patches, diagnostics, bug reports, and technical articles
Compliant with emerging industry standard development	Helps reduce the complexity and costs of enterprise management

7.3 DEVICE-INDEPENDENT MANAGEMENT APPLICATIONS

Web access to management applications is extremely important to suppliers. Once the Web interface is provided, their products can become part of a simplified and unified management architecture. This segment addresses trouble ticketing first, followed by application management, storage management, analysis, and reporting.

7.3.1 TROUBLE-TRACKING MANAGEMENT APPLICATIONS

In this segment, the most important trouble-tracking applications and their Web capabilities are shown from Clarify, Remedy, and Vantive.

7.3.1.1 ClearExpress WebSupport from Clarify

Clarify offers complete solutions for customer service and help desk management. The products give functions out of the box, and offer modular, yet tightly integrated solutions. The solutions for the full range of the customer help desk include:

- High-volume call tracking and case monitoring
- Problem resolution
- Service contracts verification
- Customer configuration management
- Defect tracking
- Inventory logistics
- Report generation
- Field service management

- Return Material Authorization
- Commitment tracking
- Automatic notifications and escalations
- Security

With hooks to leading third-party applications, Clarify products serve as the foundation for complete business management solutions. Important features of ClearExpress are:

Adaptability — designed for ease and flexibility, the products are fully adapt-able and customizable, so they fit existing business processes and can be modified easily as processes evolve without programming or knowledge of Structured Query Language (SQL). Furthermore, due to the architecture, the latest release of the software can be easily implemented without the need for re-implementation.

Scalability — because they are based on a client/server architecture, the products deliver high performance and scalability from the smallest LAN to the largest WAN or enterprise environment, from ten users to thousand of users, over dedicated or dial-up lines. They also scale in terms of func-tionality, allowing customers to add new processes — such as multilayer support — as the users need them. That means they grow with the organi-zation and evolve to meet changing environments.

Portability — the entire Clarify product family is built to integrate easily with existing and future platforms. The software runs on UNIX and Windows NT servers with Sybase, Oracle, and Microsoft SQL databases, and Win-dows, Macintosh, and UNIX/Motif clients.

Proven solution — equally important, the products are mature and proven. Exhaustive tests are implemented prior to releases. Uptime is excellently referenced by approximately 20,000 customers worldwide.

The new product capitalizes on the growing trend among companies to distribute information over the internet using the World Wide Web. The Web's growing pop-ularity and the common interface provided by access software make it an ideal medium for customer services and support. In the near future, such a product is widely needed, as online service providers, operating system vendors, and telephone companies compete in offering internet access.

ClearExpress WebSupport is an extension of the Clarify Customer Service Man-agement (CSM) system and is the first in a family of electronic support products called ClearExpress. The product includes two key components that provide out-of-the-box functionality and integration with the Clarify system:

- WebSupport Data Server is tightly integrated with ClearSupport, which handles problem diagnostics, call handling, service contract verification, and report generation. The data server component provides a real-time, secure connection between the Web server and the server and database

used by ClearSupport. Additionally, data specific to the Web interface, such as usage and traffic are maintained for reporting purposes.
- WebSupport Forms are a set of preconfigured HTML templates that companies can use out of the box or can customize to fit their business needs. The templates include fill-in forms for new and open cases, as well as prompts to search the Clarify database.

There is a simple interface that connects users to Clarify and allows users to open a case, check status, add case notes, and best of all to obtain self help from SolutionPac and KnowledgePac.

ClearExpress WebSupport provides an effective alternative to traditional phone support. A recent survey found that 85% of technical support calls made during peak hours received a busy signal, and more than half of all callers could not get through despite repeated dialing. Even when they connected, callers often faced a long wait. By letting customers bypass deluged phone banks, companies not only improve customer satisfaction, but increase support center productivity as well.

Instead of waiting in a phone queue, customers can use the Web link to access the support organization's knowledge base and conduct their own troubleshooting. Or, they can key in a description of their problem and open a new case that is instantly transmitted to the appropriate support representative. Customers can later return to the Web site to query the case to check its status or add notes to assist in the problem-resolution process.

For support organizations, ClearExpress WebSupport helps reduce call volume — a welcome benefit for today's downsized operations. In addition, online correspondence often takes less time than a phone conversation because both parties must communicate clearly and concisely with the written word. Online communication is also inherently less argumentative, reducing stress levels for support personnel.

Important members of the product family are described below.

ClearSupport

ClearSupport is the cornerstone product for the external support organization. It allows support and field service professionals to manage all aspects of call handling. Users can log cases, set priorities, route cases, verify contracts, review case histories, manage configurations, and track case-related costs quickly and easily.

ClearSupport also records all activities related to a case and provides a full audit trail of activities, status changes, escalations, and notifications based on the business rules the users define. A comprehensive database underlying this functionality lets the users analyze the business and improve profitability.

In addition, ClearSupport includes useful administration functions. The user can change a customers' product configuration or personal information during a customer call, or add a new customer to the database directly from ClearSupport.

ClearHelpDesk

ClearHelpDesk is the core product for corporate support centers, offering rich functionality for enterprise-level help desks — from call tracking and problem management to service level agreements and reporting. Like ClearSupport, it includes an ownership model that ensures cases are assigned and analysts work together until a problem is resolved. ClearHelpDesk is a complete solution for handling any employee question or suggestion about technology, benefits, and facilities.

In addition, ClearHelpDesk interfaces with popular network and systems management platforms and tools. These platforms and tools enable inquiries to be sent directly to the help desk and create a case that will alert a technical support representative through on-screen notification, e-mail, or paging. ClearHelpDesk can be integrated with off-the-shelf knowledge bases from KnowledgeBroker and ServiceWare that contain hundreds of known problems and solutions for common desktop applications.

Problem resolution tools include:

Diagnosis Engine (DE), which turns the large amount of information captured by the Clarity system into a knowledge base that leads support specialists through a diagnostic process to find solutions to customer problems. It is a sophisticated problem-solving tool that leverages scarce and expensive expert knowledge and avoids "re-inventing the wheel." Tightly integrated with ClearSupport and ClearHelpDesk, Diagnosis Engine uses information collected in initial problem logging to begin the search for the solution. It understands the context of the case and uses deductive reasoning to prompt the user with logical questions to ask, thereby sharing the knowledge of experts with front-line staff. New solutions are easily captured, so it learns as it is used. No training or expert assistance is required to use the product. Solutions are stored in a database as separate objects from the case history, allowing them to be reused and ensuring that customers receive consistent answers. Support specialists can link individual customer cases to solution objects that include descriptions of the root cause of the problem, symptoms that describe the problem, workarounds or fixes, and product change requests, providing a complete history. This makes it easy to see the frequency with which a particular problem has been reported, giving engineers decision-making data for prioritizing fixes and new features.

Full Text Search (FTS) is particularly useful as a research tool to solve problems for the first time and seed the knowledge base used by the Diagnosis Engine. With very low setup time, FTS is useful on day one to resolve problems using existing knowledge within the Clarify database or externally — through manuals and product descriptions, CD-ROM knowledge bases, or application notes. Using FTS, support specialists can quickly and easily locate any word or phrase within any document. It is a tightly integrated system, supporting automatic generation of keywords from case data, stop words, and many preference settings.

In addition to the Diagnosis Engine and FTS, Clarify offers a simple query tool and interfaces to third-party diagnostic tools.

Integration tools

Clarify offers a suite of tools for customizing, extending, and integrating its products. Together, these tools allow the user to custom-tailor a solution for the specific needs of the customers without modifying source code or compromising upgradeability.

ClearExpress

ClearExpress enables the customers and end users to log cases, troubleshoot, and search for information online. This gives fast answers to technical, product, or service questions without requiring assistance from support professionals, and it avoids time-consuming telephone tags. It is available in four forms.

ClearExpress Online gives users access to support information and status updates via a version of ClearSupport or ClearHelpDesk that runs on their desktops. Clear-Express WebSupport lets users access Web sites to log cases, check status, add notes, or troubleshoot. And with ClearExpress Web FTS, users can quickly and easily locate online information using Full Text Search, which performs search and retrieval based on keywords. All of these applications are easily tailored to reflect business needs.

ClearEnterprise delivers database replication for customers with large, geographically dispersed, multiserver implementations. Replicating databases allows Clarify users in different locations on different servers to cooperate in solving problems by replicating cases, solutions, and change requests on demand and keeping them in synch.

Because ClearEnterprise is built on top of the Clarify application architecture and infrastructure, its implementation is independent of the underlying database. It takes advantage of a unique ownership model and workflow management to provide fast and efficient replication ideal for the support and product development environments.

ClearCustomize and ClearExtensions help to customize and extend the functions and capabilities of the Clarify product families.

ClearExpress WebSupport functionality

Combined with ClearSupport and ClearHelpDesk, WebSupport lets users log cases, check case status, add notes, and troubleshoot on their own. The following examples illustrate how the product works, both from a user's perspective and a support engineer's perspective.

Customers are usually dealing with the following tasks:

Logging in — the user begins by accessing the company's home page on the Web using the standard Web address or URL. Typically, a series of subcategories is available, one of which is support. WebSupport can easily be configured to be an option under this category, under a name such as "self help," "problem resolution," or "troubleshooting." When the user selects WebSupport, a log-on screen appears, requesting name and password, which are authenticated behind the scenes through integration with the Web security server security system.

Searching the knowledge base — WebFTS allows customers and internal users to access the company's knowledge database to find fast answers to product or technical questions. The product searches the database for key words, and quickly provides a list of all relevant information on the given topic. Users can then drill down to successive levels of detail to find the specific answer they are looking for.

Creating a case — the WebSupport interface presents a variety of activity options, one of which is to create a new case. This task is supported by a special form. The user simply fills in the fields with information about the problem or questions. Types of problems can be customized for each product or company. The user can also select the severity level, which may correlate to a prearranged, contractual service level agreement. Once finished, the new case is automatically forwarded to a support organization for resolution. The Clarify Workflow Engine then takes over in the support center, notifying the appropriate people of the arrival of the case and routing it to the correct workgroup.

Adding notes — if the user has an additional comment or question after the case has been opened, it is simple to forward this to the support engineer. The user simply queries for the case or enters the case ID, clicks the "add notes" button, adds the notes, and sends them off. This method is also used to respond to questions or requests for additional information from the support representative.

Querying cases — many calls to support centers are from customers who simply want to know what has been done so far to resolve their problem. The WebSupport case query feature allows customers to monitor case progress at their convenience. Built-in security features ensure that users can view only cases for which they are authorized, ensuring confidentiality of information.

Customer Support centers are usually dealing with the following tasks:

Managing new cases in a support workgroup — when an end user creates a new case, it is automatically forwarded to the support organization for processing. Depending on the preferences of the user or on case severity levels, incoming cases can generate audible e-mail alerts, on-screen notifications, or even digital pager messages. The support center can have cases automatically routed based on parameters such as origination point, severity, and type.

Tracking case communication — each time an action is taken on a case, notes can be quickly and easily added to the case file for access by the customer. This allows both the support engineer and the customer to review progress and monitor case status regularly and thoroughly. Additionally, customers can at any time log onto the Web and use WebSupport to query on open cases, thereby saving unnecessary phone time. Bookmarks can even be set up on a customer's Web browser to go immediately to a query of cases.

Notifying support engineers of milestone deadlines — due to the tight integration between ClearExpress, WebSupport, and Workflow Engine, all of the business rules put in place to handle escalations, notifications, and custom processes are able to act on incoming Web transactions and the subsequent Support Center activity. Support engineers are provided automatic notification when a case or additional case notes have been sent in via the Web. Escalations can be defined to assure deadlines are met, and management can be notified if cases begin to approach service level agreement thresholds.

WebSupport architectural overview

The product line includes ClearExpress Web support and WebFTS. While they provide different functionality, both products are built from the same basic components. Each component can be customized to meet specific needs and requirements. Figure 7.4 shows the architecture.

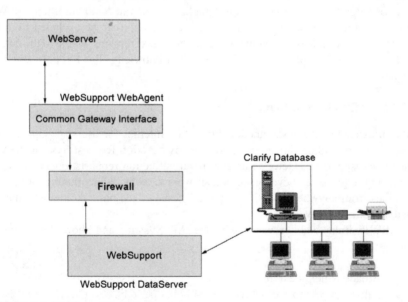

FIGURE 7.4 WebSupport architecture.

The core component is the call center interface, or the WebSupport forms. These plug-and-play templates allow the user to establish a look and feel for the support center from the World Wide Web. The basic forms require no customization, but individual forms can be customized easily in HTML without complex PERL or SQL programming, should the user wish to add attributes of corporate look.

The WebSupport data server has a real-time, persistent connection into the Clarify database and resides behind the corporate firewall. It functions as the mechanism by which data are passed into the database. Data are read out and streamed back to the other primary component, WebSupport WebAgent.

The WebAgent resides on the WebServer itself. It acts as the transport mechanism or "agent" for the Web server. It is a CGI-compliant application — compiled binary for speed and security — that passes requests sent in via WebSupport forms back to the WebSupport data server. WebAgent then listens for a return communication from the data server and presents the resulting HTML to the WebServer for output back to the user's browser.

To simplify administration, a WebSupport administrator module is provided, enabling administrators to maintain Web log-in accounts and customer information stored in the database. These accounts can be exported with the WebSupport administrator to integrate with Web server security. Using the built-in security measures, WebSupport allows users to avoid multiple log-in and authentication procedures when they want to access WebSupport. The first time the user logs in, the Clarify database is automatically searched for that log-in name, so that when the user subsequently attempts to use WebSupport, he or she is already authenticated.

WebSupport also makes it easy to specify which users are allowed to view which cases, so users see only the cases they are authorized to see. Similarly, solutions in the knowledge base can be marked as "public" or "private" and are filtered to Web users accordingly. In addition, text for internal use only can be excluded from the solution that is visible to the public, while all other text remains visible to the outside world. This allows a company to selectively filter knowledge that has been approved for publication.

7.3.1.2   ARWeb from Remedy

ARWeb expands help desk functionality to the internet for users of popular Web browsers by providing direct access to Remedy`s Action Request System. ARWeb extends the support capacity so users can submit action requests, query the status of existing requests, and even get quick answers to technical, marketing, or product questions from anywhere, anytime. Figure 7.5 shows the basic structure of the AR System from Remedy.

ARWeb links Web browsers with the AR System, and show the following features:

- Broadens help desk resources
    Allows access to the AR System 24 hours per day, seven days per week, creating an online help desk
    Turns popular Web browsers into interactive clients of the AR System
    Provides a wide range of users with direct internet access to repositories of problem solutions and information sources
    Empowers end users with self-help solutions and status information, thereby increasing end-user and help desk staff efficiency
    Offloads support burden, enabling better utilization of help desk resources
    Enhances customer satisfaction
- Integrates support processes with the internet

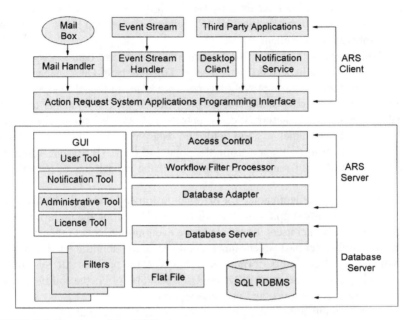

FIGURE 7.5 Structure of the AR System.

Allows users to submit help desk requests and query the AR System from
  Web browsers

Provides transparent integration of existing, familiar Web browser software with the AR System

Enables worldwide internet access for remote and occasional users

Employs existing AR System schemas, forms, and workflow processes

Uses AR System access controls and internet firewalls to assure appropriate security measures

Supports industry standards (internet and World Wide Web, CGI, HTML
  2.0, and AR System API)

• Enables a new way of doing business

Adds a new service channel, the internet, to existing channels, accommo-
  dating the use of information distribution services

Allows users to remotely find answers to technical and marketing questions, determine product availability, and access pricing information or
  whatever information made available

Offers a cost-effective service edge, providing a competitive advantage for
  businesses

ARWeb is a gateway between the AR System and a World Wide Web server. It
communicates with the AR System through AR System APIs and to the Web server
software through the industry standard Web Common Gateway Interface (CGI). As
a gateway, ARWeb performs functions such as establishing a log-in session, listing
available help desk schemas, submitting action requests, and querying databases of

problem solutions. ARWeb dynamically formats information retrieved from the AR System, so the user ultimately sees the AR System schemas and forms in their Web browser software environment.

ARWeb works with existing AR System applications and data to generate Web forms (schemas) and hyperlinks dynamically. This lets Help Desk managers focus on serving customers and improving business processes in the AR System, instead of constantly maintaining static Web pages. ARWeb also now adapts to support HTML 2.0 or greater browsers. When it detects a HTML 3.0-compatible browser, ARWeb uses HTML tables to align fields and data precisely within forms. Administrators design forms only once, using the point-and-click AR System Administration Tool. ARWeb then renders each form to fit the capabilities of virtually any browser.

ARWeb is an excellent choice for external customers or occasional AR System users. Its functionality supplements the AR System User Tool, the preferred tool for more active AR System users. Users now have even more access to their help desk. While both tools offer basic client functionality, such as submitting action requests, querying the database and performing searches with the optional AR System Full-Text Search (FTS) feature, the AR System User Tool also offers the ability to modify records, execute active links, and generate reports.

ARWeb is compatible with systems from Hewlett Packard and Sun Microsystems. The new version also adds compatibility for IBM systems.

7.3.1.3   VanWeb from Vantive Corporation

VanWeb enables anyone with a universal Web browser to interact dynamically with a Vantive database from any location around the world. Customers, partners, prospects, and employees, with sufficient permissions, can create and update data and perform complex searches as if they were using a Vantive desktop client. Interacting with data through VanWeb goes beyond mere hypertext page browsing. VanWeb leverages existing Vantive technologies, such as Vantive API and Vantive Dynamic Dictionary, to preserve workflow rules, data integrity, and permissions schemes. In contrast with static, read-only hypertext pages, VanWeb publishes client/server applications on the Web.

Vantive sees the need for a new level of interaction on the Web using sophisticated, transaction-oriented applications that produce dynamic results for users. Relational context navigation is one important key. At the same time, companies also need to control the content and display of information, depending on who the user is, what browsers they are using, and which data they want to see. By making dynamic adjustments and controlling HTML attributes, companies can provide an individualized view of data that enhances total interaction.

Web approach

Vantive seamlessly integrates two concepts of Web interaction through VanWeb: normal hypertext page linking and relational database navigation. The former provides the standard capabilities that users expect from the Web, including universal access and embedded links to other pages. The latter provides a wide range of powerful, full-featured capabilities that closely parallel the capabilities of a Vantive desktop client.

VanWeb is not only a read-only product. Users can create and update data. It does not provide one data view to everyone, but users can have different permission levels. VanWeb does not publish data to static Web page structures which limit generic browsing and fill up too quickly. Instead, users can drill-down on detail information, link data together, and use locators to set up and perform complex queries.

Open Dynamic Dictionary

The Open Dynamic Dictionary contains all necessary data from layout, field integrity, data display, and group/individual permissions information. The dictionary keeps that structural information separate from the actual data. This architecture was originally developed to ensure that changes to forms and permissions by administrators are applied immediately and uniformly to the database. The same technology is leveraged by VanWeb to provide form descriptions, field integrity (visual clues for required/read-only fields), foreign field drill-down and data display, and permissions by both group and form. Unlike most Web applications, this unique scheme makes it possible to present data in an individualized and easy-to-understand structure rich with visual navigation clues.

Web publisher and Web forms

The Web publisher leverages the Open Dynamic Dictionary to publish forms. Web designers define Web forms, user groups, permissions, data integrity, and workflow rules from within the development environment as if they were regular Vantive forms, groups, etc. The designers need not understand the internal workings of the Web. The publisher dynamically translates Vantive forms to HTML, while maintaining log-in and password security. This automatic publishing of existing Vantive forms offers customers the advantage of fast and easy publishing of Web content — virtually any Vantive form can be incorporated into any Web page. Because commercial browsers often have limitations for displaying forms, Vantive recognizes that some companies may want to simplify their Vantive forms for the Web. Using the development environment, these companies can quickly produce Web forms that work effectively with any browser by altering drop-downs and field lengths, along with other visual adjustments. In this way, companies can also adjust to an appropriate level for the Web user.

By combining the built-in navigation capabilities of Vantive Enterprise with the hypertext capabilities of the Web, a powerful data access system can be created. Below is a list of the main data types that can be displayed on a Vantive form accessed through the Web:

- Simple data like text, integers, dates, etc.
- Drop down selection boxes like selecting from a fixed set of values
- Check boxes like Boolean fields
- Links to other Vantive records with drill-down capabilities
- Links to other Web and internet documents like HTML, FTP, Gopher

- Embedded (in-line) images and graphics
- Sound and video as supported by the Web user's browser
- In-line HTML statements, which may include links to any of the above data

A Web form may be displayed in one of two modes: expanded or source. When displayed in expanded mode, all embedded Web links and images on the form are displayed. Web links are underlined or colored, and text and images are retrieved and displayed as images. In source mode, the form reverts to a standard Vantive form where all the embedded Web links are displayed as text and may be edited. In this mode, users with permission can update hypertext links in the Vantive database, or an administrator can use the Web to maintain such links. This capability also allows users to add links to their own Web pages.

In fact, any updates to the database performed through VanWeb will follow all the same rules as updates performed through a normal Vantive client. Data integrity will be checked, save rules will be triggered, escalations and automatic notifications will be performed, derived fields will be filled in, and form data will be refreshed after the save is completed. If the data integrity of a save rule prevents a save from happening, the update will be rolled back, an informational message displayed, and the form will be restored to its original state. VanWeb allows browsers to access the Vantive client/server system while preserving all the integrity and business rules of an RDBMS application. The final result is that VanWeb gives the Web user access to most of the dynamic capabilities of a normal Vantive client, and a Vantive client user will feel completely comfortable using a Web browser to access data through VanWeb.

VanWeb architecture

The architecture is shown in Figure 7.6. It integrates all the available technologies supported by Vantive. The WebAgent handles communication between a company's

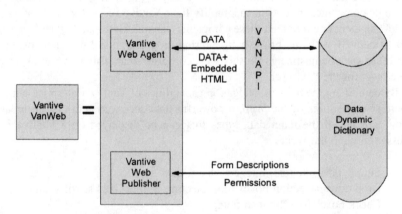

FIGURE 7.6 VanWeb architecture.

Web server and the enterprise server through the Common Gateway Interface (CGI). The WebAgent accesses information from the database using VanAPI, hence all business rules defined in the database are strictly enforced. Notifications and escalations are triggered as if the information was entered through a standard Vantive client. The WebAgent has multiple connections, as displayed in Figure 7.7.

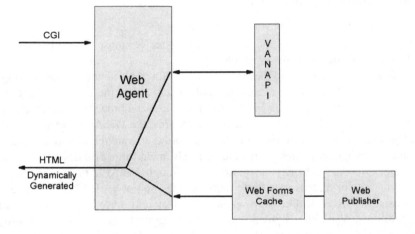

FIGURE 7.7 Connections of WebAgent.

If the user issues a search, the results will be represented on Web forms dynamically created on demand by the WebAgent. The WebAgent retrieves form information from the Forms Cache, keeping database access to a minimum. If a form is not available in the cache, or has been updated since it was cached, the WebAgent invokes the Web publisher. The Web publisher will check permission levels and dynamically create an HTML form for inserting new data (cases, trouble tickets, literature requests, etc.) or searching for existing data (resolutions, cases, etc.). The Web publisher reads the form information directly from the Open Dynamic Directory and publishes forms directly into the Form Cache.

To maximize the flexibility of Web deployment, the Vantive WebAgent can be invoked in one of three modes:

- Log-in mode — in this mode the WebAgent has no information about the user of the Web browser and will publish the default log-in screen. If the WebAgent is called without any input or command line arguments this mode is invoked automatically.
- Navigation mode — in this mode, the Web user has logged on. The WebAgent maintains user log-in and password information, letting the user browse and update Vantive data based on the group permissions.
- Anonymous mode — in this mode, the WebAgent skips the log-in screen and displays a certain database record. The form and permissions are defined by the default VanWeb anonymous access group; if no such group

has been defined this mode is unavailable. The main benefit of anonymous mode is that external Web pages can link to specific records in the Vantive database.

The WebAgent allows designers to control the display attributes of a form's HTML page so Web designers can assign different visual clues, such as backgrounds and font colors, to particular forms.

Dynamic Web interaction and navigation

In order to support present and also future browser versions, Vantive has made the Web publisher dynamically adaptable.

When a user connects to the WebAgent, the browser is identified. The WebAgent dynamically adapts to the extensions and limitations of the browser being used, generating the optimal forms without excluding low-end browsers from proper form layouts and a full functionality set. In other words, the WebAgent will use HTML extensions, but only those recognized by the browser. VanWeb provides "relational context" navigation to Web users at three levels: main form, drill down, and locator.

Because data integrity is maintained through VanAPI, users can navigate dynamic sets of records with "safe links" so they do not get led to empty pages or nonexistent URLs. Unlike Web applications that only have hypertext navigation capabilities, VanWeb's dynamic navigation features are designed for browsing/searching the large sets of data which are typical of corporate information systems.

VanWeb also extends the hypertext capabilities of the Web to the Vantive database. External documents can link to records in the Vantive database using the WebAgent's anonymous access group. Data in the Vantive database can also be linked to external Web pages, images, sounds, and even video.

In fact, VanWeb can embed complete HTML statements and URLs within Vantive data. This enables the Vantive database to cross-reference data throughout the Web. With a single step, Vantive users will be able to download FTP files, search WAIS or Gopher databases, and access the resolution databases of partners, vendors, and other third parties.

7.3.2 PatrolWatch for Web Browsers from BMC

Patrol products are known to support applications management. Applications management means ensuring that applications are online, available to users, and performing optimally. It is best accomplished by automatically monitoring and managing the applications, internet/intranet servers, databases, middleware, and underlying resources that affect application availability.

Patrol application management products shift that administration focus away from managing individual components, such as systems and networks, to an application management approach that looks at the entire environment, from business processes and end-user tools to lower-level resources. Figure 7.8 shows the architecture from Patrol. Key components are:

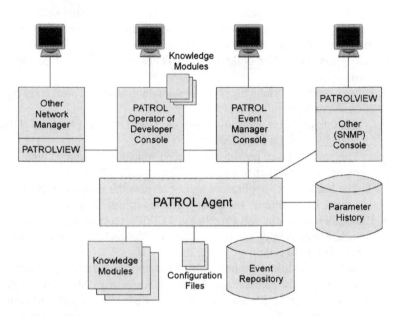

FIGURE 7.8 Architecture of Patrol.

- Patrol Agents — these are small, independent programs that run on each managed server. The agent is able to run autonomously — without console connection — because it is essentially self-contained. All of the application discovery and management rules the agent needs are contained in "plug-in" libraries of information called Knowledge Modules (KMs). These KMs reside on each managed server along with the agent. Using information from the KMs a single Patrol Agent collects data about managed resources. The multitasking agent can potentially monitor hundreds of parameters on each object instance, interpret the data, store the data locally in history files, and implement predetermined corrective actions. Because the agent is autonomous, it can do this without any communication with a console.
- Event Manager — the Event Manager is part of the Patrol Agent architecture. It is accessed through the Patrol Console as a stand-alone Patrol Event Manager console of a third-party management framework. The console allows administrators to focus on and control specified events through advanced event filtering, sorting, control, and escalation capabilities.
- Patrol Consoles — by providing true multiconsole support, management information remains consistent across the enterprise, with each connected console receiving an identical view of monitored objects and metrics. Since the Patrol Agent-to-Console communication protocol is so efficient and scalable, a large number of console connections will have only minimal impact on the agent's performance. Tests have measured only marginal performance degradation, even when more than 100 consoles are

attached to a single agent. Another important aspect of true multiconsole support is that each console is able to maintain its own view of the monitored objects, sharing either the same view as other consoles or a customized view. The desktop layout is also fully user-configurable for each console.

- Patrol Communications Elements — communication in Patrol takes place at three conceptual levels:

  System level communications use the User Datagram Protocol (UDP) layer for speed and availability

  The session layer provides the added reliability features common to higher-level protocols

  The higher-level application layer provides the transfer of parameter values, object status, and other requested information

- Patrol, however, can still establish a TCP/IP connection, and can even provide monitoring of the higher-level TCP/IP and RPC (remote procedure call) transactions.

- Knowledge Modules — much of the Patrol application management products' extensibility comes from the use of Knowledge Modules — plug-in, product-specific libraries of expertise. KMs contain the information used by the agents to discover and monitor the key components of a distributed environment. Patrol KMs also provide the product-specific expertise administrators need to effectively leverage their management skills across new operating systems, databases, and third-party applications with a minimum investment in training or new staff. Due to its modular structure, KMs can be easily adapted to new releases of a given application. The KM library is continuously being updated, providing administrators with the flexible management tools they need to manage constantly changing technologies with the shortest possible learning curve.

- User interfaces — the Patrol interface, with an intuitive, hierarchical structure and flexible customization operations, plays an important role in the product's user-friendly look and feel. It provides a clear, coherent view of processes taking place at many levels of the managed environment. The processes monitored and displayed may range from the performance characteristics of the operating system kernel, to the locks of other resources held by an individual user. The interface can be extensively customized to meet organizational requirements. Access by Web browsers will further simplify and unify the user interface.

PatrolWatch for Web browsers provides a simple and cost-effective solution to the requirements of distributed administration today. Key features and functions include:

- Minimal requirements — administrators can view Patrol-managed objects and events across the network using standard PCs running NT or Windows 95 or higher, or across the internet using a leading Web browser
- Anytime, anywhere access — administrators can check on the status of the environment from virtually any desktop in the organization, or from any remote site that has secure internet access, without needing a management console.
- Enhanced productivity — administrators no longer need to waste time trying to locate a management console or returning to the office simply to check on the status of their environment. They can respond more rapidly.
- Cost effective and efficient — PatrolWatch is a low-cost product with minimal resource demand, providing a flexible, distributed option to meet administrative access requirements.

It leverages the growing availability of the internet to provide authorized access to an event-based, graphical view of Patrol objects in the managed environment. Its interface displays a hierarchical tree structure of items being monitored, options for the type of information to be viewed, details on each item's status, and explanations of error messages. Event information on time, object, type, and parameter is also included. In addition to supporting the new Web-based management standards, it also uses Java from Sun Microsystems and JavaScripts from Netscape. PatrolWatch is loaded on a Web server. The Web browser is used on the client to view information collected by PatrolWatch. No additional software is required on the client. Part of PatrolWatch for Web browsers is actually a Java applet that is downloaded from the server only when requested by the application. PatrolWatch in the Web server uses a command line interface to interact with all of the managed Patrol agents in the computing environment. This means that PatrolWatch can be used to monitor any server in the environment, including those that are Web servers, as well as those that aren't. Patrol products must be installed in the computing environment, so that PatrolWatch has the necessary information to display. But, besides that, the server on which PatrolWatch runs does not need any other Patrol software. It is assumed that the Common Gateway Interface (CGI) comes as a standard part of the Web software.

7.3.3 STORAGE MANAGEMENT APPLICATIONS

The internet and intranets may be utilized for management applications that were considered just for dedicated private networks before. WebStor and SmartStor from Network Associates are good examples for these types of applications.

WebStor is a personal backup and file management solution providing internet-enabled backup, restore, and file management capabilities for PCs running Windows 95 and higher. It will automatically and transparently back up the most important files. By using the simple drag and drop capability in the Explorer Interface, the user can retrieve files quickly and easily. With WebStor, the most important files can follow the user wherever he or she goes because they can be backed up to an internet repository. WebStor can use existing private networks of the users, the internet, or intranets to safely store data.

According to industry analysts, 90% of all data restore requests originating from users are not the result of disasters, but are instead caused by the loss of a single file, such as a Word document, a PowerPoint presentation, or Excel spread-sheets. WebStor is specifically optimized to leverage the internet and intranets to address the unique backup requirements of these smaller and more dynamic data files. For full systems backups, WebStor integrates a disaster recovery module called ImageStor, that utilizes image-based — as opposed to file-based — backup tech-nology to create a baseline snapshot of the entire primary storage system.

WebStor simplifies the backup and recovery process by fully integrating within the Microsoft Explorer interface. Files are dragged to or from destinations while backing up or restoring. Any remote storage source that can be recognized by the operating system as a logical device can be used as a source or destination for backups. Supported sources and destinations include remote FTP sites, tape drives, hard drives, and rewriteable optical devices.

WebStor includes Protection Manager, a feature that helps the user identify personal data files that need to be backed up on a regular basis. Once these files have been identified, WebStor can automatically launch unattended backups on a scheduled basis. Using the internet or intranets, WebStor offers near instantaneous backup and retrieval of personal data files. It relieves users from the session-orien-tation of traditional tape-based solutions by supporting tape-less backups over the internet. While tape solutions require users to remember the date, time, and version of a backup to retrieve a data file, WebStor allows users to perform on-demand requests by file name. WebStor's support of random access searches also allows it to retrieve files faster than tape drives, which can only perform sequential searches.

SmartStor offers the same data protection, data management, and disaster recov-ery features as WebStor plus the advanced storage technology of an installable file system (IFS). IFS installs a tape drive like a logical device. This allows the user to view and manipulate files as if they were stored on a disk drive.

WebStor and SmartStor both integrate a disaster recovery module called ImageStor, which utilizes logical image-based backup technology to create a baseline snapshot of the entire disk. It is recommended to use ImageStor for full backups and WebStor for individual data files. ImageStor supports tape and other rewriteable storage media. Key features are:

- Personal backup/restore protection leveraging the internet/intranets
- Fully automated backup operations with right mouse click menu options
- Explorer integration with the ability to drag and drop files selectively
- Schedule backups any time — during idle time, or on-demand
- Setup Wizard provides step-by-step installation, data selection and con-figuration for backup options
- Complete disaster recovery protection with ImageStor application

The combination of easy and cost-efficient backup and recovery using the inter-net or intranets makes this solution a viable alternative to existing techniques.

7.3.4 ANALYSIS AND REPORTING

Web-based analysis and reporting have been popular from the early days of utilizing the Web technology to support management functions. The basic idea is to publish results in HTML format and to make results available to a broad user community. Everybody with the proper authorization can access information from a universal Web browser. This technology addresses the presentation side, and not how data are collected and processed. The large majority of vendors in the monitoring, analysis, tuning, and reporting business have extended their products with Web capabilities. The basic technology is passive, indicating that users are expected to look and search for information. In future developments, selected information may be pushed to the right destination addresses.

Practical examples are shown with PerfAgent from Quallaby, Domainmeter from Technically Elite, and Health Monitor from Concord Communications.

7.3.4.1 PerfAgent from Quallaby

Quallaby's PerfAgent is the first self-refining service level performance tool for networks that gives an enterprise-wide picture of health and availability. Exception-based reports and summaries can be in real-time for immediate problem identification, or they can be automatic and report historical levels for good trending. Perf-Agent continuously synchronizes the database with custom indicators, building a "living" knowledge base of concise information to refine baseline trend targets.

The PerfAgent advantage

- Automatic reports — exception, summary and detail reports give concise information to quickly assess information on how the network supports the business needs of the organization and customers.
- Data management — the system automatically collects SNMP and RMON data and sends them to any SQL database. PerfAgent regularly synchs the data with the network to build and manage a smart database of minimal size and save time.
- Intuitive and easy, plug and play ease of use saves time and effort. The system is standards-based, open, flexible, and adaptable to ensure interoperability and long-term investment protection.

The PerfAgent system is the first premier flexible and adaptable service-level reporting solution for NT and UNIX, whose platform is open and adaptable. It is able to support service level management (SLM) and quality of service (QoS) in the true sense, not only because it analyzes and reports on captured SNMP and RMON data, but also because PerfAgent builds an intelligent knowledge base from which concise information is delivered, enabling smart business decision making.

Its architecture is comprised of a Requests Manager that configures and manages parameters and thresholds so you end up over time with only pertinent, smart data in a database of minimal size. PerfAgent tracks and reports through a custom tailored dashboard only the pertinent information that the operator needs to support and guarantees specific network and system service levels. The goal of the PerfAgent performance analysis and reporting system is to report useful metrics in useful forms. The sophisticated and rich analytical capabilities of the software, combined with its intuitive interface, allow the wide range of reports to be as simple or complex as one desires. Some of the categories of reports that PerfAgent offers are:

- Exception reports and tiering show a view of the special service level circumstances where thresholds have been crossed. They present a summary of networks and systems performance in a concise and actionable way with second-tier data providing relative detail. Trends can then be corrected proactively early on to ensure the contracted or guaranteed quality of service.
- Trending and summary reports show tracked trends, automate predictive analysis and corrective action and provide a historical view of performance indicators. This information ensures fulfillment of SLAs and helps to define thresholds for exception reporting.
- Detail reports provide a view of resource availability and utilization. Both real-time and historical views of performance address immediate problems or long-term trends and allow for resource optimization.
- Web Reporter is an intelligent Web link providing a view of high-level reports and can show anything from service fulfillments to a detailed event.

The Helix Data Model (HDM) is a three-tier application framework based on a distributed, scalable management architecture. This model has a lot of advantages that work together. Distributing portions of business application software into a separate layer opens opportunities for big improvements in the business applications themselves and increases the scalability of the network. Further distributing of a portion of the user interface toward the client is particularly effective when realized using browser technology for a slim/universal client. Lastly, in unique fashion, the HDM architecture is built from an object engine (PerfAgent's Request Manager) that can adjust and refine its parameters based on the analysis of previously gathered data, as defined by PerfAgent's Formula Editor. Therein, this flexible and adaptable resource allows for proactive management applications.

There are a lot of ways to implement the three-tier model. An increasingly popular implementation is shown in Figure 7.9. In this scheme, the user interface can be implemented using internet/Web page technology such as HTML and JAVA or the traditional fat client approach. In the case of PerfAgent/Q WebReporter, the application is managed entirely from browser software (slim client) and the application interfaces are accessed dynamically from a Web server. The network connections are realized using standards-based intranet or internet technology.

In the HDM architecture, data are gathered and sent to the Requests Manager Engine (RME) where parameters are configured, set, and stored in an SQL database for further processing. For each parameter, the RME can configure the IP address, the collecting agenda, the collecting frequency, the threshold, and the command linked to the given threshold. Based on the continuous change of trending results, the RME is capable of automatically reconfiguring its reference model based on

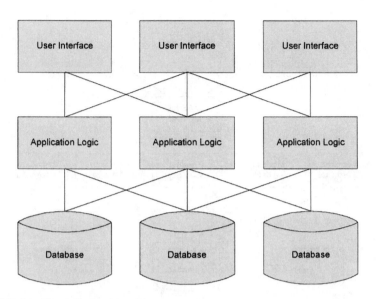

FIGURE 7.9 The Helix Data Model.

each analysis, cleaning away data now deemed useless based on the results of the analysis. This process happens continuously to provide good, smart trending and promotes improvement of the quality of services. In this way, the RME can handle complex management tasks and leads to a high degree of scalability.

The HDM architecture, as a whole, is designed to allow greater reliability and simplification, particularly in long-term trending and analysis. The implementation of the Requests Manager Engine in the HDM architecture will be a significant value-add over the three-tier distributed architecture that most other enterprise management platforms offer today. The HDM architecture helps IS organizations deliver a consistent quality of network service and at the same time allows for continuous improvement by constantly redefining the new quality baseline goals.

PerfAgent is built around the following functions (Figure 7.10):

- Managing quality indicators: creating, editing, saving, and viewing standard or user-enhanced indicators
- Collecting data from target devices and storing them in the SQL database using the Request Manager
- Real-time dashboards which allow the administrator to view all of the desired quality indicators in real time
- Creating fully customizable enhanced reports
- The WebReport module gives access to PerfAgent reports through the internet or an intranet
- The Import/Export function allows PerfAgent to be interfaced with data sources or with other PerfAgent servers

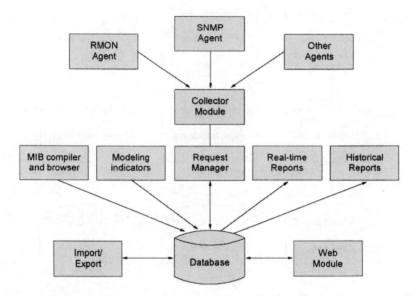

FIGURE 7.10 Architecture of PerfAgent.

Parameters play the most important role in monitoring quality of service. An indicator corresponds to a type of information or data that the administrator wishes to monitor in order to:

- View changes over time and set values in relationship to technical or qualitative objectives
- Compare changes during a given period in relation to a past period (reference sample)
- View its immediate value and be able to compare it to an acceptable value

There are a number of different types of parameters:

- Technical parameters, for example:
    Percent of IP packets lost on a router
    Percent of collision rate on a local area network
- Quality parameters, for example:
    Availability rate of a local Ethernet network
    Percent of available bandwidth on a WAN line
- Financial indicators, for example:
    Number of X.25 or Frame Relay packets transmitted between two sites

A parameter always results from an operation carried out on target hardware device MIB objects (routers, hubs, probes, servers, databases). PerfAgent's parameter module allows the manager to:

- Select from the predefined parameters which are supplied with PerfAgent
  LAN parameters for the most common hardware devices
  Frame Relay WAN parameters
  NT Server parameter
- Define new parameters or edit the predefined parameters; new parameters
  can be immediately tested on the target hardware devices when they are
  created.
- The MIB compiler module can recognize MIBs associated with any new
  SNMP agent.

The Request Manager module is used to manage all collected parameters, the
frequency of data storage, the desired instances, and, above all, the target devices.
The administrator can set a threshold for each parameter. If this threshold is
exceeded, he or she can then use the following standard functions or set the program
to:

- Generate an SNMP trap for any other network management or error
  management program
- Send a message to a pager
- Send a user-definable message to a proprietary event management program (Tivoli, CA, Candle, etc.)

In addition the administrator can also set other actions to be carried out on the
PerfAgent program itself. For example: a report can be printed for the entire day X
for the indicator when Y has exceeded the threshold which has been defined for the
day X. Using this method, only those reports associated with exceptions will be
printed, instead of printing all reports for all hardware devices. In addition, this
module handles data management in an SQL database using an advanced handling
for aggregating, purging, and saving data selected.

Data collected by PerfAgent are stored and saved in the SQL database with no
limit on either time or capacity. Where intervals of one minute are desirable for
creating daily reports, this degree of precision would be superfluous for weekly or
monthly reports. PerfAgent can aggregate and consolidate this data automatically
in order to save only the average values or extreme values for a given hour or day,
while still saving all the base source data. This method allows for a wide variety of
possible uses. PerfAgent also allows programming of tasks on request or according
to daily, weekly, or monthly periods. These tasks may be aggregations (a variety of
operations based on averages, minimums, and maximums are available) and/or
purges on selected parameters.

This aggregation is started by an internal calendar-based scheduler which allows
the user to select the period for the cycle: daily, weekly, monthly; or alternatively
at a given time, or on a given day.

This module lets the manager:

- Have an overview of changes in a quality indicator over a long period of time and thus stay on top of future needs.
- Define "quality profiles" which can be used as yardstick references for new reports.
- Save detailed information for more comprehensive analysis at a later date.
- Create a "Network Reference" which can be used to evaluate the advisability of new investment or upgrades to new technology.

PerfAgent is a solution that allows the network manager to monitor the quality of service for any type of network (reports, baselines, etc.). Real-time surveillance of quality parameters is a key additional function to carry out this monitoring.

- If the quality parameters are technical parameters, the manager must be informed of any error in real time:
  Examples
  Percent of collisions on a local network
  Percent of IP packets lost
- The manager needs to be alerted if these thresholds are exceeded but also needs to be able to take control of the system in real time
- If a scheduled report shows an abnormal change in a parameter that has been detected repeatedly and is isolated in time (for example, every Wednesday afternoon), the manager can use this information to investigate the problem. He can use the same time basis (polling period) and the same parameters (formulas) to dynamically verify the evolution of the problem the following Wednesday afternoon.

Reports are created from data that are collected and stored in the database. This may be for selected parameters or aggregations. The manager can create reports using:

- Parameters calculated from collected data
- Aggregated parameters — averages, minimums, maximums for a given period (hour, day) which are calculated automatically by PerfAgent
- Other types of data imported by PerfAgent (ASCII files, data from other platforms such as HP OpenView, Tivoli TME, and Bull ISM)

This module allows the manager to:

- Either generate reports using the predefined templates that are supplied with PerfAgent, such as
  Frame Relay report template
  Brand X IP Router report template
  Agent Y UNIX server template

- Or create reports using templates that may be fully defined by the manager to suit his or her operational model
  Type A site report template
  Type B site report template
  Device Z report template

PerfAgent can also be used to create generic reports. The manager can then make groups of reports by simply specifying for each of them: the list of devices, a presentation period for the report, and the instances associated with the selected parameters. A group of reports can be generated for a site or for a given device.

Finally, this module allows the user to view any difference between the current activity profile for a given parameter, and the reference profile which has been previously selected by the manager: this is the "Baseline" function.

7.3.4.2 Domainmeter from Technically Elite

Domainmeter collects and processes management information from third-party RMON probes or SNMP agents on multiple segments. Network managers can gather statistics from anywhere on the Web using any PC or laptop with a Web browser There are two application areas for this product:

1. It can supplement an enterprise management console by collecting and interpreting SNMP and RMON statistics
2. It can support smaller users with an affordable alternative to a high-end workstation

Domainmeter consists of a UNIX server loaded with the Enterprise Meterware software, an SNMP and RMON data polling engine, a report builder, and a database. The device is installed at every site in the enterprise to collect SNMP and RMON data from probes and agents on each LAN segment. Domainmeter works with the vendor's own RMON agents and with all Ethernet, token ring, and FDDI RMON compliant probes. It also can gather information from probes supporting RMON2 capabilities. Figure 7.11 shows the architecture of the product.[12]

The Domainmeter polls network devices at regular intervals. It then analyzes the information and automatically builds reports using several prefabricated formats on the Meterware software. Network managers have several different options for viewing these reports: use of X-Terminals; use of e-mail with specific target addresses; and use of universal Web browsers.

Domainmeter acts as its own Web server, distributing reports over the internet or intranets. Graphical reports are converted into GIF files and text into HTML files. In order to support real-time reporting capabilities and security, Java applets are used. Using Java, network managers are able to run SNMP and RMON protocols natively as applets on their PCs. This allows them to query the Domainmeter for specific pieces of information, such as device statistics on utilization, errors, etc., without the need to translate SNMP and RMON data into HTML and GIF, respectively. The Java security model for user authentication is based on public key encryption.

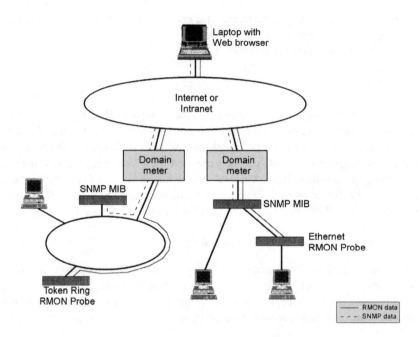

FIGURE 7.11 Architecture of Domainmeter.

7.3.4.3 Health Monitor from Concord Communications

Technology managers face increasing pressure from both budget-conscious corporate managers and technology-dependent end users to document the quality and consistency of information technology services. Provision of regular, meaningful service level metrics forms the basis of effective service level agreements between IT providers and IT customers. Today, the process of collecting, analyzing, presenting, and distributing service level information represents an enormous investment of time and expertise, yet still leaves senior management demanding more frequent, reliable, and meaningful documentation of service levels.

Network Health service level reports automate the collection, analysis, presentation, and distribution of service level information. They consist of three reports:

1. Executive report — a single-page summary of service level performance across the enterprise. Executives can review the previous period's activity with respect to their own service level definitions. The report also summarizes the monthly activity of the organization's most important business units, giving managers the relative effect of how their business units are affecting IT service.

2. IT manager report — an immediate summary report on service levels across the IT environment, from clear visibility of long-term trends at the enterprise level, to general service level performance by business units, down to detailed service level metrics on a device-by-device basis. IT

managers can customize the report by selecting devices and service level metrics, as well as a specific time frame for inclusion in the report.

3. Service customer report — a single-page, site-specific, monthly summary of service level information for service customers. This report identifies long-term service trends, provides a customer-wide service level trend, as measured by exception totals, and details service level for each of the customer's IT devices.

While supporting automated service level calculation and reporting at an aggregate level, the service level reports maintain the ability to deliver information on individual IT elements, such as routers, WAN lines, Frame Relay circuits, or servers. Through custom element tables, the reports calculate and report on service level, measured by availability, latency, bandwidth distribution, among other metrics, on individual network or server devices. Management information provided include the following metrics:

- Availability — measures how often IT resources are available to IT customers; it is one of the most important metrics for evaluating IT effectiveness.
- Latency — measures how fast the network moves information, a critical indicator of service level for technology end users.
- Bandwidth distribution — provides a key measurement of IT service levels, as high bandwidth utilization is closely linked to poor IT service.
- Network volume — measures network traffic trends by enterprise or region; a key indicator of overall usage trends of IT resources.
- Exception trends — sums and trends the volume of network health exceptions over time. By defining thresholds to trigger exceptions of service level, IT managers can manage overall service level by tracking the total number of exceptions.
- Health index — measures service level enterprise-wide or by individual IT element, identifying the relative contributors to poor service (Figure 7.12).
- Technology-specific metrics — measure service level by monitoring critical performance metrics on network and systems hardware, such as errors, faults, collisions, buffer utilization, and discards.

The company has started early to offer information and all types of reports via the Web. After completing the analysis, report content is converted into HTML pages and housed on Web servers. Besides service level reports, the following additional reports are available:

- LAN/WAN reports analyzing the traffic on network infrastructures, reporting on the performance of individual segments, rings, and WAN circuits.
- Frame Relay reports extend the scope of LAN/WAN reports, and help to manage cost-effectiveness on Frame Relay investments.

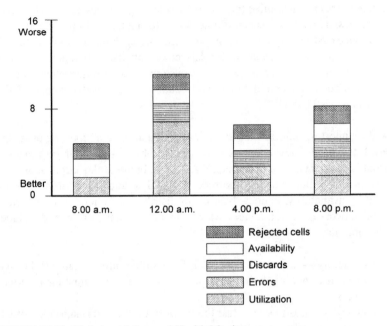

FIGURE 7.12 Health index of Concord Health Monitor.

- Router/switch reports analyze how efficiently inter-networking devices are managing the network load, and help to pinpoint specific devices causing problems.
- Server reports measure the availability of servers on which key applications reside. They also report on key server performance metrics, including CPU, memory, disk, and communication utilization.
- ATM reports help to maximize ATM deployment with quality of service measurements and usage information.
- Traffic Accountant reports look at RMON2 and application layer data to identify users, groups, and applications driving traffic (Figures 7.13 and 7.14).

Network Health understands the information IT managers need and automatically collects, analyzes, and distills the information down to key points. Without visibility across different vendor's devices and technologies, it is difficult to make informed, enterprise-wide capacity planning and investment decisions. Network Health delivers automation on three levels.

Automation of device discovery and configuration

It automatically discovers network devices and configures itself. It supports standards like SNMP, MIB II, RMON1, and RMON2, coupled with an extensive library of supported devices, saves operations team time and resources. And, with new devices constantly being added to the Network Health list of supported equipment, managers

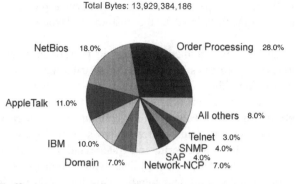

Total Bytes: 13,929,384,186

FIGURE 7.13 Traffic Accountant daily applications.

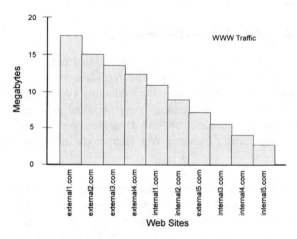

FIGURE 7.14 Traffic Accountant top Web sites daily summary.

are assured that Network Health will grow with them and continue to support deployment of new technologies as networks expand.

Automatic trend analysis

It collects and applies key analytics to condense data into only the critical information needed to optimize network performance. Network managers eliminate hours typically spent in writing programs to access and collect key data as well as time often spent to further analyze and present the information to management. Its colorful, easy-to-understand formats enable network managers to easily assess the status of their network, identify potential problems, and recognize their trends.

Automatic report distribution

It allows the IT or network management organization to tailor the content, distribution, and presentation of valuable information to fit the requirements of just about any internal process. Service level reports are usually delivered via the Web. Managers responsible for specific regions or devices receive daily reports that highlight exceptions and trends based upon their existing business processes and are customized to the needs of their specific environments. Service providers can send out reports to their customers, tailored to the customer's resources and service level goals.

The Web interface gives immediate access to performance reports across the whole enterprise and automates the process of distributing reports to consumers across the organization. Clicking on the actual reports on the desktop gives users additional details on specific network elements, down to the port and interface card level. The Web interface also features online help and makes it easy to drill down for additional detail and correlation of trends across technologies.

Network Health includes a powerful, integrated relational database and a graphic console. The database stores the collected data, while the analysis engine analyzes historical resource requirements and trends as well as forecasts future resource requirements. Network Health runs on SunSparc and HP 9000 under Solaris and HP/UX. It also runs on Intel P2 under NT 4.00 SP 3 and 4.

7.3.4.4   Statistical Analysis System from SAS

SAS is one of the best-known products in the field of performance management, data warehousing, and performance reporting. SAS is a powerful database language for general purpose, and very popular with evaluating systems and network performance. SAS/IntrNet is a new extension to the original product; it supports Web publishing, dynamic database queries, and dynamic compute services.

There are many reasons for using Web technology in data warehousing and in related fields:

- Use of a universal browser as a front-end between user, SAS/IntrNet and the database. The handling of a browser is easy to learn. The average user does not need to know details about the SAS applications.
- Thin clients off load the workstations of the user significantly. It gives the choice to use network computing or older PCs for access. In both cases, resource demand on behalf of Web access is minimal.
- The use of IP supports the full-sharing of hardware and software resources. Geographically, SAS application servers, Web servers, and Web browsers can be physically deployed at different locations. Logically, they are connected via IP.
- Directory service is available to easily locate resources that are distributed in the network.

Figure 7.15 shows the structure of the SAS/IntrNet solution.[2] The Application Dispatcher is in charge of distributing the applications in the network. It is based on a Common Gateway Interface (CGI) solution and isolates the user from any kind of programming. The dispatcher is a continuous process communicating with the broker and access module. All applications can be developed on the basis of Java or HTML.

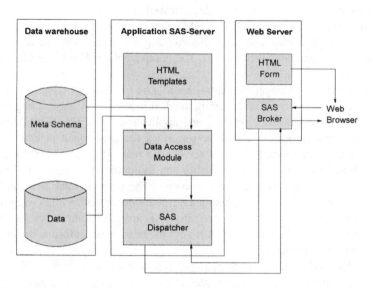

FIGURE 7.15 Structure of the SAS/IntrNet solution.

Over the long term, Java seems to be more powerful. SAS/IntrNet has Jconnect to start applications, to create data sets, to access SAS files, to analyze data and to download search results. In order to support SQL queries, Java Data base connectivity and a SAS Driver for ODBC are available. Jtunnel connects the Web server and the application server, with the result that they need not be on the same physical device. If they run on different hardware, their configurations may be sized and optimized separately.

On the other hand, HTML experiences are more widely available in enterprises. Content authoring is supported by many case tools that can be combined with SAS know-how. HTML templates may be designed with HTML tools, and they can be populated by SAS data during run-time. Most likely, a combination of Java and standard HTML guarantees the highest effectiveness.

7.3.5 INTEGRATION OF MANAGEMENT FUNCTIONS USING FRONTLINE MANAGER

FrontLine Manager unifies the management of rapidly proliferating intranet computing resources across network devices, systems, services, and applications. Designed for systems and network administrators, helpdesk agents, and others who manage on the frontline, responding to and solving user support calls. FrontLine Manager uses Web technologies to simplify day-to-day operational tasks and thus lower the cost of intranet management. It begins managing out-of-the-box by discovering and identifying resources, while creating a unified management view of the entire intranet environment. It goes beyond passive monitoring to identifying and diagnosing problems proactively. Embedded software intelligence determines the ideal operating state of each resource and notifies support staff when healthy operating conditions are exceeded. Rapid installation and ease of use are combined with low administrative overhead to maximize productivity. It is a typical first tier support tool. All management functionality and the unified management view are accessed via a standard Web browser. The components of FrontLine Manager are:

- FrontLine Manager Server — each server manages a typical LAN or LANs, supporting up to 255 network devices and systems, along with a base set of intranet services and applications. The FrontLine Manager server incorporates a Web server and a scalable object database. As a result, a distributed group of servers can manage up to 100,000 nodes.
- Web browser — all functionality and the unified management view are accessed via a standard Web browser. The browser interface simplifies the presentation of complex management information, while giving front-line managers the freedom to manage securely from anywhere, locally or remotely. An active window displays the most recent information for each managed resource.
- Managed agents — each managed resource has an associated SNMP or Java agent. Agents transmit management data to the server and can also conduct management tasks. A base set of SNMP and Java agents developed by Manage.Com are included with FrontLine Manager. Third-party SNMP agents already installed on network devices and system can also be used.

FrontLine Manager is prebuilt with key management features needed to manage the majority of intranet commuting environments. No time is wasted on complex installation, customization, or integration. Quickstart installation automatically discovers all resources and begins monitoring them so that productive management can begin immediately. It begins proactively discovering and classifying resources during installation, a process that completes within a few hours. It then associates an ideal operating state with each resource and monitors accordingly. If abnormalities are discovered, FrontLine Manager immediately begins to diagnose and isolate the causes. For maximum efficiency, it helps to identify and resolve problems before users report them. The intelligence to identify the healthy operating state of specific resources is built into the product. As a result, it is able to take samples of the intranet continually and determine its overall health. It also launches automatic analysis to diagnose and segment operating problems, often before they are reported by users. Figure 7.16 shows the principal management functions.

This Web-based solution differentiates itself from individual device- or application-dependent products, because it integrates the management of network devices, systems, services, and applications.

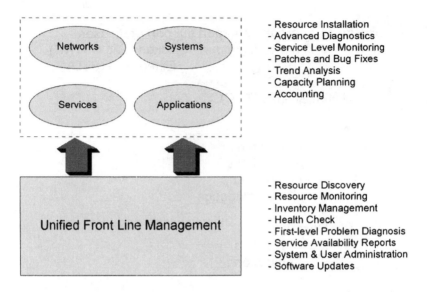

FIGURE 7.16 Architecture of Frontline Manager.

7.4 SERVICE LEVEL MANAGEMENT USING WEB TECHNOLOGIES

Service level agreements are gaining in importance. There are so many relationships between incumbent and new service providers, ISPs, VPN suppliers that without written agreements, relationships cannot be managed anymore. But, between the partners, an agreement is needed about metrics, presentation forms, and frequency of information exchange.

7.4.1 OBSERVANT FROM TERTIO

Observant from Tertio Limited[9] can help organizations figure out just how well the technology infrastructure supports actual business operations. It also lets network managers get an early read on potential problems, which means they can get an early start on fixes.

Observant is a Java-based package and runs together with management platforms, such as OpenView and TME 10. It typically runs on the same server as the network management platform. The core software is an object matrix which models the relationship between each business process and the systems and networks that support it. Collectors handle input from network management systems, and dispatchers send output to external systems, such as trouble ticketing and reporting. The model itself populates the display, which can be accessed by Web browsers, as shown in Figure 7.17.

Building the model means creating a tree-like structure that represents the dependence of one object on another, in successive levels of detail. An object is anything that requires monitoring — from the complete line of business to a system

Business Application: Airport support processes
System and network support: Token Ring C (TRC)
                               Ethernet D (ETD)

A. United Airlines (TRC)

- ● Check-In
  - x   Computers
  - x   Applications
    - -   Ticketing
    - -   Lost luggage

- ● Reservations
  - x   Computers
  - x   Applications

- ● Payroll
  - x   Computers
  - x   Applications

B. Continental Airlines (ETD)

FIGURE 7.17 Access of Observant via Web browsers.

comprising various hardware and software components to individual devices and
applications. Configuration alternatives are provided with the product.

As users view the model, Observant notes the condition of various objects, using
specific colors to indicate status. Also special SLA metrics can be defined, and their
thresholds supervised. Any parameter can be monitored, as long as it is being
measured by the underlying management system. Colors can also be changed according to behavior templates that are attached to objects. These templates can be created
with a special editor, and they help administrators define combinations of events
that determine a trouble condition. For instance, a network manager can create a
behavior template that changes an object's status to a "critical" color if a backup
circuit has been activated more than "x" times in a week. Observant can be configured
so that different users see different levels of detail. Support desk personnel might
simply be able to view the specific line of business and whether the network is
impacting business performance. But network managers can see the entire model
displayed, so they can troubleshoot early and efficiently.

7.4.2 ENTERPRISE PRO FROM INTERNATIONAL NETWORK SERVICES

Analysis, reporting, and trending are very useful functions to support performance tuning and capacity planning. But service level management (SLM) may need reports delivered in real-time. Most of the products introduced earlier offer this capability. When the company is interested in this kind of reporting but does not want to establish such a service, Enterprise Pro from International Network Services (INS) may be an interesting alternative. It differentiates itself from other products with so called quality-of-service alert capabilities. It immediately notifies network managers when network traffic exceeds a predetermined threshold. And with server monitoring, it helps get to the root cause of problems. Reports can be viewed through e-mail or via Web browsers or from OpenView consoles since INS has integrated Enterprise Pro with the OpenView management platform.

Enterprise Pro is installed on a server connected to the LAN, as shown in Figure 7.18.[18] Network managers can set performance thresholds per device, per group of devices, or per segment through a GUI. Using SNMP, the software gathers information from MIBs embedded in routers, switches, bridges, and hubs. It also can collect bandwidth-utilization data from RMON1 (Remote Monitoring) and RMON2 probes throughout the network. As soon as a threshold is exceeded, Enterprise Pro generates a report to the management console or to a browser.

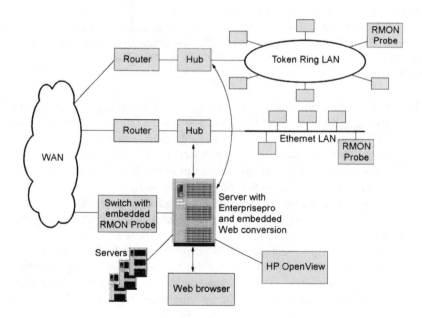

FIGURE 7.18 Architecture of Enterprise Pro.

Enterprise Pro can collect data from NT, Novell, and UNIX servers. It collects statistics on CPU load, memory utilization, and disk space utilization — information that helps to isolate and resolve problems. Instant updates help corporate networkers to start problem resolution before users notice faults or performance degradations. And all that means they have a better chance of meeting service level agreements they have signed with various external and internal users.

Enterprise Pro offers information in various levels of detail. Operators, administrators, and network managers can drill down for reports of the latest alarms, results of the last five-minute poll, or a combination of those. It is also possible to customize reports to present information for various sites or groups of devices. Reports can, for instance, be tailored to show activity on the LAN, or on all hubs, or on all routers in a specific geographical area.

Using Enterprise Pro means that certain performance management functions are outsourced to INS. Price/performance ratio is worth considering with this type of outsourcing.

7.4.3 PRONTOWATCH FROM PROACTIVE NETWORKS

ProntoWatch from Proactive Networks may also be utilized to supervise service level agreements in real-time. ProntoWatch goes beyond the capabilities of traditional network monitoring solutions, adding real-time intelligence to the problem detection process, providing proactive notification of trends that could lead to downtime, and enabling the user to isolate and eliminate soft-faults before they become serious problems. The results are higher network service levels, increased business productivity, and better competitiveness.

This Web-based, turnkey solution is offered at a very affordable price, and requires little effort on behalf of the users. Implementation times are very short. Service to users is delivered electronically over the Web. Benefits using the Pronto-Watch service include:

- Improved service levels — the intelligent early warning support solution leverages the Cognitive Alarms and 3-D Telescoping technology to predict and prevent degraded network and application service levels.
- Higher network operations productivity — real-time intelligent alarms, daily status e-mails and easy access to network performance and asset information helps streamline network operations.
- Better capacity planning decisions — ProntoWatch monitors and tracks changes in network capacity and performance data so informed planning decisions can be made.
- Savings on equipment and WAN circuit expenses — infrastructure can be optimized on the basis of complete, dependable, and timely reporting.
- Less resource drain — due to the adaptive technology and the turnkey approach, management of the underlying technology can be limited to a minimum.
- Favorable payback — fast installation and user-friendly access to information guarantee a fast payback of investments.

7.4.4 NETWORK MANAGEMENT SERVICE FROM WORLDCOM

Web-based monitoring is becoming the way for corporate networkers to keep tabs on their voice, frame relay, and internet services. Web Network Management Services (Web NMS) from Worldcom Inc. puts the customer in control. With it, customers can easily maintain a near real-time outlook on toll-free, dedicated access line and frame relay/ATM traffic. The benefits of using Web NMS are:

- Customer-controlled reconfiguration gives the power to reroute toll-free numbers directly from the computer of the customers.
- Switched trouble tickets reporting allows viewing and updating of switched trouble tickets which are sent to the Worldcom trouble ticket system mainframe via the Web.
- Real-time utilization reporting makes it easy to obtain utilization reports and statistics, such as how often toll-free calls go unanswered and average customer call duration for toll-free numbers.

Customers who sign on will be able to use Web browsers to retrieve performance statistics on their ATM ports and circuits. By reviewing utilization statistics, network managers can tell whether they are buying the right amount of bandwidth. The reports also show whether Worldcom's ATM service is performing well. Figure 7.19 shows the Web NMS with its access capabilities.[6]

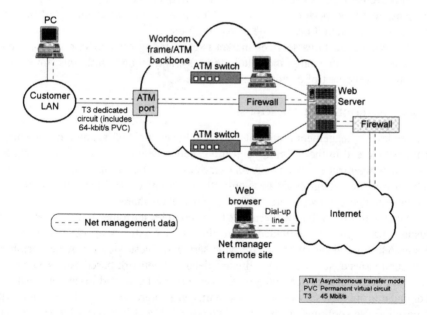

FIGURE 7.19 Web-based Network Management Service from Worldcom.

Web NMS is a significant improvement for ATM customers; before this service, they had no way to monitor their networks. Web NMS is flexible and easy to use. A customer's LAN is connected to the Worldcom frame relay/ATM backbone network over a leased line ranging from 64 Kbps to 35 Mbps. A 64 Kbps PVC (permanent virtual circuit) links customers to the Web server, which in turn is connected to several PCs that poll the carrier's ATM switches for performance data. Customers can also access the server through a much slower dial-up internet connection. With either access method, customers go through an authentication and password process and define parameters for their reports. They can view the data in three formats: graphical, tabular, and plain text. Then they set the time frame, which could be a historical look at performance going back 45 days or a recent look at traffic. Network manager can select from several reports:

- Busy hour PVC utilization
- Average PVC utilization
- Cell discard eligibility
- Port utilization
- Logical network configuration

These reports cover three ATM service classes: CBR (constant bit rate), VBR (variable bit rate), and ABR (available bit rate). More detailed reports are provided as an option on latency and average utilization on all PVCs and ports.

Improvements are expected to offer more frequent updates of Web pages. If it happens, real-time performance can also be monitored and evaluated. Also, the storage interval should be extended beyond 45 days.

The communications services market is expected to offer this or similar Web-based services. Technically, the solution is easy, and requires little investment and education on the part of customers and suppliers.

7.4.5 NETCOOL FROM MICROMUSE

Service level management represents a relatively new field of business management that has emerged in the telecommunications deregulation area. It is a fundamental concern in organizations where network service providers, internet service providers, cellular providers, large-scale mission-critical enterprises, and other telecommunications-oriented companies are competing for market shares.

Netcool offers a solution alternative to the complex customer-to-service provider business paradigm. Its distributed architecture allows network operators to custom-design real-time views of enterprise-wide services. These views provide operators with summaries of service availability and details of network-based events, enabling them to circumvent service outages. A service might be an end-to-end application, a digital transmission service, a business unit, a virtual private network, or an internet connection. Netcool runs under UNIX, Windows NT, and Java, is based on an open, client/server architecture. It features lightweight supersets of code called Probes that collect enterprise-wide event messages from over 50 different management environments in an object-based, high-speed, active database, called the ObjectServer. It normalizes the events into a common data format. Operators use drag-and-drop filtering tools to manipulate ObjectServer data to create service views and reports on service level availability.

In Netcool, Probes push event messages from management environments across the enterprise into the ObjectServer. After being formatted, multiple operators can simultaneously view them. Event messages include data such as faults, alerts, traps, exceptions, and exceeded thresholds; these are the fundamental elements of service level management. Java Event List (JEL) distributes real-time operator-specific views of systems- and network-based services to authorized users over the Web using standard browser interfaces. The views mirror the familiar color-coded EventLists that run under UNIX and MS Windows. As with traditional events lists, JEL data are filtered and arranged by each user to convey the precise information needed to represent the availability of systems and network services. Because it collects data from management platforms already installed in the customer environment, JEL is rapidly deployable. Leveraging off-the-shelf interfaces available in Netcool, JEL filters information from all Probe-enabled environments. The Java EventList fulfills a critical role by enabling distribution of clearly targeted, easy to understand views of all service monitoring to many different groups.

One of the additional benefits of using the JEL is that operators can view information in the ObjectServer without logging on to Netcool. To display a Java EventList, the user runs an applet, which connects to a Netcool ObjectServer. To start the JEL, a Java-enabled browser is necessary. In addition, a URL is needed in order to set up for displaying events. The JEL is updated automatically at time intervals with information from the ObjectServer. In addition, operators can choose to update the EventList at any point of time by selecting Refresh mode.

Netcool JEL is an interesting alternative because new and legacy type management platforms and element managers may be integrated under one event management umbrella.

7.4.6 NetExpert from Objective Systems Integrators

Web-based technology is changing how operations support systems (OSS), business support systems (BSS), and marketing support systems (MSS) work. In each of these cases, Web-technology is going to change the user interface and information distribution techniques. Due to global deregulation of telecommunications services, competitive advantages may be gained by better customer care and support functions. Web technology, including Java, can help a lot. NetExpert is considered a typical OSS, widely used in managing wireline and wireless products and services.

It consists of a series of coordinated modules that fall into three general groups: external network elements and non-NetExpert subsystem gateways, object persistence and behavior servers, and user/operator workstation/Web interfaces. NetExpert is a robust, scalable and distributable architecture that supports a high degree of configuration flexibility while maintaining individual component independence. Easy to use, easy to modify, easy to initiate, it is quick to roll out and integrate with existing platforms and systems. Its application packages provide a comprehensive subset of functions. These can be further tailored to individual customer environments. Application packages consist of various rulesets that align with the TMN management layers:[27]

- Point Integration Rules to manage specific systems and network devices, usually vendor-specific solutions.
- Domain Integration Rules to manage across multiple vendors and process boundaries, are usually network, but not device specific.
- Corporate Integration Rules to manage multiple networks and their management data. In addition, telecommunication services and business processes may be managed, as well.

The WebOperator server is a Java-based, multiplatform internet application that uses a browser to provide existing NetExpert operator functionality over the internet and the corporate intranet. It is a stand-alone Java application that runs on the same host machine as the user's internal Web server. It interfaces with NetExpert and the NetExpert database to provide NetExpert services and data to WebOperator clients. It runs on low-cost platforms, and provides network managers the ability to remotely administer their networks over a narrow-bandwidth, dial-up internet connection. This capability makes fault monitoring and identification practical on the network even when the network manager is at a remote site. Also, the ability to view a NetExpert's user interface from a PC or workstation makes WebOperator a cost-effective solution at NetExpert sites that have a large number of users. WebOperator also simplifies installing NetExpert upgrades in systems where administration of the entire network is distributed over multiple workstations. It consists of both client and server software components. The server component is a Java application, and thin-client Java applets are downloaded at runtime.

The WebOperator applet is served up to internet browsers using Web server software. Universal browsers that support Java can be used to load and execute the WebOperator applet. Displays can be customized to suit user preferences. Users can choose from a variety of alert-notification methods, including beep, flash, and auto-scroll. Users can specify the font size and style used in alert rows, as well as the color of the window heading and alert row boundary lines. Alert severity can be indicated by coloring the entire row or by using a colored dot at the beginning of the row. The status bar at the bottom of the window can be toggled on and off. All these selections — along with column definitions, sorting, and filtering options — may be saved in preferences files for reuse.

Web technology will bring the accessibility of management functions of service providers closer to the users. Customer network management (CNM) will be significantly improved by a simplified and unified common interface.

7.5   SOFTWARE DISTRIBUTION OVER THE INTERNET

Corporate IS/IT departments face significant changes as they attempt to distribute data and software filesets to a more complex group of users, including customers, vendors, and strategic partners while also distributing them over a more complex infrastructure: the internet and intranets. Neither conventional electronic software distribution models nor existing Web-based approaches meet their needs for high performance, control, accountability, and user transparency. A hybrid model, combining the best attributes of both approaches, is needed. This can be accomplished with a set of utilities that reside on the Web client and Web server. These utilities allow businesses to gain the advantages of Web-based communication, while supplementing them with automated installation and de-installation scripts, non-repudiable confirmation and failure notices, authorization by attributes mechanisms, time stamps, third-party communications triggers, and other useful features for supporting new internet-technology oriented business models.

Figure 7.20 shows different alternatives for electronic software distribution (ESD). Besides dedicated lines and packet switching services, the internet or intranets may also be utilized.

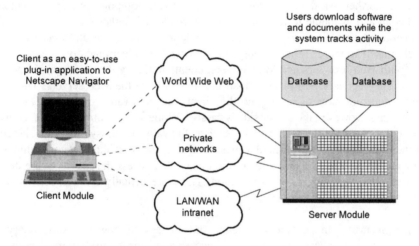

FIGURE 7.20 Alternatives for electronic software distribution.

The effective distribution of databases, documents, images or other contents, including applications or applets published by an IS/IT department, software company, entertainment company, or service provider, is a key strategic issue today. The fileset can vary greatly in complexity and size. In some cases, they may replace or update existing filesets residing on the client. They may also carry technical or business requirements, such as the presence of particular applications on the client or confirmation that payments have been made. Adding complexity to this problem is the fact that the recipients of these filesets may belong to a variety of user groups. The ability to accommodate any required distribution criteria is important in a phase when pinpoint marketing, mass customization, and organizational fluidity are driving factors. Rather than depending on the logistical conveniences of internal network topology to determine who gets what, IS/IT managers must be able to flexibly create policy-based distribution criteria for the new internet/intranet user community. Distribution to these location-indefinite populations must be verified, as well. This verification mechanism allows distribution managers to confirm that all users have, in fact, received the filesets they require, and that they are at the same version levels. Keeping users on the same iteration of a given fileset is important for smooth information processing and simplified support desk operations. Distribution criteria change very rapidly. If the distribution solutions are not flexible, they will get bogged down in the internal development backlog and quickly lose their business appeal. Security is also a key issue, since distribution over the public network infrastructure exposes corporations to security risks.

There are two basic models for dealing with software distribution. Conventional electronic software distribution takes a push approach to move filesets across the network. A distribution cycle is scheduled and executed for a set of clients over which IS/IT exercises direct control. ESD assumes that all target clients are within a given network territory, that any relevant attributes of those clients exist in a management console database, and all clients are directly reachable. Push technology assumes further that the hardware and other software components on the client are sufficient and available to receive the fileset. A client is either eligible or it is not. It cannot take an action to make itself eligible to receive a fileset, either by introducing itself to the distribution engine or paying a fee electronically.

With Web browsers and Web servers, clients initiate a whole range of interactions. They actually pull or download the filesets from the Web servers. The Web server does not have to know who the clients are in advance or how to attach to them again. However, the server side is passive. While some control can be exercised through the use of filter technologies such as firewalls and passwords, most aspects of the transaction — the particular fileset selected, the particular date and time that they are distributed, the attributes of the clients that access the fileset — are determined by the growing client population. There are actually three problems with internet-based pull-techniques:

- Security can become a problem due to lack of powerful supervisory techniques. Password control and access screening are used in most cases.
- The Web offers little in the way of transaction confirmation and version control. IS/IT can count the number of hits on a page and types of activity generated during each hit, but it cannot confirm key attributes of fileset recipients, unless it implements some manually completed forms as part of the distribution process.
- Web downloading does not offer IS/IT the ability to simplify client installation with the types of scripts commonly available under ESD. Without this feature, support and maintenance problems may occur.

Three product examples will be used to demonstrate the effectiveness of Web-based software distribution.

7.5.1 WEB TRANSPORTER FROM MEGASOFT

To achieve a balanced approach that meets the needs of corporate IS/IT, two things are necessary. First, adherence to existing standards of Web technology. The universal distribution capabilities that Web technology permits are essential to the effective movement of filesets across internal and external networks. Second, both Web servers and browsers must be equipped with the value-added utilities that provide the supplemental functions that IS/IT requires — without undermining the independence or utility of the client, who may not have any relationship to the IS/IT department besides authorized use of filesets.

Web Transporter has the following architecture shown in Figure 7.21. The server component acts as an electronic clearinghouse. It maintains software libraries, which can include data files, documents, conventional executables, or Java-based applets. It also makes it easy for managers to quickly update, modify, or withdraw files or processes from the clearinghouse. By building management into the distribution architecture, WebTransporter eliminates development and maintenance efforts. It tracks information on the number of downloads, versions and types of software and data files requested. The open architecture of the server enables links to backend databases, billing and payment systems.

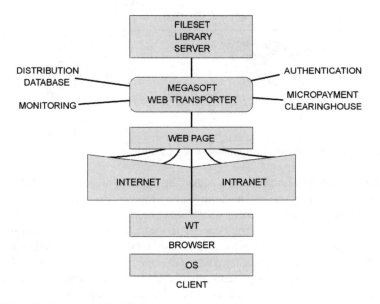

FIGURE 7.21 Structure of the Web Transporter.

It also supplies an authentication mechanism to control the downloading of library files. It monitors all online activity, giving IS/IT management full account-ability for fileset distribution. This auditing capability is essential to track down-loading activities and thereby assess the results of a particular marketing program or re-engineering project. Reports can be generated on queries by product, account number, and type of user.

On the client side, Web Transporter runs as an add-on to the user's Web browser. In conjunction with the server, the client utility serves as a security and authentication mechanism. It also automates a variety of installation and file configuration functions which simplify the use of data or software by the user. The interaction between the client and the server can also be used to implement version control and verification, which eliminates the downloading of duplicate filesets — a common capability of ESD that is often lacking in Web-based distribution models. The client module provides a graphic front-end that lets users scan lists of data files or software applications and make requests for downloading. This module executes a secure download, confirms transmission, and manages configuration and installation on the desktop computer. The client module is shown in Figure 7.22.

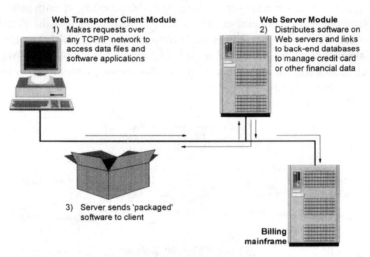

FIGURE 7.22 Operating the client module of Web Transporter.

Web Transporter also provides a packaging tool that prepares filesets for distribution from the library server. This utility suite simplifies the construction of server-ready fileset packages — including all security parameters, installation scripts, and client attribute specifications. The Packeter lets users prepare software for delivery by creating customized file types to "format" files for downloads. The client receives the packaged information and automatically executes the installation process on the remote workstation, providing secure distribution, checking available user space, and providing a transaction record when distribution is completed.

The features and benefits of Web Transporter can be summarized as follows:

- Automated installation — it is a plug-in application to automatically download and install software using Web browsers without user intervention. Web Transporter automatically manages the installation process, eliminating the need for users to administer manual set-up procedures. This allows organizations to deploy applications and other time-sensitive information without the support and administrative costs of physically facilitating these tasks with traditional production methods.
- Confirmation of receipt — it can verify software downloads were received and successfully installed on the Web client from the internet or from intranets. This is ideal for electronic commerce applications.

- Advanced security — it provides advanced software distribution functionality without compromising privacy and security. The system is designed to confirm downloads were electronically transmitted and received by the Web client. It also offers password protection, encryption, authentication and support for Secure Sockets Layer (SSL) to eliminate unauthorized user access.
- Real-time downloads — using the Web Transporter, software downloaded can be automatically installed on the local workstation in real-time, without requiring users to administer installation procedures.
- Multiplatform support — it is compatible with Windows 95, NT, Windows 3.X, UNIX, and Mac operating systems and can be integrated with Oracle, Sybase, Informix, and other relational databases.
- Use of standard Web technology — it operates as an in-line, plug-in to Netscape Navigator, to MS Internet Explorer, to ActiveX, and Java technologies.

The Web Transporter architecture fits very well with the business scenarios associated with fileset publishing. It provides mechanisms for effectively preparing filesets for distribution, executing the distribution itself in a secure manner, supporting distributed files with appropriate installation scripts and control, and reporting on distribution activity to publishing managers — all without interfering with the most desirable aspects of Web browsing. Most importantly, this product offers solutions with reasonable costs.

7.5.2 NET.DEPLOY FROM OPEN SOFTWARE ASSOCIATES

Combining the flexibility of a sophisticated cross-platform installation program with the universality of the Web, net.Deploy offers a valuable choice of software distribution and update management on an intranet. It consists of client software called Launcher and a software packaging application called Packer to distribute applications, ensuring that all components of the application are up to date each time the application is launched. For many developers, net.Deploy will eliminate the need to develop separate installation programs and make application update distribution much simpler.

The differentiator of net.Deploy is the way in which it makes downloads and installing applications from the Web a one-step process. Without net.Deploy, when users need to download the latest browser update from Netscape or Microsoft, they first go to the site and indicate which operating system they are using. Then they download a single, very large executable or compressed file and, finally, run an installation program or script. With net.Deploy, users click on a link to a script file, called a catalog, which was created by Packer. The catalog is read and interpreted by Launcher, which automatically downloads and installs only those components appropriate to the user's operating system. The catalog also specifies other operating system-dependent details, including what environmental settings to make and where to place the application icon. The application can then be launched in the usual way.

Launcher automatically checks to see if any of the application's components have been updated. If they have, only those components are downloaded.

net.Deploy solves the common problem of deployment — actually delivering the finished application to hundreds or thousands of end-users scattered throughout an enterprise. With net.Deploy, all a programmer needs to do is place the packet application on a Web server. It does not matter whether internet or intranets are in use. A single link points to the application, and each user initially runs the application by clicking on the link. From then on, users can run the application directly from their desktop or from the Web page. With this product, commercial use of the internet becomes a whole lot more realistic. It handles multiple development languages, and the widest range of desktop computers. Users get fully automatic application updates, digital signatures validate the application provider, and security digests guarantee application integrity. Its smart pull client-side technology requires no special servers, and minimizes impact on network bandwidth and client resources.

The architecture of the product is shown in Figure 7.23. This technology makes a vital difference to any enterprise that deploys applications to more than one computer.

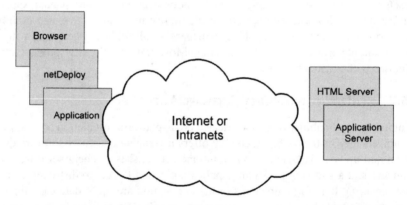

FIGURE 7.23 Architecture of net.Deploy.

SmartPull was designed from the beginning to simplify all the complex needs of application installation and updating. By comparison, SmartPull is all simplicity. There is no full-time tuner running on the client. The net.Deploy Launcher runs briefly as each cataloged application is launched. One Launcher is needed for any number of applications. There are no special protocols to break through firewalls: SmartPull requires nothing more than standard HTTP. There are no special servers for SmartPull. Application or data files can be dispensed from any standard Web server or servers. So the standard technologies that the internet or intranets provide for managing Web traffic flows — Web proxy servers, smart routers choosing servers, etc. are instantly working for use with SmartPull.

net.Deploy features include:

- Automatic version updating of applications, loading only changed files at configurable times without requiring a Web browser for updates
- Supports applications in any language or development tool
- Fast downloading of compressed filesets with MD5 cryptographic file digests providing file authorization
- Support of digital signatures
- Installs applications direct to Windows desktops in full integration with desktop services
- Allows per-component virus scanning during installation
- Catalogs single files through entire directory trees at a keystroke, and auto-updates deployment Web server
- Requires only HTTP for downloads via direct connect, HTTP proxies, or Socks proxies
- Supports conditional installation of platform-dependent modules
- Supports conditional installation of prerequisite modules

net.Deploy is a valuable Web-based product with the following major benefits:

- Simplicity — for developers, it is as simple as listing the files for the application. For users, it is as easy as clicking on a link on a Web page or desktop icon.
- Accuracy — because net.Deploy installs and runs the application, users make fewer errors, and need less support and training
- Integration — it fits right in with existing development tools and methods. There are no special requirements.
- Transparent updates — releasing updates becomes as simple as changing the files in one central location. Users automatically receive the latest version the next time they run the application.
- Minimum impact — the SmartPull technology means only changed components are downloaded, and only when actually needed. Impact on network/desktop resources is minimal.
- Security — it uses MD5 security digest to guarantee that applications reach users free of interference or corruption. Standard or enterprise-specific digital signatures verify the application supplier.
- Client/server — a single installation of net.Deploy lets users run any number of downloaded applications, whether they run stand-alone, or offer client/server connections to remote databases.
- Flexibility — any kind of application can be downloaded and run with net.Deploy, no matter how it was developed.

net.Deploy also offers software distribution solutions with reasonable costs.

7.5.3 CASTANET FROM MARIMBA

Marimba's Castanet system distributes, installs, and updates software and documents over intranets and the internet. The Castanet unit of distribution is called a channel; a channel can be an application or a Website. Channel developers create a channel's files with conventional programming or Website development tools. They use the Castanet publisher to copy a channel's files to a Castanet transmitter. Subject to security constraints, anyone can use a free Castanet tuner to subscribe to a published channel. Subscribing downloads and installs a channel's files on a user's disk, from which the channel can be launched or viewed in a Web browser, with or without a network connection. Each channel includes a developer-provided schedule which the tuner uses to automatically keep the channel current, downloading new and modified files as they are republished to the channel's transmitter. Figure 7.24 shows the structure and components of Castanet from Marimba.

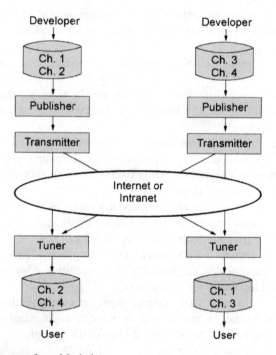

FIGURE 7.24 Castanet from Marimba.

At first glance, the Castanet system might seem similar to downloading with FTP. In fact, it goes far beyond:

- Castanet tuners do not just download software; they install it, update it automatically, and remove files that are superseded.

- Castanet transmitters are highly scalable; repeating transmitters enable channels to be distributed to thousands of users spread around the globe, with the simplicity of a single administrative site.
- Castanet channels can be multiplatform, consisting of either Java code or Web pages, or single-platform if written with Java and another language, such as C.
- Castanet channels can send feedback data for offline analysis or real-time per-user channel customization.
- Castanet transmission makes very efficient use of network bandwidth.
- Castanet security features enable sensitive channels to be sent across the internet with high assurance of integrity, authenticity, and confidentiality.

7.5.3.1   Castanet Channels

There are four types of Castanet channels:

1. An HTML channel is a Web site, meaning the Web page files subordinate to a directory.
2. A presentation channel is a scripted graphical user interface developed with Marimba's Bongo presentation builder.
3. An applet channel is a Java applet, optionally supplemented with native code.
4. An application channel is a Java application optionally supplemented with native code.

Users subscribe to channels with a Castanet tuner. They can launch subscribed channels either from the tuner or with a conventional desktop mechanism, such as a menu or icon, or from a command entered in a shell. Each subscribed channel has an automatic update frequency that is initially specified by its developer and can be changed by its users. That frequency can be as high as every few minutes or as low as monthly. When it is time to check for updates to a channel, the tuner contacts the channel's transmitter, and downloads and installs the updates, if any. If a network connection is unavailable, the tuner postpones the check. Channel developers can specify that the tuner should launch a channel when it receives an update for it. Developers can also write applet and application channels that absorb updates while they are running.

HTML channels

An HTML channel is a Web site: a collection of Web pages, including media files, rooted in a common directory, with a designated first (index) page that links to other pages. When a user directs the tuner to launch an HTML channel, the tuner passes the first page to a Web browser for display. The user interacts with the Web as usual, except that the pages are fetched from the user's disk instead of across the network. An HTML channel can contain links to pages outside itself, which will work if the network is available. Internal links work whether the computer is connected to the network or not.

A developer can designate an HTML channel as incremental. Whereas an ordinary HTML channel is downloaded as a unit when a user subscribes to it, an incremental HTML channel is downloaded page by page in response to user clicks on links. In this way, the just-subscribed channel is viewable almost immediately. After several minutes, the tuner automatically transfers the remainder of an incremental HTML channel; the user can also direct the tuner to complete the download immediately.

HTML channel developers can instrument their pages to log image displays and link clicks. These might represent advertising impressions and click-throughs, for example. Logging continues whether the user's computer is connected to the network or not. The tuner sends a channel's accumulated log to the channel's transmitter with the next update request; the log can be read offline or in real time by a transmitter plug in written by the channel developer.

Executable channels

Presentation, applet, and application channels are executable channels. By default, executable channels are deemed untrusted; more flexible trusted channels are also supported. Untrusted channels are written entirely in the Java language and are subject to the Java applet security model, which provides the best protection for unknown downloadable software. However, the applet security model is relaxed for untrusted channels in one important way: each channel can read or write one directory on the local file system; the tuner ensures that a channel can access only its designated directory. Because channels can be updated automatically and efficiently, they can be much more dynamic than traditional application software, which is typically updated once a year or so. Channels are well suited to the incremental style of software development, which gets a basic product to market quickly, then rapidly refines and extends it. Besides distributing code updates, channels are an excellent vehicle for distributing information that changes weekly, daily, hourly, or even more often. Whether channel code or information is updated with the Castanet system, developers can be confident that the updates are installed correctly without user effort.

Developers of executable channels can direct the tuner to send feedback data to the channel's transmitter via the Castanet BackChannel feature. The tuner sends the data when it asks the transmitter for updates to the channel. Anything the channel can record while it is running can be returned as BackChannel data: the users preferred language, counts of features used, and counts of errors made are a few examples. A developer-supplied channel component called a transmitter plug in can log the BackChannel data or use it to customize the update data that the transmitter returns to the tuner. Although BackChannel data is a flexible and potentially powerful way to dynamically customize channels, users who object to the feature can disable it in their tuners.

Channel launching options

When a user launches a channel from the tuner or from a desktop shortcut or alias, the channel runs without arguments. But there are other ways to launch channels that pass in arguments.

- A channel can be represented on a Web page by a URL that includes arguments for the channel. Clicking on the URL subscribes to the channel, if necessary, and launches it with the arguments in the URL.
- Channels can be launched from shells (command line interpreters) with arguments.
- A running channel can launch another channel, passing arguments to it.

Interchannel launching is one way to implement a suite of channels with a single log-in point. Suppose there's one channel called the Log-in channel. When a user launches it, the channel asks for a user ID and password, and then displays icons representing the other channels in the suite. When the user clicks on an icon, the Log-in channel launches the corresponding channel, passing in the user's ID and password as arguments.

Signed channels

Channel developers can optionally sign both executable and HTML channels. Signing a channel augments the channel with:

- A digital certificate which positively identifies the organization that developed the channel
- A digital signature which provides the basis for detecting accidental or malicious alterations to the channel

Both the certificate and the signature are security measures that are best suited to important channels that are transmitted over the internet. The certificate gives a prospective channel user confidence that a channel is in fact the work of, say, XYZ Software. The signature assures the channel user that the channel bits he or she has received are in fact identical to what the channel developer published; in other words, that the channel has not been damaged by an internet vandal situated between the transmitter and the user's tuner.

Trusted channels

Ordinary executable channels are written entirely in the Java language and are subject to runtime constraints that prevent them from damaging or revealing information on a user's computer. These untrusted channels cannot:

- Read or write the file system except for a single per-channel directory allocated by the tuner
- Connect to any network host except the one they were downloaded from
- Call any non-Java code, including operating system code

Trusted channels, by contrast, can do all of these things, just as conventional applications can. Trusted channels can read and write the user's file system, can connect to any reachable network host, and can call native code including operating system functions. Note, however, that a trusted channel that calls native code loses the platform-independence of a pure Java channel.

A channel becomes trusted when all three of the following occur:

- The channel developer nominates the channel for trusted status
- The channel developer signs the channel so the user can positively know who developed it and that it is intact
- The channel user agrees to trust the channel, that is, grants the channel permission to do what untrusted channels cannot

Note that a channel developer nominates a channel for trusted status, but only a user can confirm the nomination. A user decides to trust or not trust a channel based on the reputation of the channel's developer, and perhaps on the experience of other channel users. The Castanet tuner will not launch a channel whose developer has nominated it for trusted status until the user designates the channel as in fact trusted.

Plug ins

A channel can be more than software or a Website that is transmitted to a user's computer. An optional channel component called a plug in can reside with a transmitter. Each channel served by a transmitter can have its own plug in which serves all copies of the channel that have been downloaded from that transmitter. Plug ins can be written by developers or purchased from third parties.

A plug in processes feedback data created by instances of its channel. A transmitter invokes a channel's plug in when a tuner requests an update for the channel. The plug in can do anything with the feedback data. For example, the plug in may record the data for offline processing, or use it to perform a database lookup, or use it to select files to be returned to the requesting tuner. Notice that the combination of a channel and its plug in can operate as a client and its server.

By selecting files for transmission to the tuner, a plug in can customize or personalize a channel instance. For example, a plug in may return French files for French users and German files for German users; it may increase the difficulty of a game channel based on the user's previous score; it may send advertisements related to those the channel user has clicked on; or it may send help on features the user has employed incorrectly. There's no limit to how feedback data can be employed by plug ins. Note that although feedback data identifies the tuner that sent it, it does not disclose the identity of the tuner's user.

7.5.3.2 Tuners

The Castanet tuner is the receiver component of the Castanet distribution system. Marimba provides a tuner that is a small stand-alone application. How ever it is packaged, a tuner does four main things:

1. It subscribes to new channels, downloading and installing them on the user's disk.
2. It updates subscribed channels by pulling changes from transmitters; updates can be performed automatically or manually.

3. It sends channel feedback data back to the channel's transmitter and plug in, if the channel has one.
4. It launches and monitors the execution of channels.

Each channel includes an update schedule provided by its developer; channel users can change this schedule, and can direct the tuner to update a channel immediately. When it is time to update a channel, the tuner connects to the channel's transmitter; if the network is not available, the tuner postpones the update. The tuner and transmitter compare the files constituting the channel. If the transmitter has a newer version of a channel file, or a new file, it sends the file to the tuner. Thus, channel updates are differential: only files that have changed since the channel was last updated are transmitted to the tuner. To further conserve network bandwidth, small updates to large files are sent as editing commands which the tuner executes. If a running channel's developer has indicated that the channel can be updated on the fly, the tuner installs the new files immediately; otherwise it waits until the channel stops. Channel updates are performed automatically, like database transactions, so that a channel always has a consistent set of files, even if the power fails during an update. To conserve disk space, tuners automatically garbage collect obsolete files, and keep only one copy of files that are shared among channels.

Tuners are themselves channels, and automatically update themselves once a week if they are connected to the network.

Startup channels

To help new tuner users get started, tuners come "pre-subscribed" to two channels. The tuner launches the intro channel the first time the tuner runs; users can launch it from the tuner's Help menu whenever they like. The intro channel is a quick introduction to the tuner that explains the basics of subscribing to channels, launching, and stopping them. Companies can use the intro to substitute a company-oriented intro channel for the one supplied by Marimba. The tuner's Channel Guide channel, which launches with a button click, is like a Yahoo!™ page for channels. It lists channels selected by Marimba in categories, with a short description of each. With the Channel Guide, users can subscribe to channels without having to know transmitter names. Companies can use the Channel Guide to substitute their own Channel Guide for Marimba's.

Security features

The tuner includes user interfaces to these Castanet security features: signed and trusted channels, and secure and access-controlled transmitters. The tuner automatically detects and verifies signed channels, both when they are downloaded and when they are launched. Verifying a signed channel before launching it detects damage to the channel that may have occurred on the user's disk. A user can inspect a signed channel's certificate at any time. The tuner's subscribed channels page marks signed channels with a pen icon.

When the tuner downloads a channel that has been nominated for trusted status, it asks the user to grant or deny the developer's request for trusted status. The user can inspect the channel's certificate to ascertain the positive identity of the channel's developer. If the user denies trusted status, the tuner does not launch the channel but keeps it, in case the user wants to investigate the channel further and revisit the decision to trust it. Trusted status can be granted or revoked at any time. Trusted channels are marked with a distinguished icon on the tuner's subscribed channels page. From a user's perspective, a tuner communicates identically with secure and insecure transmitters. The only perceptible difference is speed; secure channel transmission incurs some setup overhead as the tuner checks the transmitter's certificate, and some transfer overhead as the tuner decrypts the files it receives. Secure transmitters are marked with a lock icon on the tuner's subscribed channels page; users can be assured that channels downloaded from secure transmitters were protected from internet eavesdroppers.

When a tuner user asks to see the channels of a user, the tuner asks the user for an ID and password, and passes them to the transmitter. The tuner shows the channels only if the transmitter returns them (that is, if the transmitter acknowledges that the user is authorized).

Tuner administrators

The tuner administrator is for companies that have in-house transmitters and distribute tuners from their own Web page. It has two uses: customizing the in-house tuner that the company distributes, and controlling updates to in-house tuners. These properties of a Castanet tuner can be customized with the tuner administrator:

- The URL of the intro channel; this can be changed from Marimba's intro channel to one developed by the company
- The URL of the Channel Guide channel; this can be changed from Marimba's Channel Guide to one developed by the company
- The URL of the transmitter the tuner obtains its own updates from; this can be changed from Marimba's transmitter to a company transmitter

If in-house tuners are customized to obtain their updates from an in-house transmitter, an administrator can decide when those updates occur. In particular, an administrator can verify that Marimba's latest tuner update works properly with the important channels used by employees. To control tuner updates, an administrator:

- Keeps one tuner that updates itself from Marimba's transmitter.
- Tests this tuner periodically to be sure that Marimba has not updated it with a bug
- Publishes the verified tuner's updates to the in-house transmitter

After the tuner updates have been published to the in-house transmitter, in-house tuners, which have been customized to update themselves from that transmitter, will automatically obtain the verified changes.

7.5.3.3 Transmitters

Castanet transmitters serve channel files in response to tuner requests, roughly as Web servers serve Web pages to Web browsers. Unlike Web servers, transmitters send a tuner only the files that are out of date on the tuner's machine, and they send all of the files in a single network connection. Each primary transmitter maintains a list of the channels it serves; both tuners and Web browsers can obtain the list, and users can subscribe to a channel on the list from either a tuner or a Web browser.

Repeaters

For a given channel it serves, a transmitter may play the role of primary transmitter or repeating transmitter. Repeating transmitters can be used to distribute the load of transmitting a channel among multiple transmitters which may or may not be geographically dispersed; repeating transmitters also provide a measure of fault tolerance. The channel developer designates a transmitter's role when he or she creates the channel. When the developer directs the publisher to publish the channel, the publisher updates the primary transmitter and all transmitters designated by the developer as repeaters.

A primary transmitter maintains a list of the channels it serves; both tuners and Web browsers can obtain the list, and users can subscribe to a channel on the list from either a tuner or a Web browser. When a primary transmitter receives a subscribe request from a tuner or a Web browser, it assigns the requesting tuner to itself or to one of the transmitters that has been designated as a repeater for the channel. The primary transmitter makes the assignment based on the strategy chosen by the channel developer. If a tuner is unable to contact the repeating transmitter to which it has been assigned, it returns to the primary transmitter for a new assignment.

There are two repeater assignment strategies, round-robin and geographic. The round-robin strategy distributes subscriptions evenly among transmitters, where "transmitters" include the primary and the repeating transmitters. The geographic strategy assigns each subscription to the nearest transmitter, whether it is a repeating transmitter or the primary transmitter. "Nearest" means the transmitter whose time zone is nearest to that of the requesting tuner.

Secure transmitters

A secure transmitter communicates with both publishers and tuners under the protection of SSL, the Secure Sockets Layer protocol developed by Netscape Corporation to secure Web browser commerce. Secure transmitters are analogous to secure Web servers, and tuners and publishers are analogous to SSL-equipped Web browsers. Secure transmitters are intended for transmitting sensitive channels across the internet, which is inherently insecure.

A secure transmitter offers these assurances to publisher and tuner users:

- The transmitter they intended to connect to is in fact the one they connected to; in other words, that trans.xyz.com (say) is not an impostor that may send bogus channels
- The channels sent from a publisher or downloaded to a tuner are unintelligible to internet eavesdroppers

In security terms, secure transmitters authenticate themselves, encrypt the files they send to tuners, and decrypt the files they receive from publishers. Transmitters authenticate themselves by presenting unforgettable digital certificates similar to those that are associated with signed channels. The transmitter has a built-in facility for obtaining and installing a digital certificate from VeriSign Corporation.

Controlled access transmitters

Independent of whether a transmitter uses SSL, it can be directed to show and download channels only to authorized users. Such a transmitter keeps a file of authorized user IDs and passwords. Administrators can update this file with the editor built into the transmitter, or by importing a file from an LDAP (lightweight directory access protocol) implementation.

7.5.3.4　Publishers

Developers use conventional programming or Web page development tools to create the files that constitute a channel. A channel's files are subordinate to a single directory called the base directory; any directory can be a base directory. To create a channel, a developer uses the Castanet Publisher. Creating a channel with the publisher primarily means adding a few files to the base directory. The most important file describes the channel's properties: its name, its type (HTML, application, etc.), its update frequency, and so on. The developer enters the properties in the publisher's user interface, which is a collection of tabbed pages.

The publisher's Security page captures a channel's security properties: whether it is signed, whether it is nominated for trusted status, and whether it is to be published to a secure transmitter. To sign a channel, a developer needs a channel-signing certificate. The Security page includes buttons for requesting a certificate over the internet from VeriSign Corporation, and for installing the certificate that VeriSign returns by e-mail.

In addition to specifying channel properties, the publisher is also used to publish a channel, which means to copy its files to its primary transmitter and repeating transmitters, if any. The publisher transfers the files automatically, so that any network or computer problems do not result in a malformed channel on a transmitter. Channels can be published interactively with the publisher's graphical user interface, or programmatically with a script that invokes the publisher from a shell.

To revise a channel, a developer modifies the relevant files in the channel's base directory and then publishes the channel again. The publisher differentially copies the channel's files to the channel's transmitters; that is, only new and updated files are transferred. Transmitters accept published channels on the fly. If a transmitter receives a new version of a channel at the moment when it is transmitting the old version, it continues to serve the old version to tuners that are already connected, and serves the new version to new tuner connections. Transmitters automatically garbage collect obsolete channel files.

7.5.3.5 Gateways

A transmitter runs on a dedicated network port. At sites that also run HTTP (Web) servers behind firewalls, administration would be simpler if the transmitter shared the same host and port as the HTTP server. A Castanet gateway makes a transmitter appear to run on the same host and port as a Netscape or Microsoft HTTP server. A gateway is an HTTP server plug in that forwards tuner requests to a transmitter running on a different host and/or port. In addition to making a transmitter work with a firewall that is configured for an HTTP server, a gateway provides a measure of flexibility. A transmitter can be moved (to a faster machine, for example), without disrupting tuners that have subscribed to its channels; only the gateway configuration has to be updated to forward tuner requests to the new host.

7.5.3.6 Proxies

A Castanet proxy provides a channel file cache for a collection of tuners, typically those on a local area network. Like an HTTP proxy, a Castanet proxy conserves network bandwidth and improves responsiveness. Suppose, for example, that 100 tuners on a department network subscribe to the same channel, and that one file in the channel is updated. The first tuner request for an update will pass through the proxy to the transmitter; the transmitter will return the new file to the proxy which will both pass it to the requesting tuner and add the file to its cache. Subsequent update requests will be satisfied by the proxy without requiring the transmitter to send the file again. Note that proxies send tuner feedback data to transmitters for the benefit of channel plug ins, and that plug ins can customize channels whether a proxy is present or not.

7.6 WINDOWS NT MANAGEMENT USING WEB TECHNOLOGY

The Windows NT operating system is fast becoming the platform of choice because of its power and versatility in deployment as a server or workstation. The BackOffice offering may be added, and it is no surprise that many companies are aggressively deploying NT-based systems and applications. This power and the many alternatives in which NT systems can be deployed lead to significant complexity when it comes to monitoring and managing NT systems. Also support costs may increase. This is especially true when large number of systems must be maintained or servers at remote locations must be deployed, where there is little, if any, Windows NT expertise.

7.6.1 WEB ADMINISTRATOR FROM MICROSOFT

Installing the Web Administration software on the server causes the server to publish Web pages that include forms the user can utilize to administer that particular server. Any Web browser may be used that supports either basic or Windows NT Challenge response authentication. The tasks most commonly performed by roaming administrators are supported by Web Administration. The actual interface is a series of HTML pages that the administrator navigates through using a Web browser. The interface is intended for administrators familiar with existing administration tools, such as User Manager, Control Panel, Performance Monitor, etc. The following tasks can be performed with this product:

Account management
  • Create and delete user accounts
  • View and change user information
  • Change user passwords
  • Disable user accounts
  • Create and remove groups
  • Add and remove users to and from groups
  • Add workstations to the domain
Remote access service (RAS) management
  • Grant and remove RAS dial-in permissions to users
  • Configure RAS call back options
  • View and manage RAS connections
Share management
  • View shares for all installed file services (Microsoft, Macintosh, and Netware compatible file services)
  • Change permissions on shares
  • Create new shares for all installed file services
Session management
  • View current sessions
  • Delete one or all sessions
  • Send message to current users of the server
Server management
  • Shut down (reboot) server
  • Change services/driver configuration
  • View system, application, and security log events
  • Server configuration data dump
Printer management
  • Last print queues and jobs in each queue
  • Pause queue or specific print job
  • Flush queue or specific print job

7.6.2 APPMANAGER FROM NETIQ

Microsoft provides Systems Management Server (SMS), but it focuses primarily on deployment issues such as software distribution and not on critical operational issues such as event and performance management. Microsoft also provides various stand-alone tools that come with Windows NT and each BackOffice server, but these tools are not built to manage a distributed environment.

The AppManager Suite is comprised of integrated AppManager components that are specifically designed to monitor the performance and availability of Windows

NT-based systems and Microsoft BackOffice servers such as Exchange Server and SQL Server, as well as Lotus Domino/Notes servers. Using the AppManager Console, administrators can configure monitoring functions known as Knowledge Scripts to collect performance data and monitor for simple or complex events. Corrective actions — such as send e-mail, generate an SNMP trap to a network manager, or run a corrective program — can also be easily set up to automatically execute when a specific event occurs. The result is a powerful and automated closed-loop solution for both proactive problem detection and resolution across a customer's highly distributed Windows NT environment.

The AppManager WBEM Agent is the AppManager architectural component that runs the Knowledge Scripts on Windows NT servers and workstations. It implements the WBEM technology architecture as a primary method of accessing instrumentation data and also makes its data available to other management products that support WBEM. With Windows NT 5.0 or higher, WBEM agents are automatically included.

Besides providing much needed operations management capabilities for Windows NT and Microsoft BackOffice environments, AppManager also lowers the total cost of ownership of these systems and applications by letting customers leverage scarce and valuable personnel resources. AppManager accomplishes this by automating repetitive and time-consuming tasks, providing prepackaged knowledge and business rules for managing and monitoring distributed Microsoft BackOffice environments, centralizing management of distributed and remote systems and applications, and enabling proactive notification and correction of problems before they impact the customer's business.

In order to support scalability, NetIQ provides a very flexible architecture comprised of the following components (Figure 7.25):

Console — a user-friendly program that represents systems and applications as resource icons. The Console is used to centrally define and control the execution of Knowledge Scripts on the managed NT systems and applications via simple drag-and-drop actions.

Repository Server — a central repository based on Microsoft SQL Server that stores management data.

Management Server — a service that runs on a Windows NT server that manages the event-driven communication between the Repository and the NetIQ Agents.

Agent — a highly intelligent program that runs on any Windows NT system. The Agent receives requests from the management server to either run or stop a Knowledge Script, and in turn communicates back on an exception basis any relevant data or events collected by the running Knowledge Scripts.

Web Management Server — a set of Active Server Pages that lets the user monitor the entire Windows NT environment from a Web Browser.

This robust, multi-tier architecture makes AppManager a scalable foundation for managing small- to large-scale deployment of Windows NT. AppManager is

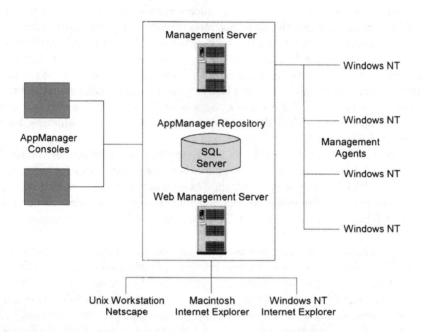

FIGURE 7.25 Architecture of AppManager.

scalable because processing is spread across multiple architectural components, enabling the Management Server to control large numbers of Agents. Push technology may be utilized to distribute AppManager agents to remote systems for easy deployment. This architecture utilizes an exception-based mechanism to communicate between its components, so no polling occurs to unnecessarily consume precious network bandwidth. This architecture is also reliable because its components have been built for continuous and autonomous operations.

The NetIQ AppManager WBEM Agent consumes and provides WBEM-based management instrumentation data via the Common Information Model (CIM), a key part of the WBEM technologies. The CIM is a method for storing management and instrumentation data in a common format. By making AppManager WBEM Agent's data available in the CIM format, the system becomes compatible with other WBEM-enabled management tools.

7.6.3 INSIGHT MANAGER XE FROM COMPAQ

Compaq integrates hardware management features and complementary management tools to provide a complete server, desktop PC, and workstation solution for the network administrator. Insight agents are installed in the managed devices that provide attribute information to an element manager. NT management technology of Compaq includes:

- Fault prevention
- Fault tolerance

- Rapid recovery, including server health logs
- Remote maintenance

The Insight Manager software architecture is typical of other SNMP-based management software and is composed of Compaq Insight Manager, Management Agents, Desktop Agents, and the Inventory Collector. The agent software executes on a manageable device such as server, desktop, or workstation and monitors the fault and performance aspects of the device. These monitored statistics, along with device configuration information, provide data to a management application using the SNMP protocol.

Insight Manager delivers intelligent monitoring and alerting, remote maintenance, and visual control of the systems. In case of NT server failures, the Manager provides a full spectrum of remote maintenance and control facilities, such as system rebooting, system configuration, and systems diagnostics.

Insight Manager provides timely system status and the means for remotely controlling NT servers through the following features:

- Comprehensive fault management
- Integration management
- Performance management
- Workstation management
- Client management
- Netelligent management
- Asset management
- Remote management
- Reporting

Insight Management Agents consist of system software that integrates Compaq manageability into SNMP-based management environments. They perform in-depth monitoring of the fault and performance aspects of the key subsystems, such as storage, memory, system processor, network interface, and the environment. In addition, agents may generate traps to notify the administrator of significant changes in the fault or performance aspects of the computer operation.

The Compaq enterprise ID (232) specifies the location of the Insight MIBs within the internet Naming Tree. The Compaq MIBs are modular, with each sub-branch representing a distinct function or subsystem supported by the Insight Agents. MIBs supported are:

- Standard PC Equipment Configuration
- System Information
- Intelligent Drive Arrays
- Server Manager
- SCSI Devices
- SCSI Storage Systems
- Server Health
- Remote Insight Board

- Drive Storage Systems
- Management Engine
- Threshold Management
- Host OS Information
- Uninterruptable Power Supply Information
- Recovery
- IDE Drive

MIBs may be added at any time by Compaq to satisfy additional needs.

Compaq Inventory Collector defines the set of manageable objects known to the Systems Management Server (SMS) from Microsoft. These files follow the Management Information Format (MIF) which is a subset of the MIF Specification from DMTF. These files collect static information only and ignore dynamic information.

The Compaq MIFs are modular, with each sub-branch representing a distinct function or subsystem supported by the Insight Agents. MIFs supported are:

- Compaq CPU
- Compaq EIS/PCI slots
- Compaq System
- Compaq Memory Modules
- Compaq Software Versions
- Compaq Drive Array Controllers
- Compaq Drive Array Logical Drive
- Compaq Drive Array Physical Drive
- Compaq Health Subsystem
- Compaq Storage System
- Compaq UPS Subsystem
- Compaq SCSI Devices

MIFs may be added any time to satisfy additional needs. Insight Manager integrates well with network and systems management platforms.

Insight agents generate a number of traps, enabling the operators to be proactive by warning them of status changes or degraded performance. The Compaq traps are grouped around the following subjects:

- Drive Array
- SCSI Devices
- System Health
- Storage Systems
- Remote Insight Boards
- User Thresholds
- Host Operating System
- Uninterruptable Power Supply
- Standby Recovery Server
- Manageable IDE Drive

- Server Manager
- System Information

The traps that can be triggered depend to a certain degree on the operating systems running on the Compaq hardware.

The Web-enabled version of Insight Manager XE makes information from multiple third-party network and systems management tools available to any browser-enabled computer. Insight Manager XE offers complete out-of-the box device discovery and fault management for both systems and network devices. It is one of the first management applications to take in data based on CIM, the data schema defined as part of the Microsoft and Intel-based WBEM initiative.

The Insight Manager XE package includes a common database repository that takes in data from a variety of sources. In addition to communicating with all Compaq systems and networking devices, the product supports third-party SNMP-managed devices and DMI-compliant equipment. The revamped application takes a different approach to the organization of management information, filtering alerts and prioritizing them based on the action that needs to be taken. Compaq made it clear that it is not trying to compete with enterprise-class frameworks. Instead, the product serves as a common point for related management information and a differentiator for Compaq customers.

7.7 WEB TECHNOLOGY FOR LEGACY MANAGEMENT

The most frequently used information source of corporations is the database. In order to share information between internal and external customers, databases are going to be opened to innovative technologies. The key is to introduce a simple front-end to various relational databases and mainframes-based proprietary data. This front-end is the Web with its universal browsers. This front-end is the way to give mainframe and client/server applications the same look and feel.

In many applications introduced earlier in this chapter, webification meant to offer access to a relational database by using a two-way-protocol converter. In generic terms, this two-way conversion shows the following weaknesses:

- Too slow for good performance due to many members in the chain of conversions
- Pulling data is always passive from the perspective of the Web server
- Many products have been tested and implemented, but few are really usable in practical environments with high volumes during peak hours
- Security filtering usually does not exist, but the corporate database, as the most valuable asset, must be carefully protected
- Inquiries by users with a Web browser are real-time; responses are expected to be real-time, too.

Practically, all players in the relational and object oriented database business are dealing with this conversion. Figure 7.26 shows the structure used by Oracle. The internet/intranet application server gives developers a powerful tool for building Web transaction systems.

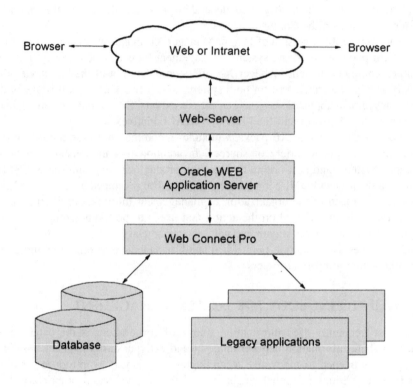

FIGURE 7.26 The role of WAS (Web Application Server).

The Web Application Server (WAS) includes an own-request broker, based on the Common Object Request Broker Architecture (CORBA), so WAS components can run on different machines for better performance. Oracle's approach is to use a Web server simply as an HTTP server that listens for browser requests. The HTTP server passes the requests to the WAS Web Request Broker, which dispatches them to applications called cartridges that execute business rules or access databases. Thus, Oracle limits the Web server to what it does best — executing HTTP requests — then offers a high-performance engine that runs application logic and uses the back-end database for transaction processing. WAS gives developers a solid basis for transaction applications and lets new Web applications work with existing Oracle data.

WAS brings the robustness and reliability of the client/server world to the Web. Process separation, an object architecture, and independent cartridge management let administrators build, manage, and service their system on a component basis. Through its independent-processing architecture, Web Request Broker guarantees that cartridges are insulated from one another, isolating failures. Applications can be constructed using components written in any language and integrated using the

Inter-Cartridge Exchange (ICX). It expands upon the power and scalability offered by traditional Web servers. This lets new breeds of business applications be delivered over the Web. Through the Web Request Broker, Oracle delivers good performance, dispatching, and acceptable accessing times even during peak traffic conditions. WAS provides a superior application environment over low-level, first generation HTTP APIs. Running all server extensions as individual processes, the Web Request Broker provides asynchronous independent processing.

Organizations running Oracle database servers are able to connect to legacy applications rapidly via Web browsers. Oracle incorporates WebConnect Pro and Open Vista technology in WAS. WebConnect Pro is implemented into a cartridge that can be plugged into WAS. To a legacy application on a mainframe, it appears to be a 3270, 5250, VT or character mode terminal operating the legacy application. Data retrieved from the mainframe are stuffed into graphical HTML Web pages before being passed along to client Web browsers. Open Vista — an additional development tool — operates on the middle-management level, allowing users to reformat the look of the material presented or combine COBOL/LL1 screens in the original application into a single graphical screen on the Web browser.

Mainframes continue to reside throughout corporations because they are reliable and they house mission-critical data. The problem is that much of their application code was written 15 to 20 years ago. Now, there is emerging what many view as a low-risk, low-effort method of modernizing host applications and data. It is achieved with information-brokering gateways — systems sitting in front of the mainframe that dynamically transform host applications and data into modern, efficient, and perhaps more relevant browser-based applications for transmission over the internet or over intranets. Such systems can even add data from non-host sources, such as Oracle, Sybase, and Informix databases, Java, and MS ActiveX components.

While managers ponder, increasingly sophisticated products are emerging to aid them if and when they decide to move forward.

Usually, applications are run on UNIX or NT and unify the roles of a Web server, Common Gateway Interface, and Object Request Broker. They take mainframe applications and fields and turn them into a set of reusable objects. The objects are then used to assemble Web pages. Users can hyperlink to specific fields and screens without going through the menu-after-menu process of the host application. The mainframe code is not touched, but the navigation is simplified, and the application and data can be presented more selectively and more efficiently. There are products on the market that simply allow network managers to make old 3270 screens look prettier by adding color, pull-down menus, and hyperlinks; 3270-to-Java tools are also available. But the effect of such products is largely cosmetic. What network managers really want is the ability to re-engineer host applications to fit in with their existing business rules and intranet infrastructure. The idea now is that the linear nature of host-based applications — where users are presented with a sequential, and often laborious, series of menu screens — must favor a more versatile logic that can selectively draw data fields and screens from host applications and also incorporate data from other relational databases.

It is not trivial when legacy applications are converted into HTML pages. There are a couple of recommendations and guidelines. Following the guidelines will

ensure consistency throughout the intranet and accelerate Web page development.
It is recommended to:[24]

- Define a standard page layout
- Standardize navigation links for easy exploration
- Divide long documents into small sections and provide navigation links
  within each sector
- Design pages for high- and low-speed access
- Create a text-only option for remote-access users
- Assemble a team to test HTML pages as end users

In addition, the following should be avoided:[24]

- Overloading pages with graphics and animation
- Exceeding a standard maximum graphic size — many HTML developers
  use thumbnails that pages load quickly
- Forgetting to give credit where it is due — otherwise copyright could
  become a problem
- Forgetting to proofread everything
- Forgetting test links for users who browse without graphics
- Writing for an updated version of a Web browser that the end users may
  not have
- Dead-end documents that leave users without an exit route from each page

The use of Web technology may unify and simplify the management of legacy
networking architectures. New management software from NetTech, Inc. promises
to let SNA users easily track network devices and troubleshoot application performance problems from any standard Web browser. EView/Web Response Time Monitor is a Java-based software tool to eliminate the need for more costly and complicated mainframe-based tools, such as NetView Performance Monitor or NetSpy. The
average user is no longer investing in mainframe-based software tools. Problem
determination and isolation are always difficult tasks in SNA environments, but as
users move to TCP/IP and the internet, SNA monitoring can become even more
difficult.

EView/Web consists of two components: an EView application on the mainframe
and EView Java applet on a local Web server. The application works by tapping into
existing SNA performance monitors on the mainframe and VTAM. EView/Web
gathers SNA and MVS system alerts and alarms, then funnels response times and
other performance data over an internet connection to the Java application. Administrators running any standard browser can then tap into the Java application locally
or remotely to check response times, for all devices in the SNA enterprise from one
screen. It lets users identify LU-to-LU sessions, specific session response times and
SNA application performance. EView/Web also has direct links to most industry
standard trouble-ticketing packages, such as AR Systems from Remedy. EView/Web
would automatically notify the system of a performance problem so the system could
cut a trouble ticket to track the occurrence.

7.8 SUMMARY

The webification of systems and network management applications is irreversible. Users require a unified and simplified front end to access management applications from universal browsers. Existing and new applications need additional conversion software that presents the necessary information in HTML format. Conversion remains hidden to users. Management applications offer this conversion in real time using extensions to HTML. In some cases, management applications are based on databases requiring an additional DB-to-HTML conversion. Using these experiences also legacy applications may be made accessible. Performance questions will be addressed in the following chapters.

8 Performance Considerations

8.1 INTRODUCTION

Users expect that the webified solution offered by platform and device vendors, and internet service providers (ISPs), respectively, are performing well, and not causing any bottlenecks in systems and networks. The performance of webified management applications depends on the content, content authoring, server efficiency, access network's throughput capabilities, and on the browser. This chapter addresses each of these areas in some depth.

The emergence of Web computing is dramatically altering the way information is accessed. The phenomenon of the World Wide Web is the most dramatic evidence of this, yet looking to the enterprise, we see the overwhelming evidence that the Web browser has become the front-end of choice into corporate information. Systems and network management solutions are no exceptions to this. The implications of the new trends are:

- All information can be viewed as Web content, accessible directly through a Web browser, a browser plug-in, or a dynamic piece of code (e.g., Java) which is downloaded automatically to the client. This content can be as varied as a static Web page, a CGI script front-ending an existing database application, or new media such as streaming audio or video.
- The information access model has changed from one in which client specific configuration is required in order to access information to one in which access is always available unless policies are explicitly defined to prevent it.
- Flash Crowds, where a certain content in the internet or intranets generates significant unexpected traffic, are frequent phenomena making traditional network design techniques (e.g., those based on measuring peak and average loads) obsolete.
- Information accessed on or through Web servers comprises the bulk of traffic on the internet (over 80%) and will do the same ultimately in intranets. Therefore, effective management of Web resources, bandwidth, and traffic is critical if users want to get acceptable quality of service for Web-based computing.

The previous chapters gave a fairly deep overview of the applicability of the Web-based technology to manage systems and networks. The roles of Web browsers and Web servers have been clarified. But, performance questions have not yet been addressed. The overall goal is to avoid performance bottlenecks that occur around

Web servers and in the access networks. Bottlenecks can occur actually in any of the components, such as the Web servers, Web browsers, the backbone and the access networks. Bottlenecks can also be caused by not well designed pages and their links to each other. Figure 8.1 shows the arrangement of components of a typical architecture.

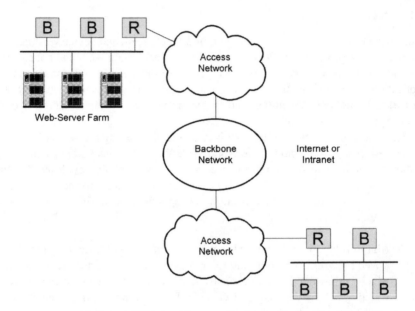

FIGURE 8.1 Architecture of Web-based systems and network management applications.

8.2   WEB PAGES CONTENT MANAGEMENT

Authoring tools present a stand-alone environment in which to build pages. While this requires learning a new program specifically for HTML creation, these tools allow users to make the most of HTML, using features that traditional word processors do not support.

Currently, there are two distinct kinds of tools Web authors can use to bring their words to the Web. Tag-based tools automate HTML syntax, allowing users to see and tweak tags without having to enter their syntax manually. In contrast, WYSIWYG tools hide HTML from the user, generating it in the background instead. If these tools do not support a specific feature of HTML, that feature must be added manually after the document's underlying code is visible, usually in a text editor. Some products use dialog boxes or palettes to accept information before displaying it as HTML code in the body of the document. Since these tools generate HTML for users, they minimize the learning curve for new Web authors and can produce syntactically perfect HTML. Many of the publicly available tools are both standard and professional features, the latter being available only in the registered or commercial version.

8.2.1 CONTENT AUTHORING

Most users are challenged by the task of information creation, management, and dissemination. These activities are time consuming and difficult to control. The internet and intranets alone cannot solve information management problems unless specific intranet solutions are implemented that directly address the need for document management. The new discipline, called content authoring or management, includes the following tasks:[20]

- Users must be able to easily add and update content on a periodic basis
- Users must be able to protect their page contents from changes by other users
- A content approval process should be defined and in place. This process should encompass ways to manage and control document revisions, especially changes to shared documents.

As policies and procedures relating to content management are formulated, it is important to designate responsibilities to specific individuals to ensure that they are properly implemented and followed. An internal style guide should be developed that provides page layout, design elements, and HTML code guidelines. Usually also case tools are involved. The style guide will help the users to maintain a consistent look and feel throughout the Web pages. Sometimes television-like techniques are helpful in this respect. The style guide should contain information on where to obtain standard icons, buttons, video and graphics, as well as guidelines on page dimensions and how to link the pages to each other. As part of the style guide, it is helpful to create Web page templates. These templates consist of HTML files, and are used to provide a starting point for anyone interested in developing Web pages or content for the intranet. Although it is very easy to create a working Web page and to publish for mass viewing, the real challenge is to maintain the page, to size the Web server, and to configure the access network.

The recommendations for Web page design can be summarized as follows:

- Use of standards for the layout of pages
- Standardization of links
- Use of navigation helps
- Segmenting log documents into small ones
- Design of pages for rapid and slow search
- Use of text pages for user with narrow bandwidth
- Test of HTML pages and links before practical use

But, users should be careful to avoid:

- Too many graphics and too much animation, which slow down operations
- Big pictures that slow down loading the pages
- Failure to obtain permissions from copyright holders
- Not proofreading

- Not checking browser compatibility
- Having one-way streets in HTML documents

8.2.2 TOOLS

The first HTML tools focused on streamlining individual page creation, simplifying the need to memorize HTML page tags and syntax while leaving site management up to the skills with a whiteboard. Although hand-coding HTML is still the preferred choice of many Web experts, developing and maintaining an entire Web site this way is very time consuming, and not recommended. A Web site's foundation is proper management of all its files, directories and links, and these seem to grow exponentially in any decent-sized site. Following this logic, the flip side to making it easier to stamp out Web pages is a tool that can manage and restructure the changing sites of the customers. As HTML authoring and site management applications mature, finding tools is getting easier. Enhancing Web sites with pre-Dynamic HTML (DHTML), Cascading Style Sheets (CSS), scripts and pre-Extensible Markup Language (XML) demand the use of powerful authoring tool environments.

Web authoring becomes increasingly complex and the internet diffuses into software; programs from word processors to databases all now export to HTML. This means the ability to both create HTML and integrate HTML from other sources grows in importance. Similarly, tools recognizing that modern Web sites are the work of many people across different departments also get support. HTML was never designed to be a precise layout language, and even now, truly accurate page layout, as with desktop publishing, is the rare exception in Web environments. To sidestep this, designers have developed numerous work arounds. The most common position tricks are old single pixel transparent GIF and the extensive use of tables.

Netscape and Microsoft disagree on the best means of achieving absolute position via cascading style sheets, which means users all have to wait before there is a single standard way to address this problem. Providing users with the means of simple HTML page production while controlling access to that production guarantees an easier life for Webmasters. For departmental users, an easy-to-use, page focused HTML authoring package is the best choice. In the graphics area, the best tools can do on-the-fly, drag-and-drop importing and perform basic inline image touch-ups, such as resizing and resampling without the need to launch a separate graphic editing application. These are must-have tools for professional-level development; similarly, any site management-enabled tool worth the download must verify and correct links in conjunction with directory and file moves, saving time in recoding pages.

Users should take advantage of free-downloading Web authoring tools for tests. Those tests will give answers as to whether the authoring tool performs well in a particular environment. Table 8.1 summarizes some selection and test criteria for Web authoring tools.[21]

There are many tools available for generic use. Examples include PageMill from Adobe, HomePage from Claris, Dreamweaver from Macromedia, FrontPage from Microsoft, and VisualPage from Symantex. This list is not complete, and changing very dynamically. This segment focuses on site management tools, only. Two site

TABLE 8.1
Selection Criteria for Web Authoring Tools

General Features
Frames editor
Table editor
Forms editor
HTML source editor
Wizards/templates
User-defined tags
HTML source code editing
HML code validation
Multiple undo

Media and Extensibility
Java applets
Javascript
ActiveX controls

Graphics
PNG
BMP
Automatic file conversion
Client-side image maps
Server-side image maps

HTML Support and Importing
HTML version support
Font definition and support
CSS style sheets
CSS external style sheets
Dynamic HTML
Import MS Word
Import WordPerfect
Import Rich Text Format
Import spreadsheet tables

Site Management
Link verification and correction
Global search and replace
Overall site items
Modify site structure on the fly

management tools, Linkbot from Tetranet and SiteSweeper from Site/Technologies, are shown in some detail.

8.2.2.1   Linkbot from Tetranet

Linkbot is a suite of Web site management utilities that can help to track down and repair problems on Web sites. It contains all the tools the Webmasters need to automate site management and maintain an error-free site. The principal features are:

Basic Features	Description
Find and repair dead links	Improves the quality of sites by cleaning up bugs
Find unused orphan files	Recovers disk space by cleaning server of files that are no longer linked to
Find stale content	Identifies pages that have not been updated recently and may not be accurate anymore

Basic Features	Description
Find slow pages	Ensure that users with slow connections can access pages quickly
Find pages missing titles	Pages without titles will not display correctly in browsers and search engine query results
Support for work groups	Produce separate reports for subsections of the site belonging to a specific author
Interactive site mapping	Explore the structure and organization of sites in Linkbot's Explorer style interface
HTML reports	Automatically generate HTML reports detailing the site's major problem areas
Multitasking scanning	Scans large sites quickly by processing up to 30 URLs at a time
Automated scheduling	Schedule Linkbot to scan the site at regular intervals and to automatically generate HTML reports
Uses a high-performance multitasking engine	Allows for extremely fast analysis of large sites
Checks internal and external HTTP, HTTPs and FTP links	Isolates all broken links on a site
Checks for unused (orphan) files	Cleans out old unused files from Web servers
Checks for stale content	Pinpoints pages on the site that may be outdated
Checks for slow pages	Finds large pages that may be slow to download
Checks syntax of "mailto" URLs	Finds "mailto" references that may be invalid
Checks for pages with missing titles	Finds and repairs pages that are missing titles
Filters URLs from the analysis	Specifies areas of the site that Linkbot should not check

Mapping and organization

Maps out the structure of site in an "Explorer" style interface	Allows webmasters to interactively explore the organization of a site in a familiar interface
Shows links in and out of a selected URL	Makes editing bad links easier by showing all the links that are pointing to a selected URL

Basic Features	**Description**
Sorts the site's URL list by title, description, author, size, last modified date and type	Isolates pages with missing titles, finds all the documents published by a specific author, finds old and new files, finds large files with slow download times
Provides advanced filters for viewing subsets of a site's contents	Makes it possible to view and organize smaller subsets that contain thousands of URLs

Maintenance and repair

Provides built in HTML editing	Edits and repairs problems within Linkbot's interface
Rechecks specific subsets of URLs on a site	Enables Linkbot to check targeted groups of URLs, e.g. all broken links to external sites
Allows Webmasters to export results to a delimited file	Allows the results of Linkbot's analysis to be exported to a file and then imported into a database

HTML reports

Creates nine customizable HTML reports	Summarizes the site's problem areas and statistics. Automatically generates detailed reports of broken links, broken pages, warnings, orphaned URLs, and on new, old, and slow pages

Workgroup features

Creates reports listing the site's problems by author	Makes it easier for authors in workgroup to repair the problems in their pages

Automation/scheduling

Automates maintenance with customizable scheduling options	Allows Linkbot to be programmed to turn itself on, check a site and produce a report

8.2.2.2   SiteSweeper from Site/Technologies

Web professionals are challenged to maintain the integrity of mission-critical Web-based business applications. SiteSweeper performs time consuming quality assurance tasks for the webmaster and provides the additional information needed to ensure the smooth operation of any Web site.

Large images with slow download times are a major source of frustration for Web site users. SiteSweeper helps make sites more efficient by automating the process of determining the total download sizes of all the pages on the site. It even estimates the download times at different connection speeds for easy analysis and comparison. Time-intensive searches for bad links are also automated with Side-Sweeper, helping webmasters to identify and resolve problem areas before they escalate. Types of bad links such as "not found", "unauthorized" and "moved permanently" are identified and described in the reports of the product.

Informed decisions may be made about the state of the Web site. The following data are available:

- Properties of each page
- Aggregate site statistics
- Links to and from each page
- Links to external sites
- Catalog of images
- Pages with bad links
- Total download size of each page
- Thumbnails and size of all images

In order to use this product, the user simply enters the home page into the interface. Then, SiteSweeper sweeps the site following each of the links identified. Along the way, it visits all the pages in the particular site that are linked together, and tests the validity of all links to external Web sites. It gathers important data about each page it visits, including size, last modified date, and expiration date. When finished, it generates a series of reports, as specified by the webmaster via the reporting interface. Since the reports are generated in HTML, they can easily be published and shared by the webmaster.

Key features of the product are:

- Detailed reports on demand or by schedule
- Support for multiple servers
- Authentication for access to password protected sites
- Parallel processing provides fast sweeping
- Proxy server support

SiteSweeper is an industrial-strength application suitable for corporate internet and intranet sites of any size. Multiple Web servers running on multiple platforms can be swept simultaneously.

8.2.3 PERFORMANCE OPTIMIZATION AS A SERVICE

Performance optimization of Web applications may be offered as a service. Website Garage does exactly this. For a fee, which is structured for various services, principal metrics of Web page performance can be analyzed and improved. All tuning activities are supported remotely. Depending on the service requested, the service provider determines the time it needs to fulfill the service.

The basis service is Tune Up, and consists of the following diagnostics:

- Browser compatibility check — it indicates how well the Web page is displayed by viewing it with different browsers.
- Readiness check — it investigates whether the Web page is set up to be indexed correctly by search engines and directories.

- Load time check — it measures how long it takes for the site to load up with an average modem.
- Dead link check — detects hard to find dead links on the customer's page.
- Link popularity check — finds out how many Web sites are linking to a particular Web site.
- Spell check — discovers and highlights spelling mistakes.
- HTML design check finds out how the site's HTML design compares to the best in practice.

Tune Up Plus offers more. Users work hard to get traffic to their Web sites. Tune Up Plus ensures an efficient way of monitoring the quality of Web sites. This service is offered for more Web pages in comparison with the basic service. The most comprehensive service is Turbocharge with the following portfolio: Register-It service registers the Web site with the top 100 search engines and directories on the internet. This service includes:

- Automatic registration
- Selective registration (only selected directories are included)
- Free registration
- Free updates
- Status tracking

While most services only provide one-time registration, this service provides re-registration and updates at no cost to the users. The company updates the top search engines' lists constantly and keeps abreast of the best search tools on the internet.

The browser snapshot provides a snapshot of how the particular site actually looks on different versions of major browsers, platforms, and screen sizes. This service helps to verify that the particular site is compatible with all the various browsers on the internet. This service includes:

- 18 screenshots in Netscape and Microsoft Internet Explorer on both Macintosh and Windows platforms
- Yearly license allows taking multiple screenshots over time
- Free updates include updates to the system, including the support for additional browsers, platforms, and screen sizes

Estimates indicate that 30% of the sites on the internet may suffer from browser compatibility issues. Getting visitors to a particular site can be expensive and time consuming. By using this service, users can verify that users viewing the particular site from the various browsers see an accurate and complete picture. Also the development of the site can be observed with this service.

Many search engines and directories use META tags to index Web sites. Users can greatly increase the odds that search engines will put the particular site near the top of the category by using the right META tags in the HTML code. META tags consist of two items:

1. Keywords — these should match the words that someone would enter in a search to find a particular site. Include the following: company name, products, product category, the plural of these words, and possible misspellings.
2. Description — this is the description that will show with a particular listing in the search engine. The description should make the users want to visit the site or solve a problem for the visitor.

GIF Lube helps pages load faster by reducing the size of an image. It reduces image size by reducing the number of colors in the image. GIF Lube also allows users to compress and convert images into GIF or JPG formats.

8.3 SERVER MANAGEMENT

The Web server farm is expected to host systems and network management applications. It is further assumed that browsers can be everywhere, both local and remote.

The server farm is responsible for maintaining the home pages for management platforms and eventually for managed devices. But, in the second case, more distribution is expected when Web servers are embedded into managed objects. In both pull and push implementations, members of the server farm are accessed by authorized users very frequently. Besides the usual OS-related metrics, such as

- CPU utilization
- CPU queue lengths
- Processes wait information
- Number of processes active
- Disk utilization
- Disk queue depth and process wait data
- Physical and logical I/O rates
- Memory utilization
- Swap utilization
- Network packet rates
- Printer usage

specific Web-related metrics must also be defined and supervised. In most cases, home page hits, home page misses, access delay within the Web server, read time, and frequency of page links are important.

Web server monitors and management tools concentrate how the Web server is utilized and how performance goals can be met. In addition to these tools, other tools are required that are able to continue the analysis using log files. This segment is devoted to log file analyzer tools that are able to give the necessary data for usage analysis.

Figure 8.2 shows the information flow to and from log file analyzers. In most cases, performance and accounting management are the primary targets. Usage analysis is a means of understanding what is happening on an internet or intranet server such as a Web server. Usage analysis tools piece together data fragments to create a coherent picture of server activity.

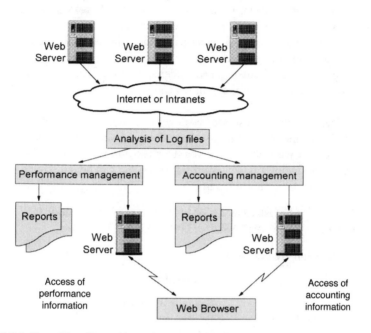

FIGURE 8.2 Use of log file analyzers for usage statistics.

Usage analysis can answer the following questions:

- How many individual users visited the site on a particular day?
- What day of the week is the site busiest?
- How many visitors are from a certain country?
- How long do visitors remain on the site?
- How many errors do visitors encounter?
- Where do visitors enter and leave the site?
- How long did it take most visitors to view the home page?
- Which links on other sites send the most visitors to this site?
- Which search engines send the most visitors to this site?

Reports can span any length of time, making it possible to see trends. They can also display any degree of granularity, allowing users to see both broad-ranging reports and detailed reports. Usage analysis is most frequently thought of in terms of Web servers. The reports created by usage analysis tools can be used throughout organizations to help people make informed decisions. For example:

- Web developers use these tools to gauge the effects of site design changes. Using this information they can make further refinements to the design of the site to maximize its effectiveness.

- Marketers use these tools to analyze the effectiveness of marketing programs and online ads.
- Site administrators can spot Web pages that are causing errors, determine future server hardware needs, and track FTP and Proxy server activity.
- Sales persons can gather information about prospects, including their geographic location, how many pages they viewed, and how they found the site in the first place.
- Executives use the intelligence gathered with log analyzers as a resource when making a broad range of decisions.

Each time a visitor accesses a resource on a Web server — whether it is an image, an HTML file, or a script — the activity is usually recorded as a line in a text file associated with the Web server. This text file is known as the Web server log file. A single line of a typical Web server log file can be interpreted as follows.
Record of the server log file entry:

foo.bar.com --(31/Oct/1998:23:31:44+ 500) "GET home.html HTTP/1.0" 200 1031 http://www.yahoo.com/"Mozilla/3.0 (Win32;U)"

Interpretation by elements

Element	Interpretation
foo.bar.com	Host name of the visitor's computer
31/Oct/1998:23:31:44	Date and time
GET	Method used to request the resource
home.html	Name of the requested resource
HTTP/1.0	Protocol used to request the resource
200	Status code "200" means that the request was successful
1031	Number of bytes transferred to satisfy the request
http://www.logfile.ana.html	Web page that referred the visitor to this page
Mozilla/3.0	Visitor's Web browser and version
Win32	Visitor"s operating system

Most Web servers write out log files in the Combined Log Format. It differs from an older Common Log Format in that it contains browser and referral information. Referral information is important to determine what sites are sending most traffic to the target address and what sites might have out of date links pointing to specific user sites. Referral information is also critical for gauging the effectiveness of online ads. Other information that can be included in a log file includes:

Cookie	A persistent identification code assigned to a user which allows the user to be tracked across several visits
Session identifier	Tracks each visitor for the length of the visit only
Amount of time the request took to fulfill	Enables server performance reporting

Figure 8.3 shows a full configuration of an instrumented intranet with Net.Medic from VitalSigns. By installing Net.Medic at multiple sites on a corporate intranet, IT professionals can automatically monitor Web site performance from different access points. ISPs can use this product to regularly test Web sites of their customers and to ensure high service quality. Data from multiple access points enable the user to compare application performance as experienced by customers accessing applications from different areas of the intranet, track Web server availability and response, identify leading indicators or emerging issues, and proactively address problems.

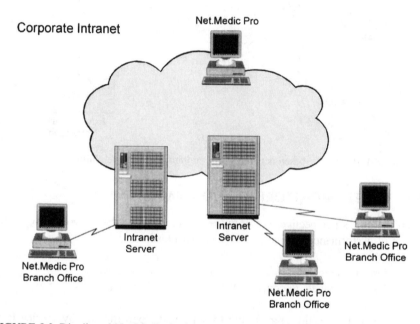

FIGURE 8.3 Distributed Net.Medic for intranet management.

Basically, there are two types of usage analyzer tools: software-based and on-the-wire collectors. On the high end of usage analysis tools are packet sniffers which offer on-the-wire reporting by installing an agent against the kernel of the operating system of the Web server. They run as root in the kernel of the operating system on the Web server. Furthermore, they require that a network runs in promiscuous mode in order to expose network traffic to the agent. Usually, there are very few reports packet sniffers can create that log file analyzers cannot. Log file analyzers can create reports on the usage of secure/encrypted communications, which packet sniffers cannot. Packet sniffers are more expensive, offer fewer reports, and offer just a few report distribution capabilities.

Figure 8.4 displays an average configuration with WebSniffer from Network Associates. In the center, the repository receives and distributes data to various target addresses, such as the IT center and alarm centers.

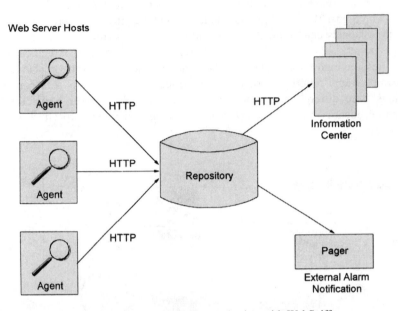

FIGURE 8.4 Repository-based network traffic monitoring with WebSniffer.

8.4 TRAFFIC MONITORING AND ANALYSIS

From the user's perspective, not only the server, but also the networks can be the source of performance problems. There are two basic cases:

- Use of the internet including ISPs for the access network
- Use of intranets to connect Web servers and browsers.

In the first case, the user is able to control the performance by service level agreements signed with the ISPs. Usually, the access networks cause performance bottlenecks by not providing enough bandwidth.

In the second case, the user has full control, and can significantly improve the performance by properly sizing networking components and by resolving the necessary bandwidth for transmission.

Web traffic poses a significant number of challenges to existing internet and intranet infrastructures. Most Web sessions are short lived. As such, they have fewer TCP packets compared to batch mode operations such as file transfer. In addition, HTTP traffic tends to spike and fall radically. This creates instant demand for hot content which in turn causes network and server congestion. When Web technology is used to support systems and network management, transport paths are shared between productive traffic and management traffic. Management traffic is even more sensitive to bottlenecks. Web site traffic is highly mobile in that a unique event on a particular Web site could trigger a significantly high hit rate within a very short period of time. This would be typical in cases with periodic management report distribution and major systems and network outages.

Web traffic behavior is significantly different from today's client/server paradigm. It has the following unique characteristics:

- The amount of data sent from a server is significantly larger (5:1) than the amount of data sent from a client to a server. This suggests that optimization of server to client traffic has more significant impact to the internet and that client request redirection to the best-fit server could have significant performance advantages for Web traffic flows.

- The median transfer size for Web server documents is small (e.g., 5 KB). This implies that Web flows are mostly short-lived flows. They are more likely to create instantaneous congestion due to their "bursty" nature. This suggests a resource management model must deal appropriately with short-lived flows. Even though HTTP supports persistent connections, due to interoperability issues with existing network caches, it is unclear how widespread deployment will be, or how soon.

- The top 10% of Web server files are accessed 90% of the time and are accountable for 90% of the bytes transferred. This suggests that Web server selection, caching and content replication schemes that focus on this top 10% will yield the greatest gain.

- A significant percentage (e.g., 15% to 40%) of the files and bytes accessed are accessed only once. That is, some small number of large files often consumes a disproportionate amount of total server and network bandwidth. In addition, servers suffer performance degradation when subject to significant job size variation. This is due primarily to memory fragmentation, which occurs when buffering variable size data in fixed length blocks. Furthermore, subjecting servers to workloads consisting of both hot and one-time requests will result in lower performance due to frequent cache invalidation of the hot objects. Therefore, a server selection strategy that takes into account content, job size, and server cache coherency can significantly improve network and server resource allocation and performance. In addition, requests for large files may be good candidates for redirection to a server that has a shorter round trip time to the client.

- Hosts on many networks access Web servers, but 10% of the networks are responsible for over 75% of this usage. This suggests that resource management strategies that focus on specific client populations may yield positive results in some cases.

- Real time traffic is becoming an increasingly significant proportion of Web traffic. Web Site resource management strategies must take into account an increasing demand for support of real time applications such as voice, distance learning, and streaming media. To deal with both legacy and Web traffic as well as real time Web traffic, these strategies will need to include admission control as well as bandwidth and buffer allocation components.

The emergence of Web computing and Web traffic over the internet or intranets has created some unique new problems. It is estimated that over 80% of internet traffic is related to Web-based HTTP traffic. Even applications, such as FTP and RealAudio, which run over TCP and UDP, respectively, typically use HTTP to set up the transfer. Since HTTP is an application protocol that runs over TCP, LAN switches and routers, which run Layer 2, 3 and 4, have very limited ability to influence Web traffic behavior. This burden is left to Web servers, which take on the function of TCP/HTTP connection management and, in some cases, the responsibility to distribute HTTP requests to servers within a server farm. This creates inevitable scaling problems as Web sites grow.

The current internet can be described using a model where local bandwidth is plentiful in the premise LAN located at the edge of the internet. However, the uplink from LAN or remote user to the internet is often severely bandwidth constrained by orders of magnitude. Although congestion can occur anywhere in the internet path between a client and a server, the most frequent culprits are the WAN connection between the client and the internet and the WAN connection between the Web farm and the internet. Actions taken to insure that this bandwidth is not over committed will help improve end-to-end performance.

Instantaneous bandwidth mismatches can occur for a network device that functions as a demarcation point between the public internet and the Web farm. Examples are:

- The incoming link of the traffic is a faster media type (e.g., fast Ethernet) and the outgoing link is a slower type (e.g., T1 or T3).
- The instantaneous fan-in, i.e., the number of flows being sent at the same time to the same output port can vary dynamically from one instant to the next.
- A number of traffic sources (e.g., outbound server traffic) may be sharing the bandwidth of a 45 Mbps T3 pipe in a "bursty" manner over a very high speed switching fabric (e.g., 10 Gbps). This creates a need to regulate flow admission into a slower pipe from multiple higher speed traffic sources.

Since HTTP runs on top of TCP, TCP's behavior as a Web transport protocol deserves careful study. TCP provides some inherent flow control via end-to-end acknowledgments and TCP window size adjustments between two application end points. This mechanism allows applications to detect packet losses due to varying network conditions and rate-adapts automatically. However, this built-in flow control mechanism was designed originally for long-lived flows over very low bandwidth, long haul pipes. In that scenario, the number of unacknowledged packets traveling through the pipe at any instant in time is small. This limits the number of packets that may have to be resent in the case of packet loss. In situations where TCP packets travel through higher speed links or over longer delay end-to-end paths, the number of unacknowledged packets becomes large, and TCP becomes more susceptible to expensive packet loss recovery. This problem is exacerbated by TCP's congestion avoidance mechanisms, which can result in oscillation between congested and uncongested conditions on busy links. TCP also exhibits behavior that is commonly referred to as greedy source. For long-lived flows, TCP will continue to grow the number of unacknowledged bytes outstanding (or window size) until it occupies all the bandwidth available in the connection. This process is called slow start and can take several round trip times to complete. The bandwidth the flow will consume is limited only by the speed of the lowest speed link in the path of the connection with other flows sharing the pipe.

TCP cannot distinguish between congestion caused by a sudden traffic burst at the edge and that caused by true network congestion at the core of the internet. Instead, it simply assumes the latter in all cases. To deal with burst-related congestion at the edge for short-lived flows, the best strategy is for the networking device at the edge (i.e. between the Web farm and the internet) to allocate enough buffers to cope with them. For these flows, allocating additional buffers during a burst has the effect of smoothing out packet processing load for the switch without the side effect of over-allocating buffers at the expense of other active flows. The explanation for this is as follows: if a flow is short-lived, its net buffer requirements will peak only for a transient moment. If flows can be classified according to size, bandwidth, and type, it is possible to allocate buffer, switch, and uplink bandwidth resources accordingly.

Bandwidth borrowing on the basis of class-based queuing (CBS) is getting very popular. Figure 8.5 shows this hierarchy with a likely dialog for the process of borrowing bandwidth.

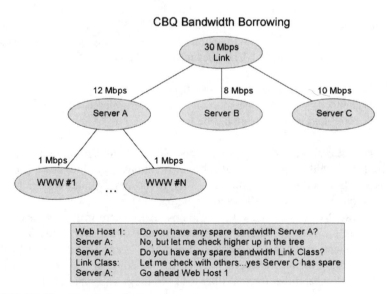

FIGURE 8.5 Class-based queuing.

Most TCP buffers will not be the cure for all TCP problems, however. For long-lived flows, fairness issues and suspectibility to packet loss recovery must be carefully considered. In early ATM switches and in routers, the same conclusion was reached, i.e., throwing buffers at it does not solve the problem.

Rate shaping techniques, in which a networking device in the data path intercepts TCP acknowledgments and alters their pacing and advertised window size show promise, but suffer scaling limitations when deployed at the termination point for large numbers of flows (i.e., at the uplink for a large Web site). This is due to the requirement to maintain state information in the networking device for each flow. In addition, these techniques provide very little benefit for typical, short-lived Web flows. These flows are often just completing slow start around the time the flow terminates. Hence, window management techniques never have opportunity to kick in. Obviously, these techniques only apply to TCP traffic. Although more research is required, these techniques appear most useful at a slow speed WAN demarcation point such as might be found between an enterprise network and the internet, where it may be useful to rate limit long-lived flows. In the Web farm, the most useful technique for managing WAN and switch resources is to ensure that sufficient bandwidth and buffers are available to support the lowest speed bottleneck link in the flow path. Admission control procedures can ensure that sufficient local switch, buffer, and bandwidth resources are available for admitted flows.

Information about the use of Web pages, their users, the frequency of access, resource utilization and about traffic volumes can also be collected in the network or at the interfaces of the network. In many cases, the borders between tools and techniques in the server and networking segments are not clear. Tools are different from each other; the differentiators are data collection technologies, performance metrics used, and reports offered.

In the internet and intranet area, effective bandwidth management is a critical success factor. The role of network planners is going to be redefined. Real-time and near-real-time bandwidth allocation definitions are needed. Network managers agree that load balancers are needed. The questions are whether:

- Hardware- or software-based load balancers are better
- Embedded or stand-alone solutions should be preferenced
- A combination of both should be used

In the first case, considering high-traffic volumes, hardware solutions should be preferred. Software solutions in critical load situations may slow down processes, and risk performance. At this time, there are no accurate guidelines for tolerable workload, but a range up to 5% seems to be reasonable.

Switches, routers, and firewalls are almost everywhere in internet access networks and in intranets. To embed traffic control and sharing functions would save extra components, but would — as stated earlier — generate additional load and may impair the principal functions. The embedded solution may also include the use of RMON capabilities for real-time load profiling. The stand-alone solution is sensitive to a single point of failure, but would offer overhead-free traffic and load management. The following attributes may play an important role when evaluating alternatives.[19]

Load-balancing switch

Benefits:

- Load balancing is performed in a device that is needed anyway in the network
- Centralized management
- Good opportunity to control and guarantee quality of service

Disadvantages:

- Performance may be impacted by management functions
- Single point of failure for both switch and management functions

Load-balancing firewall

Benefits:

- Load balancing is performed in a device that is needed anyway in most networks
- Centralized management
- Includes special functions and services, such as traffic management and application-based load balancing

Disadvantages:

- Switches are still needed
- Single point of failure for both firewall and management functions
- Performance depends on hardware and operating system configuration

Load-balancing traffic shaper

Benefits:

- Load balancing is performed by a device most likely present in the network anyway
- Centralized management
- Offers traffic shaping and balancing for internet or intranet access in addition to server access

Disadvantages:

- In most cases, switches and firewalls are needed in addition to these devices
- Single point of failure for both traffic shaping and load balancing
- Little experience yet with performance and scalability

Figure 8.6 shows this last alternative with PacketShaper from Packeteer. It resides behind WAN devices, enabling network managers to control bandwidth for inbound and outbound traffic flows.

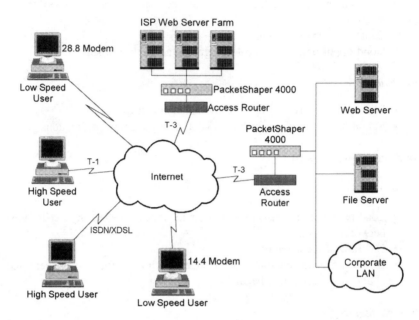

FIGURE 8.6 Stand-alone traffic manager from Packeteer.

8.5   CONTENT SMART RESOURCE MANAGEMENT

While Web server performance improvements are part of the performance optimization solution, they must be accompanied by improvements in network and content management technology to have a true impact on WWW scaling and performance. Specifically, developments in the following three areas are critically important:

- Content distribution and replication — by pushing content closer to the access points where users are located, backbone bandwidth requirements can be reduced and response time to the user can be improved. Content can be proactively replicated in the network under operator control or dynamically replicated by network elements. Caching servers are an example of network elements that can facilitate the dynamic replication of content. Other devices and models are likely to emerge over time.
- Content request distribution — when multiple instances of content exist in a network, the network elements must cooperate to direct a content request to the "best fit" server at any moment in time. This requires an

increasing level of "content intelligence" in the network elements themselves.

- Content-driven Web farm resource measurement — a server or cache in a server farm ultimately services a specific content request. Local server, switching, and uplink bandwidth are precious resources which need to be carefully managed to provide appropriate service levels for Web traffic.

8.5.1 CONTENT SMART QUALITY OF SERVICE AND RESOURCE MANAGEMENT

In a typical Web site, the top 10% of Web server files are accessed 90% of the time and are accountable for 90% of the bytes transferred. Therefore, techniques that optimize performance for these files will have the most significant impact on total Web site performance. This requires that the network itself be keenly aware of which content is hot and which servers can provide it. Since content can be hot one instant and cold the next, content smart switches must learn about hot content by tracking content access history as it processes content requests and responses.

To effectively manage Web site servers, network, and bandwidth resources, something must also be known about the content size and quality of service (QoS) requirements. These content attributes can be gleaned through the processing of active flows, through proactively probing servers, or through administrative definitions. In addition, it is important to track server performance relative to specific pieces of content. All of this information can be maintained in a content database that provides an analogous function to a routing table in a router or switch. Content smart switches make a content routing decision based on the information contained in the database, connecting a client to a best fit server in either a local or remote server farm. This enables the emergence of a business model based on replicating content in distributed data centers, with overflow content delivery capacity and backup in the case of a partial communications failure. Additionally, overflow content capacity intelligence minimizes the need to build out to handle flash crowds for highly requested content.

8.5.2 CONTENT SMART FLOW ADMISSION CONTROL

Two factors often contribute to congestion in a server farm. One is that servers are not up to the task of handling the amount of incoming traffic. The other is that the link bandwidth from servers to the internet is overwhelmed by the combination of inbound and outbound traffic; this is complicated by the fact that the amount of outbound traffic from servers is on average about five times that of the inbound. As a result, a TCP/HTTP connection could be made successfully only to find out that the server could not be allocated the necessary bandwidth to deliver the requested content. To make matters worse, some server implementations come to a grinding halt when presented with an excessive number of TCP/HTTP connections — sometimes requiring a hard reboot.

Content smart flow admission control is explicitly aware of:

- The requested content's attributes (e.g., size, location, QoS requirements, and access frequency)
- The capabilities of all servers to service a particular piece of content
- Switch and buffer resources
- Uplink bandwidth out of the Web farm

Therefore, a content smart switch can make an intelligent decision whether to admit, reject, or redirect the flow. Using information about content size and client bandwidth, a precise additive bandwidth management model can be built. Using this model, flexible services can be defined which meet the differing service level requirements of both service providers and enterprises. Using this additive bandwidth management model, oversubscription related system resource problems can be avoided by allowing definable thresholds on per customer, per server, and/or per content bases. Content smart admission control can also be used to tag specific flows with specific precedence values. These tags can be used by other routers and switches in the path to preserve quality of service end-to-end. This is compatible with the current direction in differentiated services going on in the Internet Engineering Task Force.

8.5.3 Content Smart Link Management

This technique can ensure that more flows are not admitted than can be handled through the switch or on the uplinks on average. It is still critical, however, to deal appropriately with traffic bursts and temporary congestion on these links to ensure that Web flows get the appropriate quality of service. Priority queuing provides a way to prioritize requests based on their type precedence. Fair queuing and weighted queuing methods improve over the priority queuing scheme by addressing the low priority traffic starvation problem with a scheme that separates traffic into well-identified flows so that each receives a "fair" or "weighted fair" share of transmission bandwidth.

Class-based queuing (CBQ) was developed by the Network Research Group at Lawrence Berkeley laboratory, as an improvement upon these existing bandwidth management techniques. It proposes a model in which traffic is categorized in hierarchical classes. Flows inherit their flow characteristics from their parent flow class tree and can have local characteristics of their own. Flows are identified based on the IP address and the inner attributes within the IP header and payload. CBQ provides more granular control of transmission bandwidth and distributes it to member flow classes in accordance with their allocation policies. The model itself is independent of the scheduling techniques that run underneath it, therefore implementation details will vary based on the target architecture.

Content smart link management borrows concepts from CBQ. However, where CBQ is a model that operates on a packet-by-packet basis based on layer 3 and 4 classification techniques, Content smart link management classifies flows at admission time based upon the content requested, its attributes, and configured policies.

These policies support the enterprise and service provider service models described in an earlier section of this chapter. This facilitates the classification of flows in a two-level hierarchy which includes owners (or customers) and content. Actual scheduling of flows is managed by a hardware-based flow scheduler which supports guaranteed bandwidth flows, prioritized/weighted flows, and best effort flows. Hardware-based scheduling is critical in order to scale the Web farm.

8.5.4 CONTENT SMART LOAD BALANCING

Simple load-balancing techniques such as round robin, weighted round robin, and least connections are inadequate for Web traffic. For example, Web traffic load balancers must support "sticky" connections, which allow a particular server to be selected regardless of server load due to content locality or transaction integrity. Because of the disproportionate ratio of hot content files to total content (1:10), it is highly desirable to support a content replication model that does not require that content be equally and fully mirrored among servers in a server farm. This means a load-balancing technique must be intelligent enough to recognize if content is available on a particular server before making the selection decision.

Content smart load balancing takes into account several factors that have a significant impact on the overall performance and cost of a Web server farm:

- Server cache hit rate — directing requests for hot content to a server that has recently serviced that content ensures that cache hit rate reduces disk access latency for the most frequently accessed content. Since a significant percentage (15% to 40%) of the files are accessed only once and 90% of the files are accessed only once or not accessed at all, it is important to keep those infrequently accessed files from thrashing a server cache. That is, an infrequently accessed file should be invalidated in server cache promptly to increase the chances that a more frequently accessed file can remain in cache.
- Burst distribution — short-lived, "bursty" flows can best be handled by distributing them among eligible servers so long as the servers have been performing below a defined threshold for a period of time.
- Web flow duration — most Web flows are short lived. However, a relatively small number of infrequent, long-lived flows have a far significant impact on overall bandwidth and server resource consumption. For that reason, long-lived flows should be separated from short-lived flows from a load-balancing perspective and short-lived flows of similar QoS requirements should be aggregated together to increase TCP flow intensity and reduce per flow resource allocation overheads.
- Content based server performance measurement — current server loading can best be measured by examining the request/response time interval of a server as it handles requests. This measurement is most accurate when connection between the switch and the server is direct. In addition, server performance is not uniform across all content. For example, computer intensive applications may perform better on one server than another.

Other servers may perform better for other types of content. Server performance information needs to be qualified by content.

In summary, content smart techniques contribute to fine tune the performance
of Web-based solutions. In the area of Web-based systems and network management,
content smart decisions are extremely significant, because management is usually
sharing the bandwidth with other — in most cases — productive applications.

8.6   LOOK-THROUGH MEASUREMENTS

End-to-end service level monitoring is getting extremely popular with Web-based
applications. Monitoring is targeting availability and response time measurements.
Element-centric management platforms "look-down" and manage elements.
Response time monitoring tools "look through" the infrastructure from one end to
the other. Typical look-through products work on the same principle. Java applets
in combination with C++ scripts are distributed to various selected end points on
the network. These agents generate synthetic transactions against targeted applications, such as databases or intranet Web pages. Response times for these scripts —
including the response times over each individual hop along the route — are logged
on a management server, which assembles and organizes the collected data. The
data are then available to users through a client-side Java interface.

This new type of network instrumentation closely mimics the end user's actual
experience since it measures the end-to-end responsiveness of an application from
one or more outlying LAN nodes to the application server and back again. By doing
so, it delivers a metric that accurately reflects application and service performance
levels on the network.

8.7   BROWSER ADMINISTRATION

In a fully managed environment, the browsers should also be included. It is very
unlikely that they are the reason for performance bottlenecks. But, still, certain
attributes should be carefully evaluated. All experiences with desktop management
can be utilized here. Chapter 2 has shown one example with the Management
Information Format from the DMI standard.

The performance of a browser has more impact on both the perceived and the
actual system performance than any other component. The operating systems are
frequently the same or similar from the same supplier as with Web servers. In these
cases, coordination between the two is much easier. When the Web browser is
running on an old PC with limited RAM, performance may be impacted. It cannot
accept and display data as fast as the Web server and the network are supplying it.
At times, it is cheaper and more practical to upgrade the browser by adding more
RAM or a co-processor. The protocol software can also affect the performance. A
full seven-layer stack requires considerable resources to run. Even with more user-
friendly protocols, performance problems may occur depending on how they select
packet sizes, transfer buffers, and translate addresses. The browser executes the

network's protocols through its driver software; a faster browser will add to the performance. One factor to consider is whether the browser should contain a disk drive of its own or not. Obviously, a diskless browser will ease the budget and improve security somewhat. But diskless browsers have their own set of costs. For one, these browsers are dependent on shared resources. If the work being performed at the browser does not involve sharing resources, a browser with its own disk may be more appropriate. Moreover, diskless browsers add to the network traffic.

In a Java environment, the browser should be able to accommodate all the applets transferred from the Web server for execution locally.

8.8 SUMMARY

Performance bottlenecks can occur in any of the components of a Web-based management environment. This chapter has addressed specific items of content authoring and auditing, and generic items of server and network management. Even in the server farms and network environments, content smart resource management can be very helpful. Look-through measurements help to quantify the time, home page inquiries spent in systems and network components. Besides the bottlenecks, tools also have been introduced that may help to highlight and eliminate the problems detected in various components. Web-based management related tools and applications are expected to work very professionally and highly efficiently, and do not cause any performance impacts on productive resource components.

9 Summary and Trends

Managers, administrators, and operators have been facing a number of manageability problems for many years. Seamless integration of management applications into management platforms, remote configuration of networking devices, remote management capabilities, distribution of management software to element managers and to management agents, real-time performance data reduction, security of accessing management information, version control, are high priority, just to name a few. There is big hope that Web-based technology will help to solve most of these management shortcomings.

Web-based technology has been employed in systems and network management for a number of years. Practical examples are available for the following cases:

- Web-based access to individual devices: Web-server capabilities are embedded into the device and offer in most cases status information and unsophisticated configuration change capabilities. Access is by universal browsers. Devices can be managed individually without maintaining status and performance data.
- Web-based access to management platforms: Web-server capabilities are embedded into the platform by using common gateway interfaces (CGIs) or proxy agents. They offer status information on managed devices and access to the database of the platform. Access is by universal browsers.
- Implementation of Java-based applets into Web-servers and/or management platforms: it promotes the use of universal browsers as thin clients. Status information on Web pages is near real-time and being created dynamically. Users can customize pages to report on their specific domains of responsibility.

Almost everybody in the management business offers one of these options. There are many evaluations available that compare the capabilities of the leading management protocol, simple network management protocol (SNMP) with the Web-based technology. Table 9.1 compares the two by listing advantages and disadvantages of Web-based technology. But this comparison is actually not necessary. The best results can be accomplished when both alternatives are used in combination with each other. The new technology should be considered as complementary and should concentrate on eliminating SNMP weaknesses.

SNMP and RMON are the strongest to collect data to support fault and performance management. No changes are needed here. Web technology helps to unify the access to these data. But configuration management, remote diagnosis, remote

TABLE 9.1
Advantages and Disadvantages of Web-Based Technology

Advantages of Web-Based Technology for Systems and Network Management

No specialized management software is necessary to configure and monitor the device

Practically no versions problems; the front-end is easy to maintain

Platform and location independence for the application

Seamless integration with online documentation

Transport of large amounts of management information is supported

Better security solutions borrowed from other Web applications

Use of universal browsers instead of workstations

Support of workflow

Disadvantages of Web-Based Technology for Systems and Network Management

Latency of HTTP when used for small transactions

Inefficiency of HTTP

Overhead in device to provide information in HTML pages

Requirement for a TCP implementation

Data collection is difficult

Data moves and data manipulation are inefficient

troubleshooting and manager-to-manager communication could be significantly improved by Web-based solutions.

Combination of both technologies is helpful, but may increase complexity. If the same managed device is supporting two agents, one for SNMP/RMON and one for HTML, overhead may become too high. The solution is the use of one combined SNMP/HTTP stack, usually deployed in the form of middleware. The trend is that a number of vendors improve the manageability of their devices by this combination. Chapter 7 has shown solutions with 3Com, Ungermann-Bass, Cisco, and Bay for their sophisticated management systems.

Most enterprises must build a business case prior to deciding for webification. It is not the intention of this book to build specific scenarios for sample enterprises. But some input for cost justification is useful. Some of the items on the cost justification list can be quantified, others cannot.

Webification promotes intercompany collaboration efforts by offering a universal platform for information exchange. Similarly to workflow concepts, it promotes teamwork and helps to avoid unnecessary paperwork.

Many information sources can be unified by using the webified platform. Trouble tickets, problem logs, performance information, resource utilization, change requests, work orders, etc. can be exchanged by the webified front-end using Web documentation standards.

There is absolutely no need for custom software for browsers. Most enterprises concentrate on one or two browsers. The functionality of leading browsers — mostly Netscape and Microsoft — is very similar. Browsers can be implemented on existing PCs, Macs, or UNIX workstations.

Due to the webified solutions, additional resource requirements, such as for disk and memory, are minimal.

Not only browsers, but also Web servers require few resources, with the result that the number of high-end platforms and workstations can be reduced.

Using webified front-ends, information exchange takes another form and reduces the number of phone calls, e-mails, faxes and the need for mail services, with the result of additional savings.

The use of browsers anytime from anywhere enables operators and administrators to work at different locations with the result of less travel to particular management sites.

The use of Web technology will change the corporate culture of using development and deployment tools. Unification can be accomplished, which reduces training times significantly. Most large enterprises train one to five console operators to become subject matter experts in management. They are the only ones who can use the enterprise console, interpret management information and perform near real-time analysis. Web-based tools offer more flexibility, and less training. As a result of the simple and unified front-ends, job rotation is getting much easier.

Web-based tools should also take a fraction of the time to deploy, configure, and integrate compared with current enterprise-scale management tools. Given that ease of adoption is one of the biggest challenges faced by vendors and users implementing enterprise management solutions, this presents a really good opportunity.

Users can also benefit from new pricing models vendors may be requested to offer. Most enterprise management applications are licensed on a per-seat basis. With Web-based management applications throughout the enterprise, vendors will have to seriously consider per-server pricing models. This would allow a more widespread use of management tools.

But this technology is not coming free. The following cost components must be considered:

- Browser software
- Web server software
- Conversion software (e.g., CGI)
- Content authoring and auditing
- Use of log analyzers to optimize usage
- Initial Web training for a broad user community

In most cases, the benefits of using this technology and potential cost savings outweigh the expenditures by far.

Vendors should also use Web innovations from areas other than systems and network management. Security standards developed for electronic commerce, for example, could ensure that Web-based management offers better security than SNMP over UDP. Web-based management solutions should look to incorporate Secure Sockets Layer protocol, which ensures a secure socket connection between a browser and Web server. There is also Secure-HTTP, an extension of HTTP for authentication and data encryption between a Web server and Web browser. Even public and private key technologies can be leveraged to control access to management systems and managed devices. In summary, security innovations include:[5]

- Secure Socket Layer (SSL) protocol
- Secure HyperText Transfer Protocol (S-HTTP)
- Public or private key technologies to control access to management systems

Another Web innovation that benefits management applications is the use of "push" technologies to deliver critical, real-time information to a browser. Today, the majority of applications relies on the "pull" model represented by SNMP. There are multiple alternatives. One model is a server-based Java application that listens to device-generated SNMP change traps and, in turn, pushes any changes to the active management browser. By using the push technology, vendors can start to deliver dynamic device and enterprise management information in real time to network operators and IT business users. The other model is dealing with a manager who is pushing an intelligent agent to a network client to perform designated tasks, without user interaction. As the mobile agent carries out its mission, it reports status to the agent manager. This could be used for common operations such as data collection or firmware updates. In summary,

- Use of push technology to deliver critical, real-time information to a browser
- Use of agent technology to automate designated tasks

In order to further deploy Web-based technology, the two standardization trends, Web-based enterprise management (WBEM) and Java Management application programming interface (JMAPI) should be combined with each other. JMAPI is more advanced in work aimed at instrumenting devices to deliver management information, and in developing a common look and feel for browser-based consoles. WBEM is further along in developing a meta-schema, which is a common repository for various types of management data. Each brings something valuable to the solution. Rather than each side re-creating work the other has already done, they should work together to implement critical components that already exist, and put the differences aside. In summary,

- Use parts of JMAPI for better device instrumentation, and build universal user interfaces
- Use parts of WBEM to better organize the repository

The management software market is moving rapidly to support Web standards and technologies as the basis of future management solutions. Web-based systems and network management is a flexible, lightweight approach for tool integration that focuses on quick results. This approach offers a universal front-end to management tools and data that can be hyperlinked easily. By these hyperlinks between various databases, different management tools on management intranets can be built. These management intranets provide application launching, data and management function integration among multiple management applications, including Web servers, embedded in network elements. Data integration and concentration is always a problem with management architectures. The DEN initiative is addressing the integration of application and user level directory information with network management, building open standards such as LDAP and WBEM-CIM. This combination helps to provide solutions not only for reacting well to problems and MAC requests, but also for proactive monitoring and capacity planning. This combination is also the prerequisite of a policy-based, business priority-driven approach to network, systems, and service management.

Web technology brings great potential to unify and simplify systems and network management. In addition, total cost of ownership (TCO) of management gear can be significantly reduced. However, questions still remain: what is the right update frequency of Web pages, whether and how Java may be used for interactive updating, how can the information exchange between Web and DBMS servers be made more efficient, and how the Common Information Model helps to structure performance data.

References

1. Arlitt, M. and Williamson, C., Internet Web servers: workload characterization and performance implications, *IEEE/ACM Transactions on Networking*, Vol. 5, no. 5, October 1997.
2. Bulow, D., Dynamic Compute Services, Datacom, 7/1998, p. 58-61, Bergheim, Germany.
3. Case, J., Finding the Right Job, www.nwfusion.com, April 21, 1997.
4. DeTeBerkom, Intelligent Agents: Concepts, Architectures, and Applications, Part 2: Impact of IA Concepts on the Telecommunications Environment, June 1995.
5. Forbath, T., Web-based management: a recipe for success, *Network World*, May 5, 1997.
6. Gareiss, R., Casting the Web over ATM, *Data Communications*, June 1997, p. 35-36.
7. Ghetie, I. G., *Networks and Systems Management — Platforms, Analysis and Evaluation*, Kluwer Academic Publishers, Boston, 1997.
8. Herman, J., Web-based net management is coming, *Data Communications*, October 1997, p. 139-141.
9. Heywood, P., An impartial interpreter of service-level agreements, *Data Communications*, November 1997, p. 32-34.
10. Huntington-Lee, J., Terplan, K., Gibson, J., *HP OpenView*, McGraw-Hill Series on Computer Communications, McGraw-Hill, New York, 1996.
11. Jander, M., Distributed net management — in search of solutions, *Data Communications*, February 1996, p. 101-112.
12. Larsen, A. K., Mastering distributed domains via the Web, *Data Communications*, May 21, 1996, p. 36-38.
13. Lemay, L. L., *Web Publishing with HTML*, SAMS Publishing, Indianapolis, 1995.
14. Megadanz, T., Rohermel, K., and Krause, S., Intelligent Agents: An Emerging Technology for Next Generation Telecommunications, Research Paper with GMD Fokus, Berlin, Germany, 1997.
15. Nair, R., Hunt, D., Malis, A., Robust Flow Control for Legacy Applications over Integrated Services ATM Networks, *Proceedings of Global Information Infrastructure, Evolution Internetworking Issues*, Nara Japan IOS Press, Amsterdam, 1996, p. 312-321.
16. Powell, T., The power of the DOM, *InternetWeek*, September 29, 1997, p. 61-74.
17. Powell, T., An XML primer, *InternetWeek*, November 24, 1997, p. 47-49.
18. Reardon, M., Need management that fast?, *Data Communications*, 1998, p. 30-31.
19. Roberts, E., Load balancing: on a different track, *Data Communications*, May 1998, p. 119-126.
20. Rubinson, T. and Terplan, K., *Data Network Design Management and Technical Perspectives*, CRC Press, Boca Raton, 1998.
21. Santalesa, R., Weaving the Web fantastic — review of authoring tools, *InternetWeek*, November 17, 1997, p. 73-87.
22. Spero, S., Analysis of HTTP Performance Problems, www.w3.org/ Protocols /HTTP-NG/http-prob.html
23. Stevens, W. R., *TCP/IP Illustrated*, Addison-Wesley Reading, MA, 1994.
24. Tate, D., Picking through piles of Web pages, *LanTimes*, February 17, 1997, p. 30.

25. Terplan, K., *Benchmarking for Effective Network Management*, McGraw-Hill, New York, 1994.
26. Terplan, K., *Effective Management of Local Area Networks*, McGraw-Hill Series on Computer Communications, McGraw-Hill, New York, 1996.
27. Terplan, K., *Telecom Operations Management Solutions with NetExpert*, CRC Press, Boca Raton, FL, 1998.
28. Thaler, D. and Ravishankar, C., Using name-based mappings to increase hit rates, *IEEE/ACM Transactions on Networking*, Vol. 6, no. 6, February 1998.

Abbreviations

4GL	Fourth-generation language
ACD	Automated call distributor
API	Application programming interface
ARM	Admin runtime module
ARP	Address resolution protocol
ATM	Asynchronous transfer mode
AVM	Admin view module
AWT	Abstract window toolkit
BSS	Business support system
BUI	Browser user interface
CBS	Class based queuing
CDF	Channel definition format
CGI	Common gateway interface
CIM	Common information model
CLI	Command line interface
CMIP	Common management information protocol
CMISE	Common management information service element
CNM	Customer network management
COM	Common object model
CORBA	Common object resource broker application
CSS	Cascading style sheets
CTI	Computer telephony integrated
DATM	Distributed application transaction measurement
DCE	Distributed computing environment
DCOM	Distributed common object model
DDM	Distributed database manager
DEN	Directory enabled networks
DHTML	Dynamic HyperText Markup Language
DME	Distributed management environment
DMI	Desktop management interface
DMTF	Desktop management task force
DNS	Domain name service
DOM	Document object model
DSSSL	Document style and semantics specification language
DTD	Document type definition
ESD	Electronic software distribution
FTP	File transfer protocol
FTS	Full text search
GUI	Graphical user interface
HMMP	HyperMedia Management Protocol
HMMS	HyperMedia Management Schema

HMOM	HyperMedia Object Manager
HTML	HyperText Markup Language
HTTP	HyperText Transport Protocol
ICMP	Internet control message protocol
IFS	Installable file system
IIS	Internet information server
IMT	Inductive modeling technology
IP	Internet processing
ISP	Internet service provider
ISV	Independent software vendor
ITA	Information technology administration
ITO	Information technology operations
JDBC	Java Database Connectivity
JEL	Java Event List
JMC	Java Management Console
JMI	Java Management Interface
LAN	Local area network
LDAP	Lightweight directory access protocol
MA	Management application
MAC	Media access
MIB	Management information base
MIF	Management information format
MO	Managed object
MOF	Managed object format
MSS	Microsoft Structured Query Language Server
	Marketing support system
NMS	Network management service
NNM	Network node manager
NT	Next generation
ODBC	Open database connectivity
OEM	Original equipment manufacturer
OM	Object manager
OSD	Open software description
OSI	Open systems interconnected
OSS	Operations support system
PDU	Protocol data unit
PERL	Practical Extraction and Report Language
QoS	Quality of service
RAS	Remote access service
RDBMS	Relational database management system
RDF	Resource definition framework
RME	Request manager engine
RMI	Remote method invocation
RMON	Remote monitoring
RPC	Remote procedure call
RSVP	Reserve bandwidth reservation protocol

SDK	Software development kit
SDN	Software defined network
SGML	Standardized Generalized Markup Language
SLA	Service level agreement
SLM	Service level management
SMI	Structured management information
SMIL	Synchronous Multimedia Integrated Language
SMS	Server management service
SNM	Solstice SunNet manager
SNMP	Simple network management protocol
SQL	Structured Query Language
SSL	Secure socket layer
TCL	Tool Command Language
TCP	Transmission control protocol
TME	Tivoli Management Environment
TMN	Telecommunications management network
TNG	The next generation
TOC	Table of content
UDP	User datagram protocol
UML	Unified Modeling Language
URC	Universal resource citations
URI	Universal request indicator
URL	Universal resource locator
URN	Universal resource names
VLAN	Virtual local area network
VPN	Virtual private network
VRML	Virtual Reality Modeling Language
WAN	Wide area network
WAS	Web application server
WBEM	Web-based enterprise management
WDM	Windows driver model
WMI	Windows management instrumentation
WWW	World Wide Web
XLL	Extensible Linking Language
XML	Extensible MarkUp Language
XSL	Extensible Style Language

Index